CONSERVATIVE
IN BRITAIN AND
STAT

The shock waves of conservative advances have reached into every corner of American and British politics. Parties of the right have prospered, while parties of the left have stumbled, retreated, and are now regrouping. The agenda for both right and left is set by the terms of the free-market doctrines that have displaced the post-war consensus politics of liberal capitalism.

Conservative Capitalism in Britain and the United States describes and challenges the ideological basis of the free-market right. Though critiques of the policies of the Reagan and Thatcher governments are hardly in short supply, this major new study offers the most thorough and up-to-date analysis available. No other book considers in such depth conservative ideas and policies on both sides of the Atlantic. It provides the first clear account of the distinction between conservative and other forms of capitalism. It also examines the fault lines dividing opposing camps within conservative capitalism and their consequences for domestic policy in Britain and the US. Linking political theory and public policy, it is one of the few critical appraisals of the New Right based on a clear understanding of what the arguments for the free market really are.

Finally, Hoover and Plant demonstrate what the left needs to learn from its failures, how to remould its understanding of the relationship between politics and the market, and how to recapture the lost initiative in British and American politics. This original and important book will be of great interest to all observers of the contemporary political scene as well as students and scholars of political science, political theory, and comparative government.

Foreword by Gar Alperovitz, National Center for Economic Alternatives, Washington, DC.

Afterword by Roy Hattersley, MP, Deputy Leader of the Labour Party.

Kenneth Hoover is Chairman of the Political Science Department at Western Washington University, Bellingham, Washington. Raymond Plant is Professor of Politics, University of Southampton.

CONSERVATIVE CAPITALISM IN BRITAIN AND THE UNITED STATES

A Critical Appraisal

KENNETH HOOVER

and

RAYMOND PLANT

ROUTLEDGE
London and New York

First published in 1989 by
Routledge
11 New Fetter Lane, London EC4P 4EE
29 West 35th Street, New York NY 10001

© 1989 Kenneth Hoover and Raymond Plant

Set in Baskerville by Input Typesetting Ltd, London
Printed in Great Britain by the Guernsey Press, Guernsey

British Library Cataloguing in Publication Data

Hoover, Kenneth
Conservative capitalism in Britain and
the United States: a critical appraisal.
1. Political ideologies: Conservatism
I. Title   II. Plant, Raymond
320.5'2

Library of Congress Cataloging in Publication Data

Hoover, Kenneth R., 1940–
Conservative capitalism in Britain and the United States: a
critical appraisal/Kenneth Hoover and Raymond Plant.
p. cm.
Includes index.
ISBN 0–415–01583–9.   ISBN 0–415–01584–7 (pbk.)
1. Conservatism—Great Britain.   2. Conservatism—United States.
3. Great Britain—Economic policy—1945–.   4. United States—
Economic policy—1981–.   5. Capitalism—Great Britain.
6. Capitalism—United States.   I. Plant, Raymond.   II. Title.
JA84.G7H66 1988
320.5'2'0941—dc19
88–12200
CIP

To
our students

CONTENTS

FOREWORD

Both in Britain and the United States the explosion of a more aggressive, forceful, and successful conservative politics during the last decade was largely unpredicted: the rhetoric of free enterprise, individualism, and antipathy to 'Big Government' had been an ideological staple of politics in both countries for generations, but the startling success of such themes came as a surprise even to the followers of Ronald Reagan and Margaret Thatcher.

How are we to understand this success?

And – in what appear to be the waning days of the strong form of such themes in the Reagan administration – how are we to consider political options for the future?

Kenneth Hoover and Raymond Plant are first and foremost interested in the problem of ideology; they leave to other authors and other occasions the detailed exploration of economics, political organization, elections, etc. This focus is significant: an important lesson of the decade is that ideology on its own plays a powerful role in politics – an idea which had far less currency only a few years ago, especially in the United States. Just how powerful a role it will continue to play may well be the most significant question – even, in the nuclear age, a life and death question – of the remainder of the twentieth century. A dissection of ideology also opens the way for a discussion of opportunities and challenges facing those who do not share the premises of 'conservative capitalism'.

Hoover and Plant avowedly seek to provide political guidance to 'the left', but their book is a well-informed essay which will also stimulate thought among a wide range of others who do not so identify themselves. They begin by making a sharp distinction between 'individualist' and 'traditional' strains in conservative

ix

thought. The cleavage, broadly speaking, is between those who urge
unadulterated *laissez-faire* policies and those who believe 'the state'
must play a role in helping the poor, in maintaining social cohesion,
and in guiding moral and even personal behaviour. They continue
the analysis by detailing the attack on liberal-capitalist institutions
and policies that form the intellectual basis for the Reagan and
Thatcher governments. The authors make clear precisely where the
new departures originated.

The *ideological* basis for this cleavage (as distinct from its practical
and political implications) is much better understood in Britain
than in the United States. American conservatives also come in
different varieties, but the rhetoric of most is strongly libertarian in
tone. True enough, a few intellectuals and journalists – Russell Kirk
and George Will, for instance – stress the role of tradition and
of community; and the 'Moral Majority' emphasizes an activist
government to preserve moral values in connection with drugs,
sex, abortion, school prayer, etc. But in the United States, the
conservative *ideological* commitment to a strong state is far weaker
than that of the traditionalist conservatism which has much older,
aristocratic, and religious roots in Britain.

None the less, the two strains – one requiring less government,
the other more – are clearly evident on both sides of the Atlantic.
Moreover, the conflicting strains of opinion and political philosophy
have already created major problems for conservative politics in
both nations. The conflict between the radical right wing of the
Republican Party and conservative 'moderates' is obvious, and it
is bound to increase as Ronald Reagan's personal role in politics
diminishes. Hoover and Plant show that the tensions go far deeper
than superficial labels often imply. In a careful analysis of issues
of federalism and decentralization, they demonstrate the growing
conflict between those who wish to leave all matters of regulation
to state and local authorities (partly out of conviction, partly
believing that competition between diverse authorities will weaken
all regulation) – and those (often the leaders of major corporations
who need uniform ground rules for efficient economic operations)
who urge continued regulation at the national level. In Britain the
splits within Conservative ranks over issues of child welfare, public
pay, and overall economic management also suggest that the fissures
will not easily be papered over by the usual political slogans.

Hoover and Plant argue that such divisions could offer real opportunities for opponents of 'conservative capitalism' in the future. They point out, first, that most studies of Ronald Reagan's electoral successes show that the American public has been far less engaged in either brand of conservative ideology than many think. At the outset they were angered at inflation and Jimmy Carter's apparent weakness and indecision in both domestic and foreign policy. They voted *against* Carter – and, subsequently, Mondale – more than they voted *for* Ronald Reagan's ideology. In Britain, Margaret Thatcher's successes also have had a great deal to do with the weakness and failings of her opponents – and, as Hoover and Plant remind, she was in all probability saved from defeat in her second election campaign by the Falkland Islands war.

But such facts only begin to define the important political possibilities. The authors of *Conservative Capitalism* believe 'that both the Conservative and Labour parties (and the Democratic and Republican parties in the United States) have exhausted the options available to them . . .' A truly new approach is therefore needed. To exploit the growing divisions in conservative ranks, they urge the left to emphasize 'the premier value' that binds together modern societies: the work ethic. They argue that an emphasis on 'dependency' programmes has weakened progressives in both Britain and the United States, but that a new integration of full employment planning *for productive jobs*, plus a radically decentralized, community- and market-based organization of such jobs, could have powerful appeal. In the United States a recent movement in favour of a jobs-and-training emphasis in the political debate over welfare suggests the importance of this political point, but the argument goes beyond such immediate concerns:

> [The] conundrum of capitalist politics remains unsolved and awaits new conceptualizations of policy that may well lead away from an exclusive reliance on either the market or the government as the dominant agent of change. The way may now be open for a realistic consideration of how the two, together with a reordering of national–local relations, can be brought into a working arrangement that is productive for all levels of society.

Conservative Capitalism does not attempt to deal with every problem facing politics in Britain and America. Nor does the existence of opportunity mean automatic success: there are many additional

obstacles standing in the way of a progressive politics which might
not only win office, but which hopes to govern positively once its
candidates are elected. In emphasizing the ideological issues which
must be confronted, Hoover and Plant also necessarily leave aside
many specifics of policy – and such questions as the relative importance of race, geographic size, and of global foreign policy commitments in the two countries. We gain, however, from the sharp focus
– and from the authors' unyielding argument that ideology itself
plays a powerful and growing role which demands that we consider
it in its own terms.

   In Britain, this book will be a significant addition to an ongoing
dialogue on these matters – especially in its analysis of the lessons
of the Reagan and Thatcher years. In America, where the issue of
ideology is still often considered secondary, *Conservative Capitalism*
offers a primer on a subject which is bound to become increasingly
important as we approach the end of the twentieth century.

   In both countries, the book makes a useful contribution to the
reconstruction of a longer-term politics which places humane values
– and a coherent political philosophy concerning what is required
to nurture and sustain such values – at the heart of the debate over
strategy.

Gar Alperovitz
National Center for Economic
Alternatives, Washington, DC

PREFACE AND
ACKNOWLEDGEMENTS

Critiques of the policies of the Reagan and Thatcher governments
are hardly in short supply as the citations in this book will demonstrate. The particular analysis we bring to the subject is to focus
on the role of ideology. Seldom in recent memory has ideology been
as close to the visible surface of politics as it is presently.

The premise of this analysis is that all policies – and those of the
Reagan and Thatcher governments in particular – emerge from
conflicting motivations. Some of these motivations are ideological
in the classical sense that proposals for action are derived from a
systematic world view. Other motivations are not directly ideological, though even the recipient of a subsidy who simply wants
'more' is inclined to dignify the claim by some larger frame of
justification. To the extent that political action is purposive,
ideology reflects on the deepest levels of intention.

Consequently ideological analysis brings to the study of policy a
feel for the justificatory framework within which policy is argued. In
addition, our sense of the evidence (see chapter 1) is that ideological
conceptions, whether vague or precise, are powerful carriers of
political meaning and thus must be accounted for in assessing
political behaviour. Ideologies are important keys to the evocation
of demands and supports, arousal and quiescence, that provides the
fundamental rhythms of politics. Consequently we find ideological
analysis useful for understanding these two governments as well as
for estimating ways that the left can adapt its ideological commitments to currents of mass public opinion. Ideology is not divorced
from the practical and empirical dimensions of politics; the two are
interdependent as we hope to illustrate in the chapters that follow.

It happens that these two governments provide particularly

xiii

strong examples of the influence of ideology. Not since the 1930s in the United States and the post-Second World War Labour Government in Great Britain have governments come to power with such self-consciously ideological programmes. Indeed it is the reversal of the New Deal and of Labour Party socialist initiatives that are the objectives of these conservative governments. Ideological analysis provides perspectives on the basic thrust of policy in both countries.

At a second level, however, the story of the role of ideology is one of conflict within both the Reagan and Thatcher governments over which of two versions of conservatism should be dominant. The frustration of initiatives, the struggles with implementation, and the reaction of other centres of power cannot be fully understood without attention to the nature of the ideological struggle within conservatism – as well as the response without on the part of the left.

This book is confined to the analysis of domestic policy and, within that, largely to issues of distributive equity in the United States and in Britain. It is here that the essential battleground of rival ideologies is located, and here that fundamental political forces are shaped and changed. There are, however, significant dimensions of ideological struggle that remain to be illuminated in other areas of domestic policy and of foreign policy. Our hope is that this work will contribute to that larger enterprise.

The origins of this book on the American side are in Kenneth Hoover's research that began in 1981 as the impact of ideologically based conceptions of policy began to be felt in the budgetary priorities of the Reagan administration. The first fruit of this project was a paper delivered to a conference titled 'Whither America?' at Aalborg University in Denmark in August 1982. The paper was published in the proceedings and in a revised and expanded form in *Grus*, a Danish journal of politics.

The comparative dimensions of the topic soon became apparent, and the research was broadened to include analysis of the Thatcher government. The striking similarities in internal tensions over policy formation between individualists and conservatives were the topic of a paper prepared for the World Congress of the International Political Science Association in Paris in the summer of 1985. As a longer time perspective became possible, the objective became a more precise formulation of the concept of 'conservative capitalism' and of its uses in tracing the rise of Reagan and Thatcher. The results are in *Comparative Studies in Society and History* (1987), Cambridge University Press, vol. 29, no. 2.

The project has now reached a certain maturity as the original agendas of both governments have run their courses and a serious assessment is under way. By collaborating across the Atlantic, the two authors hope to advance that assessment. The literature that has developed over the last few years has, as well, allowed a more comprehensive understanding of the dynamics at work. It is time to explore the further consequences of the ideological wave that Reagan and Thatcher did so much to encourage and to begin to consider what sort of responses it might engender from the left.

On the British side Raymond Plant became interested in the issues posed in this book when at work on a different project, on the contribution of Anthony Crosland to British socialist thought. During a sabbatical year at Nuffield College, Oxford, supported by an ESRC Personal Research Grant (for which grateful thanks are due), it soon became clear that most of the assumptions about the role of the state in relation to society which Crosland took for granted, and which seemed to him to be irreversible, were under direct challenge, not just in Britain by the Thatcher government but also in the United States and in many countries in Western Europe and beyond. It seemed therefore that a preparatory study would need to be done before any critical appraisal of Croslandite socialism could be attempted, and Plant conceived the idea of writing a short study of the underlying assumptions of the growth of free-market views and the challenge they posed to the social democratic consensus on the left which Crosland so clearly represented. A meeting in a restaurant in Charlotte Street two summers ago with Kenneth Hoover convinced him that this study should be much longer than he had envisaged and that it would be best done in a comparative perspective. The present book is the result of this co-operation.

One of the other major elements of interest of the book for Plant was that it provided an opportunity to pursue an intellectual interest close to his heart, namely the attempt to bring political theory into closer contact with issues of government and public policy. No doubt political-theory specialists will be dismayed that theoretical arguments are not always pursued to the end and specialists in British government and public policy will find much with which to take issue. However, risks have to be taken if political science is

going to remain a unitary discipline, and this book is offered as a
modest contribution towards that end.

During the writing of his part of the book Plant has incurred
many debts. First of all, to the Warden and Fellows of Nuffield
College for an interesting and stimulating year and to his colleagues
in the Politics Department in Southampton University for providing
such a congenial academic environment and for their tolerance on
finding that a political science department was presented with a
philosopher as a professor. He hopes the book will show that he
has tried to come to grips with the institutional and empirical side
of the discipline. He has found a good deal of stimulation in talking
to academics and politicians across disciplines and the political
spectrum, and he would particularly like to thank the following for
their stimulus: Ian Forbes, Roy Hattersley, Bryan Gould, Austin
Mitchell, Samuel Brittan, John Lloyd, David Miller, Julian Le
Grand, David Marquand, Lord Harris of High Cross, Arthur
Seldon, Ken Minogue, Dilys Hill, members of the Socialist Philosophy Group and the Fabian Society. He would also like to thank
Nathan Glazer and Irving Horowitz for insights into the market-
based right in the United States where he participated in a
symposium with them on markets and planning in Washington
1987. Finally, thanks are due to Liz Jones and Jo Fluck for dealing
with his appalling writing, and to Katherine and their sons, Nicholas, Matthew, and Richard, for their uncommon tolerance of his
preoccupations.

Along the way, there have been individuals of particular significance for the evolution of Kenneth Hoover's research – among them:
Terence Ball of the University of Minnesota, Norman Cloutier of
the University of Wisconsin-Parkside, Kenneth Dolbeare of Ever-
green State College, Ib Jorgensen of Aalborg University, Jytte
Klausen formerly of Aarhus University, Mark Kann of the University of Southern California, Thomas Trautmann of the University
of Michigan, and Archbishop Rembert Weakland. He is particularly
grateful to Samuel Pernacciaro of the University of Wisconsin-
Parkside for his support and assistance and to the Committee on
Research and Creative Activity for a travel grant. Cynthia Kuiper,
Sheryl Lahti, and Corby Anderson have supplied research and
clerical assistance with care and good humour. Judith Hoover
reviewed these chapters with thoughtful attention to argument and
evidence.

To all of these we are very grateful even as differences of interpretation remain.

Kenneth Hoover
Western Washington University

Raymond Plant
Southampton University

Part One

CONSERVATIVE CAPITALISM AS IDEOLOGY

Chapter One

CONSERVATIVE CAPITALISM AND ITS ADVERSARIES

The shock waves of contemporary conservative advances have reached into every corner of American and British politics. Parties of the right have prospered. Parties of the left have stumbled, retreated, and are now regrouping as the popularity of conservative policies is placed at risk by economic uncertainties. The agenda for both the right and the left is set by the terms of free-market doctrines that have displaced Keynesian and socialist conceptions in the discourse of modern political economy.

The advance of this ideological wave depends on three realities that become increasingly apparent as the further reaches of its effects are realized: the economic consequences of monetarism and supply-side economics, internal splits among conservatives over policy issues, and the public response to the conservative critique of the welfare state. At the further shore lies an opportunity for the left to learn from its failures, remould its understanding of the relationship between politics and the market, and recapture the lost initiative in British and American politics.

The phrase 'conservative capitalism' is meant to convey the essential meanings of the movements that have propelled Reagan and Thatcher to power. Both leaders have resolutely embraced capitalism as not only efficient, but as a morally superior form of political economy. Yet their version of capitalism differs markedly from that of their predecessors of both parties. They have sought to implement an explicitly conservative form of capitalism where the role of government in smoothing out the consequences of economic inequality is sharply reduced. The restoration of the market-place is presented by Reagan and Thatcher as the nation's saviour from the perils of too much government.

The Reagan–Thatcher policies make it quite clear that conservative capitalism is indeed different from the liberal and social democratic versions. Rather than dealing incrementally within a general
consensus on reformist policies, they have advocated tax cuts,
shifted resources away from human-service programmes, resusci-
tated traditionalist prescriptions for personal behaviour, and
advanced the apparent substitution of the market for government
as the key institution of the society. Inequality of ability, income,
and status is openly accepted and even celebrated as the key to a
competitive world where the best will succeed, hopefully to the
advantage of all.

Privatization and *laissez-faire* have become the favoured remedies
for every social problem. Social services are contracted out privately
to improve efficiency. In the United States, as the Iran–Contra
affair reveals, foreign policy itself was carried on by private means.
In Britain the most recent election brought Conservative proposals
to privatize more of the basic utilities and even to allow local schools
to operate independently of local control.

Denationalization, deregulation, and devolution of governmental
functions have, in varying degrees, been the watchwords of this new
version of conservatism. 'Statism' has become the object of
strenuous criticism by a new generation of conservative politicians,
despite some residual elements of traditionalist regard for the uses
of state authority.

The purpose of this appraisal is to explore the origins of conservative capitalism, the ideological elements of its appeal, the splits
within the movement, and the ways that its implementation has
met with mixed results. This will lead to an understanding of the
potential and the limitations of conservative capitalism's political
role. The internal dynamics of conservative capitalism as a movement have a considerable effect on the way that the public has come
to perceive the market as an institutional rival to government. This
admixture of conservatism and capitalism will be seen to involve
conflicts between various kinds of conservatism that are not easily
resolved. These explorations will open the way for a reassessment, in
the final chapters, of the relationship of the market to the democratic
programme of the left.

We will find that conservative capitalism has been from the
beginning a movement with serious internal divisions between
elements we will identify as individualist and traditionalist, and

that the impacts of its policies are serving to exacerbate these divisions. As the consequences of conservative-capitalist economic and social policies become more apparent, it is likely that the ability of the movement to legitimize the market as the premier societal institution will weaken.

This book is designed to move from an analysis of origins and implementation to a discussion of alternatives. Part 1 presents the ideological components of conservative capitalism: the attack on Keynesianism and on the conventional politics of conservative traditionalists by market-based conservatives who advocate monetarism and supply-side economics. Part 1 concludes with an analysis of the critique of the welfare state that paved the way for the rise of conservative capitalism, and an exploration of internal tensions within the movement between individualists and traditionalists.

In Part 2, we review the political origins of the movement and the implementation of its programme in the United States and Great Britain. The focus is on policies such as income security, taxation, and privatization that were most clearly influenced by ideological considerations. Part 3 explores some possible responses from the left. What new ways can be found to advance the historic commitment to a more equitable framework for human development? What has been learned about the appropriate roles of the state and the market in meeting this commitment?

The breaking-point of public confidence in conservative domestic-policy initiatives in both countries may well lie in issues of distributive equity. The public has a right to be suspicious that conservative economics add up to a redistribution of income and power from the poor to the rich. Indeed, as we shall see, government data on income distribution provide grounds for that suspicion. As the consequences of massive debt financing in the United States impact on the distribution of income, we may expect ever greater inequality. As Senator Daniel Moynihan points out:

> The national debt is now so large that for an indefinite period it will require a third to a half of all revenue from the personal income tax to pay the interest. If the personal income tax is taken as an elemental tax on labor, and debt service an elemental return to capital, we have here the largest transfer of

wealth from workers to owners in the history of our political economy.[1]

There is evidence, and it will be reviewed in the concluding chapters, that this transfer is under way.

By the end of the decade a rising tide of inequality, deprivation, and unrest may well unseat the practitioners of conservative appeals. Yet one suspects that this will be seen not as a discrediting of the market-place itself, but rather one more negative mark on the record of government, the market's institutional rival. It is politicians that brought us the promises of the new conservatism, it was the actions of government that implemented it, and it is to government that its adverse consequences may well attach.

The quandary for the left becomes clear: how to meet the public desire for more humane and progressive policies when the means of doing so, governmental action, are derided and discredited by powerful and effective conservative leaders. The initial step is to understand where these leaders get their power and what ideological currents swept them into office.

THE FATE OF LIBERAL CAPITALISM AND SOCIAL DEMOCRACY

For the rise of conservative capitalism to be understood, it first has to be seen in the context of political developments dating back to the New Deal in the United States and, in Britain, to the post-war rise to power of the Labour Party. These structural revolutions altered the symbolic and substantive framework of British and American politics. Just as the New Deal and, later, the Labour Party's entry into government were widely perceived as remedies to the failures of the market-place in the depression, so the market is now presented as the cure for an over-indulgence in governmental control.

Modern liberal reformers and social democrats believe that all people are entitled to the prerequisites for competition in a market society. The disadvantaged should, by governmental programmes and regulations, be given the means of competing: education, health care, job-training, the right to bargain collectively with management, freedom from various forms of discrimination, and protection from the abuse of power, whether economic (as in job safety and environmental programmes) or political (as in civil liberties). Added to these forms of governmental intervention was Keynesian economics with its recipes for stimulating demand by government spending in times of recession and the converse in times of inflation. These policies comprise the core of liberal capitalism in the United States, and, with the additional elements of nationalization and expanded social provision, social democracy in Britain.

It is instructive to note that the New Deal succeeded more in doctrine than in policy. The specific policies of the New Deal, and the assistance agencies that were created to provide jobs, really failed to do very much more than improve morale. Their substantive impact was widely evaluated as minimal since the resources that were committed were not very substantial and the jobs were mainly non-productive for the economy. It is the consensus that a far larger government investment in the economy, namely the Second World War, was required to restore the health of the system. In the same way we will see how conservative capitalism has changed the fundamental symbolic parameters of politics, even while achieving decidedly mixed results from its policies.

The New Deal represented not so much a dramatic shift in patterns of expenditure as a rearrangement of authority from local levels of government to state levels in consequence of federal financial and administrative policy initiatives.[2] These bitterly contested structural changes provided the architecture for the next forty years of social policy. Every social problem acquired its 'iron triangle' of organized lobby, institutionalized interest in the bureaucracy, and legislative protection in the form of a powerful political patron. It is precisely the role of the national government that has been the focal point of conservative attack since the origins of the New Deal. That the assault finally has succeeded in the United States was signalled by the fact that the federal government now is perceived as the least effective of the three levels of government, according to the US Advisory Commission on Intergovernmental Relations annual poll. The poll, taken every year since 1972, revealed this key shift for the first time in 1984.[3]

This upward redistribution of power in the federal system during the New Deal is the reverse image of President Reagan's New Federalism, just as initiatives toward privatization in Great Britain reverse the structural initiatives of the post-war Labour governments. The aim of the New Federalism was not just a rearrangement of power, but a structural change that would alter policy over the long term. It was intended that the pre-Depression role of minimalist government be restored, and that the economy be freed thereby of the 'shackles of government regulation'. For this reason, we will come to see the New Federalism as the domestic-policy face of the economic doctrine of supply-side incentives for increased production through the reduction of taxes to stimulate investment.

In Britain post-war Labour governments legitimized a public role in looking after basic human needs through the establishment of the National Health Service and numerous other measures. While these reforms have waxed and waned in public popularity, the welfare state did provide, until the rise of Margaret Thatcher, the common agenda for both Labour and Conservative programmes. The market was not abandoned for the full socialist programme of nationalization, though inroads were made on some key institutions. Attempts were made to implement Keynesian policies to shore up an economy badly undercut by the loss of empire and the enormous cost of the Second World War. Yet the forces that weakened Britain's economy were stronger than those that added strength and the general context of decline created an opening for the development of the conservative-capitalist initiative.

According to Samuel Beer, the 'class decomposition' that accompanied the post-war modernization of British society was, in this context, replaced with a fierce struggle between rival groups intent on economic gains at the public expense. This set off a struggle of 'Britain against herself' which paralysed the left as well as the traditional right.[4]

The fact that the historical and comparative evidence is quite unclear as to whether the growth of public spending was the principal culprit in Britain's economic performance was lost in the search for a doctrine that offered a fresh vision for the beleaguered British economy. In the early post-war experience, growth rates improved as public-sector expenditures increased; in the later period, economic decline preceded new advancements in the public sector; and European states with larger public sectors did better than Britain.[5] Yet there was a crisis in that government was not able to respond effectively to the economic decline that beset the average citizen. Thus ideology, with its powerful appeals to symbolic themes of threat and reassurance, played a crucial role in the changeover from liberal to conservative capitalism. It is this ideological change-over that requires explanation.

While it is true that liberal reformers and social democrats never assaulted the basic system of production for profit, they did at least try to bridge the gap between the inegalitarian results of capitalism and the demands for equity arising from an increasingly democratic political system. Conservative capitalists mounted a direct challenge that questioned not only the effects of these policies, but also their wisdom and moral basis as well. Yet the movement speaks with more than one voice on these issues and it is important to separate out the strands that have come together under its banner.

THE TERMS OF THE DEBATE

Conservative capitalism is a hybrid of two tendencies: the one oriented to the market-place and *laissez-faire*, and the other to institutions that constrain personal freedom in the name of order. We identify the movement toward *laissez-faire* policies in contemporary politics as *individualist conservatism*.[6] It is reliance on the market for all manner of economic, political, and social decisions that characterizes the policies of these newly empowered conservative activists in both countries. Free marketeers such as Ayn Rand and Murray Rothbard have popularized these ideas, and self-avowed classical liberals (or 'old Whigs'), such as Friedrich Hayek and Milton Friedman, have sponsored the revival by conservative politicians of *laissez-faire* policies.[7]

Yet classical liberalism has been altered by individualist conservatives in that they elevate private self-interest to a position of dominance over nearly all forms of the public interest. Classical liberals in general, and Hayek and Friedman in particular, do acknowledge a slightly wider role for public authority than the free-market preference for just enforcing the law, delivering the mail, and defending the shores. Classical liberals such as Locke and Mill, however, at least acknowledged human need as a principle in distribution – a concern that is missing in Hayek and Friedman. And the latter are certainly distinct from the other children of classical liberalism: the reform liberals for whom the social and economic role of government is extensive indeed.

By reason of their acceptance of inequality, Hayek, Friedman, Rand, and Rothbard can all be included as conservatives. By reason of their preferred means for determining who deserves what, namely the maximization of personal freedom of action in the market-place, they are individualist conservatives.

There is a second strand to the movement. *Traditional conservatives* continue to be a potent force both as allies of the moralists who have advanced a politicized form of Christian evangelism, and as critics of the policy excesses of market-based conservatives in leaving too many matters to individual choice. The American 'moral majority' movement and its affiliation with the television evangelism of self-avowed conservative preachers have generated a political agenda that amounts to the restriction of individual freedom in areas of personal morality. The programme of this movement bears striking resemblance to the traditionalist view of the need for institutional restraints on personal behaviour. In Britain the call for a return to 'Victorian values' speaks to the same alliance between the moral face of traditionalism and the popular appeal of the virtues of hearth and home.

As we will see in the next chapter, the differences between traditionalists and individualists extend to such issues as the proper role of government, the deference to be accorded to élites, as well as to the limits on doctrine as a guide to policy-making. Differences among conservatives over income-security programmes will later be seen to have helped undermine the progress of the movement itself.

The labels applied to the adversaries of conservative capitalism differ as between Britain and the United States. For Reagan, it was the reform liberal variant of capitalism that was the problem. In his view, and in generally accepted usage among conservatives in the United States, liberals were nothing more than statists whose institutional remedies to the inequities of capitalism in fact worsened the problems by stultifying free enterprise and encouraging false expectations of social justice.

In Britain the target of Thatcher's critique is more properly labelled social democratic capitalism. The statist direction of policy in the post-war period arose from a direct accommodation between capitalism and socialism, rather than from a revision of liberal doctrines in the form of a 'New Deal'.[8] To the degree that socialist policies, such as nationalization and social provision of necessities, were implemented, however, they were not undertaken through a wholesale conversion to economic planning by government. Indeed, as we shall see, there was a certain affinity between the institution-

10

alist orientation of traditional conservatism and Labour's elaboration of the welfare state. The political result was a form of social democracy that became the convention of British politics. While conservative governments prior to Mrs Thatcher's criticized the doctrinal impetus of welfare state measures, they did not attempt to undo the framework of social democracy. Nor did Labour succeed in displacing the primary role of private capital in the market-place.

To be sure, there are important differences between reform liberalism in the United States and social democracy in England. The former has relied upon the regulatory power of the state to control the excesses of the market, while the latter has moved directly into ownership as well as control. However, from the point of view of market-based conservatives, the common sin is statism, mortal in the case of British social democracy and more nearly venial in US reform liberalism.

In describing the struggle between the market and the state, the phrase 'democratic capitalism' will be avoided for two reasons. It isn't self-evident that democracy fits hand in glove with capitalism. Democracy makes decisions on the basis of the vote and through participation in politics; capitalism is a system in which the principal sources of power rest with those who own and control the means of production.[9] The effort to combine both institutions in one symbolic expression creates the second problem: the symbol is used for quite different purposes by left and right.

On the right, conservatives such as Michael Novak use the phrase 'democratic capitalism' to convey the message that democratic political norms legitimize the inequalities produced by the economic results of capitalism.[10] Novak suggests that the spirit of individualism that is essential to democracy is consonant with the ethos of capitalism. The emphasis on entrepreneurship and competition is but a celebration of the uniqueness of the individual. He points out that capitalism has prospered only in countries characterized by democratic political systems; and that the reverse is also true. Capitalism, in his view, reinforces democracy. By this device of argument, socialism appears as anti-democratic.

On the left, the phrase is an entry into the argument that democracy has altered capitalism in fundamental ways and that the current struggle is about the reassertion of capitalist control over democracy.[11] The view of history here is quite different from Novak's: democratic movements appear as the antagonists of capitalism, seeking to control its abuses. The argument is that, in the 1960s and 1970s, Anglo-American political reformers, in the eyes of capitalist élites, went 'too far' in the direction of the regulation of the market through government action. The threat to the hegemony of the class that controls capital was sufficient to evoke the response represented by the policies of Reagan and Thatcher. In the name of economic efficiency, poverty programmes have been cut, regulatory systems dismantled, and entitlements reduced.

The agenda of the Reagan–Thatcher forces, from the point of view of the left, is to widen the distance between capitalists and workers so that labour will feel the discipline of the market-place more directly. Frances Fox Piven and Richard Cloward, along with other proponents of this view, see the left as the true carriers of the democratic tradition.[12] They argue that the response must be to strengthen democratic initiatives from the neighbourhood through to the national level and to increase political accountability for economic decisions. Only through the democratic control of investment decisions can communities capture the means of shaping their own futures. Elements of this argument will be addressed in later chapters.

Both of these interpretations of the relationship of democracy to capitalism reveal interesting aspects of ideology. However, our intent is to distinguish more clearly than the phrase 'democratic capitalism' allows just what the ideological variations in the presentation of capitalism mean for policy and politics. Our purpose here is to confront ideology directly.

The phrase 'New Right' has been applied variously to the movement for moral traditionalism and to the advocacy of the free market. The term was introduced in the United States by Kevin Phillips in 1974 and referred primarily to the moral dimension of the conservative movement, though in later usage on both sides of the Atlantic it came to stand for an amalgam of modern conservative political prescriptions.[13] What the phrase conceals is the sense in which the belief in moral restraint is finally inconsistent with a programme of unrestrained economic liberty – a contradiction which is left open for consideration by the phrase 'conservative capitalism'. Thus we find that the phrase 'New Right' contributes little to clarifying what in fact is being advanced by way of policy by conservatives and so have avoided it.

12

IDEOLOGY MEETS POLITICS

Since our topic is ideology, a brief definitional note is in order. The various general definitions used by scholars centre on ideology as a view of the human condition associated with a programme of political action. For a more precise working definition, we will follow A. James Reichley's formulation and conceive of ideology as 'a distinct and broadly coherent structure of values, beliefs, and attitudes with implications for social order'.[14] The view of the human condition may not be precise or detailed, nor the programme of action clearly derived from it – other than in the mind of the believer. What is essential is that ideology shapes both expectations and perceptions of what politics is about, and what it should become.

While it is popular to label as ideology that which *someone else* believes, the phenomenon of ideology appears to be pervasive. Recent research has begun to challenge the generalization, made on the basis of early behavioural studies, that the public knows or cares little about ideology. It is becoming apparent that at least a third of the population has a general grasp of ideological distinctions, another third has a rather confused picture, and the remaining third haven't given it much thought – or won't respond to the questionnaire. Given the difficulties of eliciting responses to complex phenomena such as ideologies, it may be that this survey understates the extent to which ideological benefits are present.[15] For a significant segment of the population, ideologies do appear to constrain their views on specific issues and to influence voting decisions.[16]

Ideology does not have to be clearly articulated or consistent to be powerful. It is likely that large sectors of the mass public have a *set* of ideologies rather than a single ideology, and that elements of this set are mobilized in response to particular cues.[17] The impact of an ideologically ambivalent public upon contemporary policy is one of the underlying questions explored in this book.

Whatever the state of public awareness of ideology, there is clear evidence that ideology among élites matters in terms of policy results. A cross-national study of 116 regimes and their policies by Bruce Moon and William Dixon recently concluded that the ideology of élites does indeed have an impact on the provision for basic needs – particularly in those countries where government is strong:

> There can be little doubt that the more dominant a leftist state the greater the welfare accomplishments, whereas state power under the control of rightist regimes carries just the opposite effect.[18]

While much of this book will be concerned with the question of how ideology and policy interact at the élite level, it will also become clear what the consequences of this mixture are for the public. In the conclusion, we will return to the question of public understandings of ideology as a way of canvassing the prospects for changing the current directions taken by conservative capitalists. The question for the left will be 'How can this ideological ambivalence be addressed in a manner that is sufficiently credible to produce a change in the direction of policy?'

Chapter Two

THE POLITICAL ECONOMY OF CONSERVATIVE CAPITALISM

According to the system of natural liberty, the sovereign has only three duties to attend to: . . . first the duty of protecting the society from the violence and invasion of other independent societies; secondly the duty of protecting as far as possible, every member of the society from the injustice or oppression of every other member of it, or the duty of establishing an exact administration of justice; and, thirdly, the duty of erecting and maintaining certain public works and certain public institutions, which it can never be for the interest of any individual or small group of individuals, to erect and maintain; because the profit could never repay the expense to any individual, or small number of individuals, though it may frequently do much more than repay it to a great society.

(Adam Smith)

In both Britain and the United States conservatives have had different attitudes to the state and its role in economic management and welfare.[1] However, it is only in the last ten to fifteen years that the free-market anti-state case has come to attain intellectual and, to some extent, political ascendancy and has come to challenge in both theory and practice what is seen as the dominance of the statist, collectivist approaches to political problems, particularly since the Second World War. Hence it is only possible to understand the growth of the ideas of conservative capitalism in the light of its critique of these post-war developments. In the view of defenders of the free-market form of conservatism, both the parties of the left and successive Conservative governments in Britain from Churchill to Heath and Republican administrations in the United States from

15

Eisenhower to Ford were major contributors to the consensus about the role of the state and public expenditure which modern free-market forms of conservatism are set to challenge. As Nigel Lawson, currently Chancellor of the Exchequer in Mrs Thatcher's government, put the point in relation to the proper understanding of the Conservative election victory in 1979:

> the fact is that the Conservative Party was swept into office on a programme which seemed to mark a conscious change of direction, not merely from that charted by its political opponents but from that followed by all governments since the war, including its own Conservative predecessors.[2]

This point was stated in almost the exact same terms by the engineers of the Reagan revolution. Reagan ran against Nixon in the primaries in 1972, against Ford in the primaries of 1976, and in 1980 against George Bush, later his Vice-President, on the proposition that the time had come for ending the growth of the state. Reagan, along with free-market conservatives in Britain, advocated monetarist fiscal policies as a corrective to slow economic growth and adopted aspects of the newly enunciated supply-side doctrine to argue for cuts in taxation as the key to economic growth. In both countries the growth of the state and public expenditure were seen as major restrictions on economic performance and, alongside monetarism and supply-side theories, these conservatives developed a view about a more limited role for government, one that sought to undermine the ideas, principles, and values which had contributed to the growth of government and state expenditure in both countries since the war. In this sense therefore it is appropriate to talk about the political economy of conservative capitalism because, although it does depend upon limited technical economic assumptions, it was always much more than this, embodying a critique of the institutions of modern western societies, and in particular of the extended role of the state, and the expectations which this role created among citizens, and the impact of these on economic policy and economic performance.

The aim of this chapter and the next is to outline the basis of the free-market case as it has been developed in recent years by both academic theorists and practical politicians. This will be done in two parts. First of all, we outline the basis of economic doctrines characteristic of conservative capitalism, particularly monetarism

16

and supply-side theories, exploring the ways in which these differ from the interventionist Keynesian approach of the post-war world. Second, we look at the free-market critique of the role of government as it has grown up in relation to Keynesian economic doctrines and political practices. The aim is to produce a clear account of the theoretical basis of conservative capitalism before going on in subsequent chapters to draw attention to the ways in which these ideas have been developed in conservativism in each country and the ways in which they have been implemented. Clearly a political movement within conservatism in each country which explicitly seeks to undermine some of the achievements of post-war governments, including Conservative and Republican ones, is going to set up stresses and strains within conservatism itself and a discussion of this will be the major theme of chapter 4. In chapter 4 we shall be allowing protagonists of the free-market approach to speak for themselves rather than interweaving a critical appraisal which will be left until later in the book, because we believe that it is very important that the scope and coherence of conservative capitalism are fully understood before they are submitted to detailed criticism.

CONSERVATIVE CAPITALISM: ECONOMIC THEORIES

The analysis of the new form of conservatism that has energized both British and American parties of the right requires a brief study of the essentials of three economic doctrines: monetarism, supply-side theories, and Keynesianism. The debates over these doctrines, carried out in the context of claims for the efficiency of the market as opposed to government as the allocator of values and resources, are at the heart of the revival of free-market conservatism. We shall be concerned only with the Anglo-American versions of these debates, though clearly they had international repercussions. We shall discuss monetarism first, and largely in the British context, although most of the monetarist analysis is also accepted by free-market conservatives in the United States. However, first of all monetarist theories have to be considered in the light of the prevailing Keynesian orthodoxy because it was Keynesianism in both academic and political terms which monetarist doctrines rejected. In Britain Sir Keith Joseph, who can in many respects be regarded as the political catalyst for the growth of these views within the Conservative Party, sounded the revisionist free-market position when he argued that:

> Though some die-hard exponents of pseudo-Keynesianism – ideas fathered onto Keynes after his death – refuse to admit error but go on throwing good money after bad, the intellectual climate is changing and critics of printing press economics are no longer regarded as a heretical minority, or worse still hard-faced men who choose to inflict unemployment and stagnation out of sheer malice or doctrine.[3]

There are two important allusions in this passage. The first is to the change in the intellectual climate. During the 1950s and 1960s the works of academic defenders of the market such as Milton Friedman and F. A. Hayek, against the inroads of government, were effectively marginalized by the intellectual and political hegemony of Keynesian ideas, whereas Sir Keith points out quite correctly that the intellectual climate on these issues has changed fundamentally since the 1970s. The second important allusion is to unemployment, in that in Britain the most important indicator of the official acceptance of Keynesian ideas, and all that flowed from them in terms of the role of government and public expenditure, was the 1944 White Paper on unemployment which accepted the basic analysis and prescription of Keynesian ideas in this field. A fuller account of the political acceptance of these ideas in Britain will be left for a later chapter, but it is necessary at this point, when we are considering the basic theoretical ideas of conservative capitalism, to consider the general thrust of Keynesian ideas so that we consider the fundamental change in the intellectual climate to which Sir Keith refers.

After the experiences in the 1930s when both Britain and the United States had experienced a major recession and very high levels of unemployment, it was natural that governments should cast around for new mechanisms for securing full employment and a more predictable economic environment. The fate of the Conservative Party in losing the 1945 general election had convinced majority opinion on the right that governments could no longer survive by a passive acceptance of the levels of employment thrown up by the free operation of the market. The legitimacy of government itself was at stake in relation to employment, and Keynesian theories provided a basis for arguing that government had definite positive responsibilities in this area and also that it had the competence to act in relation to the economy in the light of these responsibilities and the tools with which to intervene in a positive way in the economy. These assumptions produced a profound change in the conception of the role of government on the right, a view which was already accepted by and congenial to those on the left.

In his *General Theory of Employment, Interest and Money* Keynes said 'the ultimate object of our analysis is to discover what determines the volume of employment.'[4] Keynes rejected the view that full employment can be either maintained or restored after a slump by the market mechanism on its own. Levels of employment, at least in the short run, are determined by output: when output in a firm is running at a high level, then that firm will have an incentive to employ more workers. In its turn output is determined by effective demand, which is demand backed by money and resources. Effective demand has two features: individual consumption and investment by firms. In Keynes' view economic recession and consequent unemployment such as was experienced in the 1930s is the result of a deficiency in demand. Not enough goods are being bought and sold and there is not sufficient investment. In its turn this is subject to a multiplier effect so that, for example, a lack of demand for heavy industrial goods will create a consequential decline in demand for other goods and services in the economy. In so far as the economy is left to its own devices, free of government intervention, this depression in demand will intensify in a downward spiral until such time as a demand for the goods which initiated the multiplier effect picks up. Keynes rejected this passive *laissez-faire* approach. Government, in his view, should seek to expand demand in both its consumption and investment aspects and stimulate it by a variety of means which are directly under the control of the central government. It could use its (that is to say, the taxpayer's) resources to increase investment to break the downward spiral of demand, engage in programmes of public works, lower interest rates by the use of the central bank, lower taxes, give subsidies, and increase its own spending. It could therefore increase demand by pumping money into the economy and do this at least in the short term by running a budget deficit. Deficit financing was contrary to orthodoxy in both Britain and the United States at least until the period of the New Deal in the 1930s.

Government could also seek to redistribute income as a way of increasing demand, because money redistributed to the worst-off members of society would be likely to be spent rather than saved, and thus demand for goods and services would be increased. Keynes also believed that, when there is an excess of demand rather than under-consumption, then the government could aim at a budget surplus.

So macro economic management was to become a central function of government. With this would come a change in the role and extent of government, but, perhaps more importantly, a change in public perceptions about what government could do, what it is capable of doing, and what its responsibilities are. Keynes was very clear about these when he wrote in the *General Theory*: 'the central controls necessary to secure full employment will . . . involve a large extension of the traditional functions of government.'[5] This change would extend the proper role of government far beyond what was seen in the classical liberal tradition as being its legitimate function, a good example of which is given in the quotation from Adam Smith, the founding father of classical liberalism given at the head of this chapter, and endorsed by Milton Friedman in *Free to Choose*,[6] a trenchant American defence of the free-market case. The classical liberal case was that the role of government should be restricted to external defence, the provision of a framework of law and order to prevent mutual coercion, and the provision of certain public goods which would not be supplied by the market. Classical liberal theories of the role of government have been an important intellectual influence on the growth of conservative capitalism, and it can be seen immediately how uncongenial they would be to Keynes' economic theories which are predicated on a rejection of the classical liberal view of the efficiency of markets, together with a very limited role for government. Keynes rejected this view and argued on the contrary for a role for and a competence in central government which free-market conservatives reject.

Keynes was not a believer in economic planning in the direct sense of government's having detailed policies about prices and wages and setting precise targets for industry to fulfil. Rather, he assumed that demand management and the fiscal and monetary policies outlined above would be sufficient. Nevertheless a more direct approach to planning was a natural political consequence of Keynes' ideas and here it has seemed to many that the experience of the war was crucial. From the wartime experience it did seem as though government was able to play an effective role in the more direct management of the economy in terms of prices and incomes, if not in the setting of targets for industrial performance. The experience of the New Deal in the United States, and even of Gosplan in the Soviet Union, led to a significant change in attitudes towards the role of government *vis-à-vis* the economy.[7] It seemed to many that there clearly were ways in which the experiences of the 1930s could be avoided in the post-war world. The intellectual power of Keynesian ideas and the experience of the war which seemed to confirm the competence of government were crucial in marginalizing the intellectual case for classical liberalism and *laissez-faire*, and the theory of limited government which went with these views. So much so that Hayek's book, *The Road to Serfdom*, published in 1944, and still a source book for conservative capitalist theories, was effectively ignored.[8]

As was pointed out earlier the political impact of these ideas could be seen most clearly in the 1944 White Paper, *Full Employment in a Free Society*.[9] This White Paper was the outcome of a very long period of gestation and discussion in which Keynesian ideas were very important, and James Meade, a subsequent Nobel Laureate in economics, a follower of Keynes and at the time a member of the War Cabinet's Economic Section, seems to have played a pivotal role. The main thrust of the argument can be seen in a paper considered by the Committee on Reconstruction which argued as follows:

> Government should not be negative or interfere unnecessarily with the growth of business organization, or seek merely to get back to 19th century *laissez-faire*, but rather to promote, by positive action, an increasing volume of employment and consumption.

Unemployment was seen as the central issue after the experience of the interwar years and the capacity to deal with it seemed to be central to the legitimacy of government. The wartime coalition of Conservative and Labour ministers accepted this assumption and with it embraced at least in part Keynesian techniques for dealing with it and the role of the state which these implied. The White Paper embodies this commitment in the following way:

The government accept as one of their primary aims and responsibilities the maintenance of a high and stable level of employment after the war. Total expenditure on goods and services must be prevented from falling to a level where general unemployment appears.[10]

The contrast with pre-war assumptions about the role, limits, responsibilities, and competence of government could hardly be greater. The rise of conservative capitalism in the past fifteen years is a direct challenge to these post-war assumptions. As Keith Middlemas says in his magisterial book on this period, *Power, Competition and the State*: 'There is little here that was not still at issue, forty muddled years later.'[11] It is in the last fifteen years that this Keynesian consensus has been broken and views which in the 1950s and 60s seemed marginalized and antediluvian have come to make the intellectual and political running in relation to economic policy and the role of the state. We need to explain how this change has come about.

The same sort of pattern was true in the United States. Following upon a period of government withdrawal from economic decisions under Eisenhower in the 1950s, John F. Kennedy made the Keynesian doctrine official in the early 1960s. In 1968 Richard Nixon, the newly elected Republican declared, 'We're all Keynesians now'. Reagan, in stark contrast, was a bitter critic of Keynes for having contributed to a deficit mentality favouring ever increasing government spending. Even after his own policies were rebuked by Wall Street in the stock market crash of October 1987, Reagan laid the blame on Keynes, remarking in his first post-crash press conference that 'Keynes did not even have a degree in economics.'

By the 1970s it appeared that Keynesian policies had run into the sand. Particularly after the rises in the oil price in the early 1970s, western economies were faced with stagnation which did not seem responsive to Keynesian remedies. In place of the demand-led view of the way out of unemployment both academic monetarists such as Milton Friedman and political monetarists in Britain such as Sir Keith Joseph, Mrs Thatcher, Sir Geoffrey Howe, Nigel Lawson, Leon Brittan, and Nicholas Ridley,[12] argued that inflation at least in the longer term is the central cause of unemployment and that inflation is largely a monetary phenomenon, which is precisely the result of government's adopting Keynesian assumptions that it was possible for governments to spend their way out of recession. The very techniques whereby government sought to secure full employment were themselves inflationary. They might well bring respite in the short term, but they actually exacerbated the problem in the longer run. Each time demand is expanded by deficit financing, a greater stimulus is required to produce smaller and smaller improvements in the rate of unemployment. The monetarist view is that the techniques which government uses (demand management and deficit financing) are actually inflationary and that these inflationary pressures would destroy the very levels of employment which they were in fact designed to protect.

This analysis seemed to many to be borne out by the simple fact that by the mid-1970s inflation was running at 25 per cent per annum and that unemployment was rising inexorably. In the view of monetarists the causes of unemployment are many and specific such as wage levels, productivity, immobility of labour, unwillingness to take the type of jobs going at realistic wages and the profitability of industry, and world trade. These are all crucial factors in the causation of unemployment. To seek to cure these with the general formula of expanding demand and deficit financing may work in the short term, but, precisely because of these specific blockages in the system, shortages will emerge in the market, prices of domestically produced goods will rise, as will the level of imports and very soon the 'stop' phase of the stop/go cycle will be reached. In this sense, state spending is the central cause of unemployment in that raising the level of aggregate demand requires the state to spend more.

So what in non-technical terms is the specifically *monetarist* element in the monetarist thesis?

TECHNICAL MONETARISM

This book is not the place for the explanation in detail of complex economic arguments that constitute a separate field of study. Nevertheless, it is very important to try to identify the 'core' features of monetarist doctrine because, as we shall see, monetarism *by itself* does not yield the conservative-capitalist critique of the post-war consensus. The policy imperatives of the core doctrine of monetarism are clearly spelled out in the foreword which Mrs Thatcher wrote to Sir Keith Joseph's lecture, *Monetarism is Not Enough*:

It is now widely realized that many of our present economic ills stem from a cardinal error, the belief that inflation and unemployment presented a choice of evils. We have found to our cost that inflationary measures designed in good faith to abate unemployment have eventually intensified it, leaving us with the worst of both worlds.[13]

Inflation causes unemployment and the cure for inflation requires a tight monetary regime.

The 'core' thesis of monetarism is based upon the quantity of money theory that, in the long run, the main determinant of monetary demand or the total level of spending, and thus the main influence upon the Gross Domestic Product (GDP), is the quantity of money circulating in the economy. This can be expressed in the following equation:

$$MV = PQ$$

M is the quantity of money in the economy. V is the average velocity with which this money circulates. Q is the output produced by the economy. P is the price of this output.

This is the thesis of the quantity theory of money. PQ is the nominal domestic product measured in cash terms. This must equal the amount of money in the economy multiplied by the velocity of its circulation. Since velocity is assumed to be nearly constant, it follows that the quantity of money equals the GDP at current prices. Hence changes in the money supply will change GDP (at current prices). It is also part of the monetarist thesis that there is a clear definition of money compared with other financial assets, and that this can be controlled by central banks and monetary authorities. Hence the relationship between money supply and GDP can be made predictable and stable.

Given the relationship between the quantity of money and GDP at current prices (PQ) in the equation, the crucial question then becomes whether an increase in the money supply causes a rise in the P(rice) or Q(uantity of Goods) part of the equation. Will the real resources generated by the economy increase, or will there simply be a rise in the price level for these real resources? It is central to monetarism that an increase in the quantity of money causes a rise in prices rather than in real output. The monetarist view is that a market economy, free of government intervention, runs at the full utilization of resources and maximum output. It follows that any increase in the supply of money divorced from increases in real output will push up prices and hence be inflationary.

Any regime which seeks to reduce or eliminate inflation will seek to expand the money supply *only* in line with increase in real output. Any increase over and above estimated real output will merely add to the P side of the equation and hence be inflationary. Clearly monetarism puts a major obligation on government in relation to the MV part of the equation for, as Samuel Brittan says:

> The government and the central bank are all the time
> influencing total spending (MV). When they determine the
> size of public sector deficits and the way they are financed, when
> they act to influence interest rates or the ability of banks to
> lend, and sometimes too when they intervene in the foreign
> exchange market.[14]

Three immediate policy issues flow from this:
1 A government should seek a neutral supply of money based upon feasible assumptions about the real growth rate in the economy.
2 Inflation, which is regarded as the long-run cause of unemployment, should be the main target of general economic policy. Since inflation is caused by increasing the money supply, both the problem and its solution lie with government. However, this requires that the government should try to stick rigidly to its monetary targets and not be seduced into a general reflation of the economy by panic over what in its view should be short-term rises in unemployment and decline in output.
3 The government and monetary authorities had to have a measure of money which was both clearly definable and within the power of government to control. Broadly speaking, there are three possible definitions in the British context: (a) Sterling M1 which consists of notes and coin in public circulation plus sterling current accounts in the private sector of the UK economy. (b) Sterling M3 which consists of M1 plus UK residents' deposit accounts and saving accounts. (c) Sterling M2 which is basically the same as M3, less bank deposits held for investment purposes. Sterling M3 was the chosen monetary indicator, although in 1980 there was a good deal of pressure to adapt the tighter definition embodied in M1.

In the view of some commentators, such as Samuel Brittan, the indicator chosen was actually less important than the need to stick to it once it was chosen. The whole aim is to provide a binding and inescapable monetary discipline such as had been imposed by the Gold Standard or fixed exchange rates. These policy provisions provide the general basis for the monetarist element in Conservative capitalism and its counter-revolution to the Keynesian model of government-economy relations. It is clear, however, that monetarism can only be a necessary condition of the free-market conservative policy, because it would still be possible to reduce government deficits and the public-sector borrowing requirement by raising taxes. To look at the other conditions which would make the whole package constitute a set of necessary and sufficient conditions for the free-market conservative strategy, we must consider their supply-side proposals and, equally important, their critique of the institutional structures and expectations which the post-war Keynesian world has engendered.

MONETARISM AND FREE-MARKET CONSERVATISM

As we have seen, monetarism as a technical doctrine, as opposed to its use in everyday political debate, has very little to say about the level of public spending in itself. It is more a theory about how it should be financed, together with a vigorous critique of the Keynesian view about its financing. The Keynesian view was that public spending has a function in increasing demand and expanding employment and that this could be achieved by deficit financing or by printing money, the latter being just another way of stating the former. The monetarist rejects this. Either the level of public spending has to be cut in order to reduce, or ideally eliminate, deficit financing; or taxation has to be raised in order wholly to finance the chosen level of public spending. Other arguments have to be deployed in order to show that the latter course will have bad consequences for the economy and that the preferred solution is to attack the level of public spending by reducing state spending as far as possible on public services or limiting it, so that as a result of economic growth public spending will decline as a percentage of GDP. Market-based conservatives have been in the forefront of this argument, both at the levels of theory and practice.

The argument has tended to fall into two parts. The distinction is somewhat artificial but does, we believe, show something about the strategy of the conservative-capitalist counter-revolution. The first is a set of economic arguments to show the deleterious effect of public spending on the private-market sector and the baleful consequences that would follow from trying to finance excessive public expenditure out of taxation. The second is more institutional than economic. Free-market conservatives are concerned to attack some of the assumptions which lie behind ever increasing public expenditure: that it is necessary to secure greater equality between citizens, secure greater economic freedom for citizens to secure greater social justice, together with false assumptions about the capacity of government. Some of the negative consequences of high levels of public expenditure are social effects such as an increase in bureaucracy and discretionary power, and a destructive sort of interest-group competition in politics which has a deleterious effect upon the legitimacy of government.

It is not surprising that the ideas of classical liberalism – derived from Adam Smith and Hume and updated by Hayek and Friedman – should have offered such a useful guide because the issue of the proper functions of government is at the very heart of their work. In Britain this has been particularly helped by the growth of 'think tanks' committed to classical liberal ideas. These include the Institute of Economic Affairs directed by Arthur Seldon and Lord Harris (ennobled by Mrs Thatcher); the Adam Smith Institute; the Centre for Policy Studies, founded by Mrs Thatcher and Sir Keith Joseph to study the social market economy; the Social Affairs Unit and in Scotland the David Hume Institute. In the United States a similar role has been played by the Hoover Institute, the American Enterprise Institute, and the Heritage Foundation. These institutions have been very important in changing the balance of argument about the role of the state away from statist assumptions towards the market, so that the market rather than the state now seems to have the persuasive edge in political argument. These institutes have tended to combine technical economic analysis, usually of a monetarist sort, with an explanation of the relevance of classical liberal ideas about the state and markets.

This free-market conservative emphasis is, in a sense, the counterpart in terms of a theory of institutions to monetarism as a more technical doctrine in economics. In this section we shall explore the main features of this doctrine and consider the ways in which free-market ideas have been incorporated into a broader doctrine of conservative capitalism. Samuel Brittan is quite right when he argues that:

> Behind the smokescreen of the monetarist controversy, therefore lies a much more serious argument between rival views of human society . . . which was papered over by several decades of good fortune and money illusion.[15]

It is vital to bring together this institutional debate with the more technical economic debate. Sir Keith Joseph is quite right when he says in the title of his famous pamphlet that *Monetarism is Not Enough*. In this chapter therefore it is important to try to identify the exact nature of these additional economic arguments which, when combined with strict monetarism, would yield the economic side of the critique of state expenditure.

Broadly speaking, these arguments concern the role of taxation and the role of public expenditure coupled with supply-side suggestions about how to improve the labour market. These suggestions, when combined with strict control of the money supply, were to lead to a longer-run improvement in employment prospects than any degree of Keynesian demand management.

SUPPLY-SIDE THEORIES

In Britain the response to the decline of Keynesianism was monetarism, whereas in the United States supply-side theories became intellectually dominant. Such theories were developed by Laffer and Wanniski and were taken up and made politically salient by David Stockman who became President Reagan's Budget Director, by Congressman Jack Kemp and, of course, by President Reagan himself. As we shall see, supply-side theories are in some respects a complement to monetarism and certainly share many of the monetarist assumptions about the nature of the capitalist economy and the nature of human motivation in the economic sphere. In the discussion of monetarism we quoted from Samuel Brittan's perceptive comment that behind the technical issues of monetarism lay a whole view about the nature of human society and its desirable form. The same is true of the supply-side theories, and David Stockman, in particular, waxes very eloquent on this point when he says in *The Triumph of Politics*:

28

> Its vision of the good society rested on the strength and
> productive potential of free men in free markets. It sought to
> encourage the unfettered production of capitalist wealth and the
> expansion of private welfare that automatically attends it.[16]

On this view, left to its own devices, free of government intervention
and the pressure group politics and pork-barrelling which necessarily accompany it, the free-market economy will produce more and
more wealth and resources. The free market is a source of dynamism
and innovation but it does depend upon individuals using their own
skills and knowledge. If it can mobilize those skills, then the
economy will be dynamic, and the supply of goods will increase,
and there will be sustained economic growth which will benefit all
sections of society including the worst off. Monetarists had been
particularly concerned with the ways in which the inflationary
consequences following from the adoption of Keynesian techniques
actually damaged the economy and led to unemployment; supply-
siders, however, were more concerned with the effect of taxation on
individual incentives and thus on economic performance, and this
in turn meant that they had a direct concern with public expenditure by the central government.

It is central to the supply-side view that people work best when
they have the economic incentive to do so, when they can keep
more of what they earn. This is very clearly set out by Stockman
when commenting upon Democratic proposals in Congress that the
Reagan administration's policies for a major tax cut should be
limited to those earning less than $50,000 a year. He says of this:

> What [they] have never been able to bring themselves to admit
> is that capitalism is the product of capitalists. It is the prospect
> of getting rich and keeping rewards that drives invention,
> innovation and entrepreneurial risk taking. It produces
> intellectual capital as well, which brings about more and more
> output and wealth from farms, factories, and workers already
> there. The idea that our supply side stimulus to capitalists had
> to be polluted with redistributive political ornaments was
> profoundly offensive to me.[17]

A dynamic economy requires individual wealth and individual
incentive if the supply of goods and services is to be increased, and
this is in the direct interests of the poorest members of society as

well as the richest. The poor will benefit more from a general increase in economic growth which would be the result of increasing incentives to individuals than they would under any other alternative which would seek to redistribute resources through state policy. Again Stockman is very clear about this:

> These charges that the Reagan programme was anti poor infuriated me. My Grand Doctrine had to do with just the opposite: it aimed to reverse both national impoverishment and the rampant injustice that characterised the Second Republic's decaying regime.[18]

The solution to the problem of poverty lies in the trickle-down effect (about which more later) whereby the poor will benefit most by the increase in the supply of goods in the economy, which will trickle down to the poor eventually, rather than through a politically led redirection and redistribution of resources which will have negative incentive effects.

Clearly this emphasis on the necessity for incentives immediately implies the supply-sider's concern with tax levels and it is on this point that the academic arguments of Laffer and Wanniski come into play. In their view cuts in taxes will have a positive effect on work incentives and this will increase the supply of goods in the economy which will, on the argument adumbrated above, be to the benefit of the poor as much as the rich. In the view of supply-siders taxation is now at a level at which it is having a heavily disincentive effect on the economy. People will work harder only if they are able to keep what they earn; otherwise they will find other things to do with their time. Only by releasing the inventive energies of individuals would wealth be created. Again Stockman is very clear about this:

> Satisfying the entrepreneurs' requirement for incentives and rewards was as important to the good society as satisfying the claims of the poor for justice. The one could not be had without – indeed was dependent upon – the satisfaction of the other.[19]

Laffer and Wanniski[20] had argued that there is a clear link and subsequent trade-off between taxation and productivity and that the central problem in tax policy is to identify that level of taxation at which both productivity and tax revenue will be maximized. It is possible for government to set tax levels so high that revenues

30

are actually less than they would be under a lower-tax and more productive regime – this is precisely what had happened in the United States: tax levels were having a disincentive effect on performance – and that the same levels of revenue could be raised by a lower level of taxation on a more productive economy. Obviously the argument depends crucially upon how convincing the theory of motivation is behind the argument about the link between productivity and incentives. However, this argument was widely accepted and lay behind the Kemp–Roth tax cutting proposals on which Stockman worked. As it stands, supply-side theory does not imply a need to cut public expenditure because the argument turns upon the idea that cutting taxes will so increase revenue from increased production that existing levels of public expenditure could be maintained. The supply-side view needs much more to turn it into a critique of public expenditure *per se*. In this sense it is rather like the position of monetarism which we discussed earlier. Monetarism is a doctrine, among other things, about how public expenditure is financed, namely by not running a budget deficit, rather than a critique of public expenditure *per se*. It is only when it is combined with arguments about various baleful economic and political effects of high levels of public expenditure, and the corresponding growth in the role of the state, that it turns into an argument for limited government and reduced expenditure. It is the combination of the technical economic arguments, both from monetarism and supply-side theories, with a critique of the values and principles which underlie public expenditure which turn both monetarism and supply-side theory into a powerful practical doctrine in political economy.

Although tax levels were the central issue for supply-siders, there are other aspects of their arguments which are important for their view about how the supply side of the economy could be made to work better. These are particularly concerned with the regulation of the economy by government. Again Stockman is instructive on this:

It implied not merely a tax cut but a whole catalogue of policy changes, ranging from natural gas deregulation, to the abolition of the minimum wage, to the repeal of milk marketing orders, to the elimination of federal certificates of 'need' for truckers, hospitals, airlines, and everyone else desiring to commit an act of economic production.[21]

Again in the view of supply-siders such regulations act as a break on economic performance and, in order to increase the supply of goods in the economy, should be rescinded. In the United States the intellectual case for this approach was developed in the Center for the Study of American Business at Washington University.[22] This centre was founded by Murray Weidenbaum who subsequently became Chairman of the President's Council of Economic Advisers from 1981 to 1982. The various studies produced by the Center argue that by 1979 the cost of federal government regulation of business had reached 102.7 billion dollars and that there was a correlation between the growth in regulation which these figures illustrate and the corresponding decline in the productivity of the US economy which between 1961 and 1965 grew at the rate of 3.6 per cent and between 1976 and 1980 grew only at the rate of 0.33 per cent. The political impact of these ideas on the Reagan administration was immense and in its early years, a vigorous programme of deregulation was carried out, particularly in relation to those agencies charged with the protection of the environment and in protecting the worker from exploitation, and during the early years of the administration significant changes were made to the role and powers of the Environmental Protection Agency, the Occupational Safety and Health Administration, and the Consumer Product Safety Council. The argument was that, instead of firms spending money in meeting these unproductive regulations, they would be able to invest in new products, new plant, and thereby increase economic growth and employment. This idea is also central to the British version of conservative capitalism and many proposals for deregulation have been introduced, for example, the abolition of wages councils in traditionally low-paid areas of employment, on the grounds that having wages artificially fixed discourages individuals from opening new businesses and may well act as a break on employment growth. Examples of these arguments abound but among the most authoritative is the place they hold in *Britain's Economic Renaissance* by Sir Alan Walters who was until recently Mrs Thatcher's Economic Adviser.[23] Enterprise Zones have been established which have abolished virtually all controls on economic activity, particularly those which have been imposed by local authorities. Among proposals being discussed are moves away from national rates of pay within the public sector to take account either of regional variations or of the relative marketability of teachers, for example, in subjects for which there is a high demand; and the abolition of rent controls in order to create greater mobility in the labour market, particularly among the poorest groups in society.

There is no incompatibility between monetarism and supply-side theories. Indeed, they complement one another. The monetarist claims that demand management by central government is inflationary and is a major cause of unemployment. The cure for inflation is a sound monetary policy whereby government borrowing is reduced progressively to zero. This can be done by raising taxes or cutting expenditure and in its narrow form is agnostic about these. The supply-sider holds that the causes of unemployment are due to a lack of output, but unlike Keynes they do not look to a government stimulation of demand to increase output, but rather a reduction of taxation and regulation. It is the view of conservative capitalists that a combination of these policies is more likely to increase growth and cure poverty than state-contrived means to do the same. Most conservative monetarists hold to the supply-side doctrines, which we have been considering, and therefore reject the theoretical option, held open within monetarist theory, to reduce budget deficits by raising taxation, because of what they see as the negative incentive effects which would follow from this. Hence a combination of monetarism and supply-side economics leads naturally into a critique of public expenditure and the principles and values which have underlain its growth since the Second World War. However, before going on to discuss this issue, we need to consider what transformed supply-side theories into Reaganomics or the proposed Reagan revolution.

FROM SUPPLY SIDE TO REAGANOMICS

As we have seen, supply-side theories of taxation presuppose the assumption that the incentive effects of lower taxation will be such as to mean that tax can be reduced, while, at the same time, revenue can be sustained because there will be an increase in productivity, and therefore of tax receipts, even at a lower level of taxation, arising out of increased incentives to work, to take risks, and be mobile. Hence, in principle, a supply-side theory could be compat-

33

ible with sustaining whatever levels of public expenditure prevailed at the time of the tax cut, so long as the rate of the tax cut was estimated to produce the same level of revenue from a lower rate of taxation. There might, of course, be some lag between the tax cut and the growth of productivity, and hence of the revenue appearing, which would pose some interim problems for financing public expenditure, and this might make it prudent to cut back, but the leading assumption is that levels of public revenue can be sustained. However, it would be much more difficult to maintain this thesis if there was to be a major projected increase in public expenditure. This though is precisely what the Reagan administration was planning in the defence sphere. It was held that American defence expenditure had been underfunded during the years of *détente*, and most particularly during the period of the Carter Administration, and that there had therefore to be a massive increase in defence expenditure, an increase which became even more pronounced in the light of the massive sums which were to be committed to the Strategic Defence Initiative.

Given that Reagan came to power on a platform of reducing taxation and increasing one central item of federal expenditure, it was clear that another plank in the programme would have to be a sharp reduction in other spheres of expenditure, notably in the welfare field. For the conservative capitalists who dominated policy opinion in the Reagan administration this was in no way a reluctant conclusion to arrive at. In their view, as we shall see in the next chapter, extensive welfare expenditure had nothing to commend it philosophically, and it had contributed greatly to the growth of government, to the tax burden, and to the regulation of the economy in the health, safety, and minimum wage field. Hence Reaganomics required the adoption of the leading ideas of the supply-side theorists and the monetarists, coupled with a detailed critique of the role of the state in relation to welfare. In their view, the welfare functions of the state had done little to help the poor, and a great deal to damage the economy. It had not benefited the poor all that much in strict financial terms and had certainly increased their sense of dependency which was not compatible with prevailing capitalist values. The poor could be helped more effectively in an indirect way by economic growth which would, as we have seen, trickle down to the poorest sections of society over time. In addition, as the passage from David Stockman showed earlier, a dynamic capitalist economy would also lead to a growth in voluntary help for the poorest sections of society, rather than welfare being seen primarily as the responsibility of government. No doubt in the United States, as in Britain, the experience of the nineteenth century was regarded as salient when, in the context of a dynamic growth in the capitalist economy, all sorts of voluntary agencies arose designed to help the less fortunate. In so far as the state had taken over this role, it was argued in both countries that there had been a disincentive for voluntary effort and charity, forms of giving which Stockman argued would automatically follow from an increase in productivity and tax cuts increasing personal wealth.

In addition, it was argued that, when the state takes on extensive welfare functions, it leads to a corruption of government, because pressure groups always arise in connection with welfare and subsidy programmes which lead to politics as a form of pork-barrel brokerage between interest groups and the turning of elections into auctions of benefits. In opposition to this as David Stockman argues:

> the central idea of the Reagan revolution . . . was minimalist government, a spare and stingy creature which offered even handed public justice but no more. . . . It envisioned a land the opposite to the coast to coast patchwork of dependencies, shelters, protections, and redistributions that the nation's politicians had brokered over the decades.[24]

Hence a critique of the welfare role of government was central to the Reagan revolution, both to allow defence expenditure to increase within the constraints imposed by a supply-side tax cut and in order to restore the health of federal government. There is a very great deal of common ground here between both the American and British forms of conservative capitalism, because, as we have seen on the view of monetarism accepted in Britain, it was not appropriate to raise taxes in order to meet a budget deficit, and therefore public expenditure had to be cut if the monetarist assumptions about inflation were to be sustained. In each case therefore it was very important for free-market capitalists to consider head-on the arguments in favour of a large welfare function for the state and to seek to undermine them. Crucial here were arguments derived largely from F. A. Hayek who was a major influence in this respect on both sides of the Atlantic. Stockman talks about himself in terms of wielding a sword 'forged in the free market smithy of F.A.

Hayek'[25] and certainly in Britain Hayek has been a major influence, as the arguments drawn from Sir Keith Joseph, which we shall consider in the next chapter, show.

However, before moving on to the conservative-capitalist critique of the welfare state and its role in public expenditure, we need to consider one further aspect of the economic argument – the way in which the growth of public expenditure crowds out the private sector and leads to a decline in its resources.

CROWDING OUT THE PRIVATE SECTOR

In 1983 the Conservative Manifesto, prepared for the election of that year, made the following point: 'We have seen how the burden of financing state industries has kept taxes and government borrowing higher than they need have been.' This statement is crucial to the supply-side approach on each side of the Atlantic and it needs some further consideration. The issue contained within it is the 'crowding-out thesis', namely that public expenditure, whether on welfare or state-owned industry, crowds out the private sector. This argument usually contains two strands: physical crowding out and financial crowding out. The physical crowding-out thesis is fairly straightforward, namely that the growth of the non-market sector of the economy produces a higher tax burden for the market sector; and, given supply-side assumptions, discussed above, about the impact of taxation on individual's incentives to productivity and firms' investment, this crowding out will lead to lower productivity and lower investment. Hence it is imperative that public expenditure should be reduced in order to free resources for the private sector in the way of incentives to both productivity and investment. In its turn the reduction of public expenditure will depend upon reducing government-funded services in the field of welfare and, to be effective, this will require not just arbitrary cuts but a full-scale attack on the intellectual case for the welfare state. It will also depend crucially upon withdrawing from state ownership of industry in Britain; limiting and ideally abandoning the place of subsidy for industry in government policy; and limiting the regulatory role for government discussed earlier. This gives the role of the privatization programme in Britain one of its central justifications.

There is also financial crowding out which has been described by Sir Alan Walters in the following way:

> Financial crowding out occurs when the government issues a bond to finance expenditure and that gilt edged security is substituted for an industrial debenture in the portfolio of the private sector. Government borrows money hitherto borrowed by private industry (or persons) and the private sector will have that much less to spend.[26]

Given finite amounts of money available in the market, the need to finance government expenditure and the nature of the security which it can offer will drive out investment in the private sector (i.e. the wealth-producing sector). The additional demand for credit by government will also drive up interest rates which will again have a deleterious effect on private-sector borrowing, given the rates of return which financial investors will demand.

This argument runs directly counter to many of the assumptions about public expenditure made during the period of Keynesian ascendancy, namely that appropriate expenditure could increase the supply of goods and services, increase economic growth, and act as a stimulus to the private sector. These assumptions still lie behind ideas on the left for a public-sector-led reflation and expansion of economic activity. These arguments are rejected by the proponents of conservative capitalism because of the supply-side argument which we discussed earlier. In Walters' view:

> such public expenditures merely increase costs of either labour or capital, this being dissipated in inefficiency or increased rents to unionised labour or capital owners.[27]

The reasons for this lie deep in the capitalist critique of nationalized industry. Walters himself argues, drawing from empirical studies, that the efficiency of resource use is usually lower in those industries than in the private sector and indeed involves a negative rate of return in many cases. He takes the example of public and private provision of bus services in cities and nationalized v. private airlines to support his case and draws from his evidence the conclusion reached by David Friedman in *The Machinery of Freedom* that 'public provision doubles the cost'.[28] The Keynesian argument that public expenditure in industry can increase supply is, in his view, flawed because of the inefficiency of such industry, its low levels of productivity, and the rates of return involved in it. Hence, on this view, financial crowding out is very serious for the private sector because there cannot be a public-sector-led recovery and economic growth.

FISCAL CRISIS AND LEGITIMATION

One way in which many of the arguments we have discussed so far could be put would be to say that both post-war Britain and the United States, following welfarist Keynesian policies, face a fiscal crisis. The revenue needed to sustain the range of public expenditure is now having a negative effect on the private wealth-creating sector on which public expenditure depends. The monetarist and supply-side theories which we have considered illustrate the impact which levels of taxation and budget deficits have on individual initiative and entrepreneurship and investment by firms. Falling productivity and investment in turn have an impact on the revenue raised for public expenditure and this creates a fiscal crisis. The central idea is that public expenditure beyond a certain level cripples the production of wealth and thus tax revenue in the private sector.

Given this analysis, it follows, on the conservative capitalist diagnosis, that the role of government has to be rethought, particularly in relation to welfare and industrial policy in both Britain and the United States, and in relation to the state ownership of industry in Britain. Certainly, as we shall see later, there have been some strenuous attempts by the Reagan and Thatcher administrations to reduce government commitments in all of these areas, to reduce the proportion of GDP taken by public expenditure. This has been a particularly difficult exercise since both governments have been in power during a recession which has increased unemployment and hence associated public expenditure in relation to unemployment benefit. In addition each government came into office determined to increase defence expenditure. Hence, if there is a fiscal crisis following from the commitment to a buoyant private-market sector, together with what is still a large public sector, then this has not been helped by the economic background they have each faced, and by their own preference to increase public expenditure in the defence sphere. Hence it has been important for each government to concentrate on trying to limit the state's role in the sphere of welfare and in relation to industrial policy when it involves public subsidy either to industries or to regions.

However, this has been a central problem in that in the United States since the New Deal and in Britain particularly since the Second World War, government has been perceived as having clear duties in this field in relation to welfare and employment. Indeed, in the case of Britain, the roots of this view go back much further, to the late nineteenth century with the growth of New or Social Liberalism[29] and the growth of the labour movement which stood in clear opposition to *laissez-faire* and minimal-state ideas. These ideas soon became politically potent and had an impact on the 1906 Liberal government which brought in some of the basic welfare legislation. In this sense the positive role of the state in relation to welfare broadly conceived has become important for its claim to legitimacy. These roles and responsibilities are now expected of government. Hence to seek to reduce in a fundamental way the role of government puts its legitimacy at risk. This aspect of the issue has been seen as crucial on the left as well as the right in politics.

We have seen how the issue has been discussed on the right and we shall look in more detail at the arguments in the rest of the book, but it is worth looking briefly at how this dilemma has been perceived on the left. In some sense the problem of fiscal crisis and legitimation is just a specific example of the Marxist claim that a welfare capitalist society of the kind which has dominated British and American public policy since the war is unstable; that a capitalist society cannot sustain high levels of welfare expenditure because both the economic and moral imperatives of so doing are incompatible. They may be compatible in periods of high economic growth, such as were experienced in the 1950s and 60s but cannot be maintained in a more limited economic climate. At the economic level the imperatives of capitalism and of the welfare state are ultimately in conflict because capitalism presupposes the opportunity for private capital accumulation, whereas the welfare state presupposes social expenditure. In a period of high growth a reasonable level of private accumulation can be sustained and welfare expenditure increased. However, in a period of recession this is not possible and the fundamental incompatibility becomes clear. Given a Marxist view about the distribution of power in a capitalist society, namely that it is held by those who own capital and the means of production, then it is clear that retrenchment will occur on the welfare rather than the accumulation side of the equation. That is, welfare will be cut back in the interest of capital accumulation. This point forms one of the main themes of O'Connor's *The Fiscal Crisis of the State*.[30] In these circumstances, in a capitalist society with an unequal distribution of power, the emphasis will be on cutting back the role of the state in welfare.

However, this does create a difficulty in legitimation because of the historic growth of expectations about the role of the state in the welfare field. Once the state has gone beyond merely providing the framework to promote capital accumulation, and free exchange, and certain public goods, as argued by Adam Smith in the epigraph to this chapter, then any attempt to cut back on the welfare function of the state will produce a legitimation problem. This is certainly how the left has seen it. In his *Legitimation Crisis* Habermas puts the point in the following way:

> Recoupling the economic to the political . . . creates an increased demand for legitimation. The state apparatus no longer, as in liberal capitalism [i.e. under classical liberalism] merely secures the general conditions of production . . . but is now actively engaged in it. It must therefore . . . be legitimated.[31]

Hence any attempt to procure a retrenchment of welfare is bound to produce legitimation problems. To go back to the assumptions of classical liberalism and narrow the role of the state means enhancing and increasing the role of the market. However, in Habermas' view, the state will run up against precisely this issue of legitimacy because of the fact that for generations the state has been thought to have a broader role in welfare to compensate for the unfairness and power relations embodied in the market. To go back to the market and limited government will be a very risky business. Issues of legitimacy will arise because of the perceived unfairness of the market:

> Since it has been recognized even among the population at large that social force is exercised in the form of economic exchange, the market has lost its credibility as a fair mechanism for the distribution of life opportunities.[32]

It is our belief that modern conservative capitalism accepts this as a problem because it accounts for two of its central features: an attack on the fundamental normative assumptions of welfare capitalism, and an attempt to rehabilitate the market as a fair system of allocation. The attempt to retrench welfare spending and to rely more and more on the market requires a full-scale critique of the moral basis for welfare provision to break the legitimating spell of the welfare state, together with a vigorous defence of the market as a fair allocative mechanism. Only by changing peoples' attitude to both the welfare state and the market can the potential legitimation deficit be overcome. The long-term success of conservative capitalism will depend crucially upon how far public values can be turned away from the state to the market, and crucial to this is the attack on welfarist values and a rehabilitation of the market, and it is to this that we now turn.

Chapter Three

THE CRITIQUE OF THE WELFARE STATE

While economic doctrines were used to reassure the voters that conservative capitalism had a viable approach to stimulating growth, there was much more to the critique that broke open the rough consensus of post-war politics. It is therefore important to try to identify the main features of this consensus in order to understand fully the successes of the conservative-capitalist movement.

The assumption that public spending must be cut in order to reduce inflation, and to produce new growth and 'real' jobs led many prominent figures in the conservative-capitalist revival to redefine the role of government from a market-based perspective. A good many of these reflections consist in a critique of interest groups and of the socialist and collectivist assumptions of the post-war world. Different arguments are used in different areas of public spending and in this chapter we shall seek to disentangle some of them. We begin with the conservative critique of the growth of the welfare state which is fundamental to the argument.

Welfare expenditure is at the heart of the growth of domestic public spending. The conservative critique involves, broadly speaking, three areas: the development of interest-group pressures around welfare issues which can in turn lead to a reduction in the authority and legitimacy of government; the socialist ideas of equality that lie behind welfare spending; finally, the necessarily bureaucratic consequences of state welfare and the growth of the discretionary power of officials and professionals.

Welfare has come to be seen as central to the legitimacy of capitalist governments. Yet the conservative capitalist wants to claim that in the long run the interest-group pressure which welfare spending generates will undermine government legitimacy. It will also have long-term inflationary effects and these will adversely effect the very people welfare spending is designed to help. Interest-group pressure is seen as related to the open-ended nature of welfare provision.

It is feared that government spending on welfare is, by nature, open ended. There can be no clear limit to the scope of government's responsibilities and thus to its spending. Health is the clearest case of this in the view of the critics. In Britain health provision is free at the point of delivery, except for prescription, dental and spectacles charges. But, even here, there are large exemptions with nearly three-quarters of the population receiving free prescriptions.

In this situation there is no clear limitation on demand but there are obvious limits on supply. In any case, demand for medical care is essentially unlimited because of the nature of medical need. There is not a limited set of medical needs which could be met at a specific level of funding. Rather, medical needs expand with the growth of technology. Until kidney dialysis was invented, for example, there was no way of helping to keep alive those in end-state renal failure. Here a medical need has expanded with technology and, when the state offers free health care or insurance, there is then great pressure to satisfy such needs through the provision of a sufficient number of dialysis machines. The problem is compounded by the growing number of elderly people whose medical needs are greater than those of younger people. In this sense it is argued that the demands on health care are in principle insatiable and will always outstrip supply. Given public provision of health care and the insatiable nature of demand, government is blamed for the failure of supply. Intense pressure is put on the government by both interest groups – patients, patient associations, doctors and nurses – and citizens at large to increase supply. This can only be done by redistributing resources from other areas of public expenditure – for example, from other areas within the health budget; or by transferring it from other programmes within the public sector – the left usually favours defence; or by borrowing to increase spending; or by raising taxes.

Because of the economic diagnosis described earlier, the right is disinclined to take either or both of these last two courses. The same kind of arguments hold true, for example, in education. The need is rather ill defined and the scope for expenditure not clearly limited. Again education, to perhaps a more limited sense than medicine, is subject to new technological needs, as with the introduction of the microcomputer. It is government which is blamed for the failure to supply satisfaction of ever increasing needs.

Many of these areas of public expenditure attract large, articulate and influential pressure groups. There are producer interest groups too, such as teachers or doctors, who are concerned not just with the provision of resources for patients, children, and students, but also with their own salaries and conditions of service. It is frequently the case that producer interest groups in the state sector put forward claims for enhancement of salary which attempt to identify their own financial interests with those of the consumers of the services. So it is claimed that less well-remunerated teachers and doctors will mean less effective services for children and patients. The role of pressure groups within the state sector is something to which we shall return because it can be put into a general theory such as Hayek's, a theory which has been influential in building up the conservative critique.

However, for the moment, a number of things have to be noted. First, given the insatiability of many of the needs to which much public expenditure is addressed, it has an in-built tendency to grow and, as Enoch Powell put the point, 'At nil price, demand is infinite.'[1] Second, once government has taken on responsibilities in these spheres, it is very difficult to escape from them. They impinge so closely upon people's lives, and these people and their supporters have votes. In this sense welfare expenditure becomes central to government legitimacy.

When proposals to cut welfare expenditure are proposed, as they must be, given the individualist conservative diagnosis of the dilemmas of modern society, these are very difficult to legitimize. This is partly because they impinge so closely upon the lives of ordinary citizens, and partly because the process of making the cuts is frequently not under the direct control of the government. They are, rather, made by the professionals involved – the producer interest groups, doctors, health and educational administrators, teachers, etc., who themselves have an economic stake in the maintenance of services as well as a professional concern with patients and students. When cuts are imposed, those who actually implement them adopt what many conservative critics of welfare have called the 'bleeding stump' strategy.[2] The cuts are made in areas which are going to have the most dramatic effect both on direct consumers and the public generally. Examples include closing wards in hospitals, or even whole hospitals, or reducing services to students, or cutting the numbers of students in universities to match decreased resources, rather than cutting in less salient areas such as administration.

Thus in the view of market-based conservatives, public expenditure in these areas has to be cut back, but the political and interest-group pressures make this very difficult to do. Even if expenditure is merely maintained in real terms, this will have the effect of cutting services because of the insatiability of the demands in the respective fields.

The specifics of the conservative-capitalist attack on the welfare state lie in several sets of arguments having to do with a critique of socialist assumptions of welfare and of egalitarianism, the notions of social and economic rights, redistributivism, bureaucracy, interest-group liberalism, and the issue of dependency. Each of these deserves careful attention.

THE SOCIALIST ASSUMPTIONS OF WELFARE

This is allied to a critique of socialist views of the role of public expenditure which many market-based conservatives (at the present time) believe were implicitly accepted by even traditionalist Tories and moderate Republicans in the 1950s and 1960s. The issue here has been most clearly posed by Sir Keith Joseph who has argued that there is a difference between seeing state welfare as providing a minimum level of provision which can be generous but limited, and seeing welfare expenditure as an instrument for social equality or social justice between classes and groups within society. The latter commitment would be inherently open ended and would lead to ever increasing public expenditure. This point, which is probably most indebted to Hayek's arguments in *The Constitution of Liberty*,[3] has been most trenchantly put by Sir Keith Joseph in *Stranded on the Middle Ground*:

We have been misled into forgetting the distinction between maintaining minimum standards and making everything uniform. This distinction has for long been peculiarly clearly understood in England; and now we want to restore it to the centre of our thinking and not let ourselves be confused by

45

muddled talk of 'welfare' and 'equality', which is not the same thing as providing for minimum standards.[4]

To be fully cogent, this attack on the *assumptions* behind 'socialist' welfare policies had to be pursued in more detail and Sir Keith Joseph attempted to do this in his book, *Equality*, co-authored with Jonathan Sumption, as did Milton Friedman in *Capitalism and Freedom*.[5]

Socialist value assumptions about welfare have been threefold: first, that without welfare, the poorest members of society would have their freedom limited by their poverty. Since a free market produces poverty, the poor have to look to welfare to secure basic freedoms which would be limited by poverty. Second, markets, left to their own devices, produce social injustice. The distributive outcomes of free markets would lead to wide discrepancies in income and wealth and these are an unacceptable injustice which can be corrected only by welfare programmes which seek to promote social justice between classes in society. Finally, since the form of social justice preferred by socialists and social democrats was greater social equality, it was argued that in a democratic society it is easier to promote greater equality by social spending through the welfare state than by a direct redistribution of money incomes and an assault on inequalities of wealth.

In a growing economy the fiscal dividends accruing to government would allow the better-off members of society to maintain their absolute position, while the dividend through public expenditure would improve the relative position of the worst off and thus secure greater social equality overall.[6] This was widely accepted on the left and was tacitly accepted as a way of reducing social division by prominent Conservatives such as R. A. B. Butler and Harold Macmillan, and by Presidents Nixon and Ford.

In order to combat this potentially inexorable growth of the welfare state, Sir Keith Joseph argued the need for an assault upon the basic socialist values presupposed by the strategy, an attack which is mirrored in Margaret Thatcher's volume of essays, *Let Our Children Grow Tall*.[7] Indeed, on the first page of these essays she quotes exclusively from Douglas Jay's justification of the welfare state in *Socialism and the New Society*, based on the assumption stated earlier, and challenges it.

Joseph presents a two-fold argument, drawn from Hayek, that

poverty does not cause a loss of liberty. First, freedom is diminished only by intentional coercion and markets do not produce intended outcomes. Thus markets cannot be coercive to the worst off. Second, he argues that there is a difference between being free to and being able to do what one wishes. The command of resources required by the latter has nothing intrinsically to do with freedom which is concerned with the former. He concludes that 'poverty is not unfreedom'.[8] Milton Friedman claims, in addition, that restrictions upon our freedom to do as we wish with our income are every bit as onerous, and even politically dangerous, as limitations on our civil liberties. Consequently excessive welfare expenditures, as a coercive tax on income, positively threaten individual freedom.[9]

These arguments are heavily indebted to Hayek and need to be expanded in more detail. In the classical liberal view of the market as expounded by Joseph, Friedman, and Hayek, the market does not produce an intentional distribution of resources which can be foreseen for individuals. In a market, millions of people act intentionally to buy or sell. At any point activity will prodice a 'distribution' of income, wealth, and other resources. 'Distribution', however, is a misnomer because there exists no agent of distribution. Rather people's possession or lack of resources is an unintentional consequence of millions of different actions with unforeseeable results for any individual. If this characterization of markets is combined with a negative view of liberty such as Joseph, Friedman, and Hayek propound, then it follows that since the distributive outcomes of markets are not intended or foreseen by people acting in markets, then the freedom of those who end up with least is not infringed. They may be poor and hard up, but their liberty is not infringed.

Second, freedom does not involve command of resources because there is a categorical difference to be drawn between 'being free from' and 'being able to'. There are many things which I am unable to do which it would be absurd to regard as a limitation on liberty because no one is stopping me. I am free to run a marathon (in the sense that no one is stopping me). I am just unable to do it. As Joseph says, 'Poverty is one kind of personal incapacity. But it is not coercion. The possession of the money one would like is not the same thing as liberty, simply because both of them are desirable.'[10] Hayek argues that it is the mistake that liberty is connected with resources which has fuelled pressure for redistribution.

So the argument is that the social democratic justification of the welfare state as a necessary condition for the more equal freedom of citizens is an illusion. It has nothing intrinsically to do with liberty. If we make the mistake and assume it, then this gives a moral justification for an ever growing welfare state.[11] Only if this connection between welfare and liberty is broken, will it become possible to restrict welfare to a much more limited level in which it is seen as a matter of benevolence or humanity that has nothing to do with liberty.

Similar arguments, drawing upon the same assumptions, apply to social justice. In the same way as freedom is to be understood as intentional coercion, so injustice can occur only as the result of an intentional action. Because we cannot identify who has been unjust, we turn government into the agent of justice and injustice. The state becomes the focus of resentment on the part of those who are less successful in the market. Interest groups will emerge around those individuals and groups who have not received what they see as their just entitlement from social resources. For example, in Britain and the United States, there are powerful old-age interest groups pressing government for increased pensions in the interest of greater social justice. As Hayek argues:

> our complaints about the outcome of the market as unjust do not usually assert that somebody has been unjust; and there is no answer to the question of who has been unjust. Society has simply become the new deity to which we complain and clamour for redress if it does not fulfill the expectations it has created.[12]

Once welfare is seen as a matter of social justice rather than minimum standards, then public expenditure in this field becomes open ended and subject to severe interest-group pressure.

This analysis suggests that the dangerous consequences are particularly acute in modern society because we lack any clear criteria for distributive justice. There is a divergence of values in society. There is no way in fact that agreement can be secured on different views of social justice – entitlement, desert, need, or the relative weighting of these in distributive terms. Even if we could agree on these, there is no way of weighting the needs of one group against another. If we take a needs view of social justice, needs may be insatiable. In the absence of such an agreement, there is bound to be competition for the limited resources of government, either to redistribute them from other areas of state expenditure, or to bid up state expenditure on one's own preferred view about what justice requires.

It is vitally important, in the view of market-based conservatives, to detach questions of welfare from meaningless questions of social justice and to define a minimum standard independent of assumptions about what a 'just' distribution of resources would be.[13]

The third value which critics regard as having driven the welfare state is that of greater equality in the sense of social equality. The political importance of this is very clear in that the pursuit of greater social equality has been at the centre of socialist arguments in Britain in the post-war world. There has been a move away from defining socialism in terms of public ownership of the means of production to defining it in terms of an egalitarian view of distributive justice.[14] Indeed, in Hayek's view, both Marxist and revisionist theories of socialism, such as those espoused in Britain by Crosland and Jay, are in fact to be characterized by their agreement that socialism is fundamentally about social justice; the disagreement between them being seen much more in terms of *means* rather than *ends*. The Marxist claims that justice requires the common ownership of the means of production; the socialist takes the view that social justice can be achieved within the mixed economy by public expenditure and the provision of services. So a rejection of equality, which Sir Keith Joseph regards as an obsession in British politics, is essential to the change in the values which would allow for a much more restrictive role for the welfare state. The first paragraph of his book reads:

> The object of this book is to challenge one of the central
> prejudices of modern British politics, the belief that it is the
> proper function of the state to influence the distribution of
> wealth.[15]

By linking redistributive schemes to socialist and Marxist views of the state, conservatives were able to turn some of the most popular reforms of the post-war period into the objects of political ridicule.

THE CRITIQUE OF EGALITARIANISM

The attack on equality is not only important in seeking to break the ideological spell of the welfare state, but also because it plays an essential role in the restoration of economic incentives. Conservative views about appropriate levels of tax, for example, also require a reinstatement of inequality such as in the strategy which resulted in the reduction of income-tax bands for the highest paid from 83 per cent to 40 per cent in Britain and similar reductions in the United States.

A defence of inequality is therefore fundamental to the conservative-capitalist argument and is carried out by leading conservative capitalists such as George Gilder whose *Wealth and Poverty*[16] had a major influence in the United States and by Sir Keith Joseph in Britain. The central object therefore is to combat the idea which has led to the fact that 'people of good will have been manipulated into confusing the ideas of eliminating poverty and of raising living standards with egalitarianism.'[17] The case here rests upon two strategies: one is a rejection of the moral case for greater equality, a position common to both individualist and traditionalist conservatives; the other is a vigorous defence by individualist conservatives of the market order.

The first aspect of the argument falls into several distinct parts which can be rehearsed briefly. First, the impulse to equality depends upon envy. Egalitarian politics consists in encouraging the politics of envy. Apart from the fact that envy is a destructive emotion, it is inherently unprincipled and in so far as the defence of equality is dependent upon it,[18] there is no clear limit to the extent of egalitarian legislation and redistribution. Second, in the view of Friedman and Joseph, the direct redistribution of resources is inefficient. It has already gone much further than is economically healthy and has eroded the incentives to create wealth that are central to economic growth, the argument central to supply-side economics as we saw earlier.[19] In addition, an egalitarian regime will involve a strong centralized state which would have to interfere continually in people's lives, displace institutions important to traditional conservatives, and prevent at least significant sorts of 'capitalist acts between consenting adults', in Nozick's phrase.

One of the basic features of egalitarian politics has been a claim that the income and the wealth of the rich are undeserved, but in

Joseph's view, it is impossible to assess merit for the reasons mentioned earlier. There are no agreed criteria of merit or desert and this applies as well to claims about undeserved wealth. Rather, in the individualist conservative view, the basis of evaluation of anyone should be what other people are prepared to pay for their goods and services. In this sense moral merit or desert does not matter. What matters is the result of a person's endeavours and whether others are prepared to pay for it. This is the only criterion of value applicable in a free society. Hence egalitarian strictures on so-called undeserved income cannot be justified.

Sir Keith Joseph also believes, given his views about incentives, that equality would, in any case, require the direction of labour:

> Moreover, the working of a free economy depends upon differentials at every level. Differentials attract people to jobs where labour is scarce; they make long training worthwhile, they require effectiveness, hard work, long work, skilled work and responsibility. Abolish them and the supply of labour for easy jobs will outrun demand, while different, dangerous or unpleasant jobs will be unfilled. How many would rush to endure the rigours and dangers of an oil rig for the pay of a postman? If rates of pay do not recognize the diverse character of jobs it is unlikely that jobs will be filled voluntarily. Direction of labour would be needed.[20]

Although the argument here is much more about the equality of incomes rather than equality in relation to the aims of the welfare state, nevertheless it is all part of a strategy, the aim of which is to argue that social equality is a destructive value and should be detached from a proper view of the role of government and the place of welfare within that role.

In this context it is also important to discuss the notion of poverty, because in the view of conservative capitalists it has become over extended, largely as the result of egalitarian pressures. It is a fundamental assumption of the Conservative critique of the welfare state that it should be concerned not with justice or equality, but with minimum standards.

How are these minimum standards to be identified? If poverty is always relative to a particular standard of income and that income is always rising, then poverty will always be present until that relativity is diminished. In a sense this was part of the social democratic strategy outlined in Crosland's *Social Democracy in Europe*:[21] to maintain the absolute standard of the better off and to bridge the relative position of the worst off by social spending. However, the Conservative critic rejects this in favour of some kind of minimum standard secured by the state, but it is not the duty of the state to seek to flatten out inequalities of income or to redress relative poverty. What is important in the context of poverty is not the *state* but the *market*: 'the market will provide a constantly rising set of minimum standards including rising minimum standards of income.'

There is, of course, a categorical difference between the market leading to this result and seeing poverty as a matter of inequality to be cured by social expenditure. Two strategies are necessary: one is the traditionalist strategy for the state to fix a poverty level which is not defined against egalitarian assumptions, and which, as a safety net, will be low enough not to act as a disincentive to people entering the labour market for low-paid jobs. The second is the strategy of setting the market free so that the economic growth of the market will directly raise living standards for all through a 'trickle down' effect. The best overall strategy would be to secure a basic minimum and leave the rest to the market.[22]

THE CRITIQUE OF SOCIAL AND ECONOMIC 'RIGHTS'

Conservative capitalists reject the idea that welfare or social and economic rights are to be regarded as basic rights of citizenship alongside rights to civil and political liberties. On T. H. Marshall's widely accepted view about the development of rights, civil and political rights developed first of all, followed by social and economic rights in this century.[23] Both advocates and critics of social and economic rights recognize that such rights sit rather uneasily with capitalism because they confer an economic status relating to citizenship independently of the market and the position an individual may achieve there.

During the 1950s and 60s this problem seemed largely theoretical because the success of the mixed economy seemed to allow for the extension of welfare rights, however much they might have been in theoretical tension with the basic philosophy of capitalism. However, with the recent economic uncertainties, this tension has come to the fore. The claim that welfare is a right has come in for much more scrutiny by philosophers and politicians. Mrs Thatcher has frequently rejected what she calls 'the entitlement society', a set of goods which citizens should have by right independently of their individual economic performance. Mrs Thatcher links this emphasis on economic rights with a degeneration of the legitimacy of government when she argues:

> pressure arises in our attempts to resolve our apparent injustices. Frequently the proper channels are discredited before they have a chance to work. . . . The lesson is quickly learnt. Before long the same tactics are applied to other groups which have been meticulous in their respect for our institutions and the rule of law. All too often direct action is taken outside the legitimate social and political framework, is buoyed up and is stimulated by an all too debased rhetoric of fairness and equality. It is 'my rights at all costs regardless of who has to pay' or 'society has a duty to me.'[24]

The theoretical and philosophical backing for this political rejection runs quite deep and depends upon the claim that there is a categorical difference between 'traditional' rights, such as civil and political rights, on the one hand and social and economic rights on the other. The logical difference between these two sorts of rights is translated into the claim that, whereas the first sort of rights are genuine and should be protected by the state, the second sort – economic and social – are not genuine and refer rather to people's wants, needs, and aspirations, rather than basic rights. Any defence of a more limited role for government in the field of welfare must therefore seek to limit the role of rights claims in this field.

The political issue has been put very sharply by Rose and Peters in the important book, *Can Government Go Bankrupt?*

> Individual wants cannot be equated with rights, for everybody wants things that the government is not yet committed to provide, and may never establish as a benefit in law. To define wants and benefits with rights is to make the latter an indiscriminate jury embracing every law on the statute book and every draft bill in the pocket of a lobbyist. Moreover, it implies that citizenship is little more than the by-product of benefits or bribes from government, expanding in meaning as well as in cash value with the growth of government spending.[25]

The political mechanics of this process have been identified very successfully by Enoch Powell, one of the earliest dissenters from the post-war consensus and one of the first defenders of an articulate conservative capitalism when he argues that:

> The translation of a want or a need into a right is one of the most widespread and dangerous of modern heresies . . . [It provides] unlimited fuel for dissatisfaction, it provides unlimited scope for the fostering of animosities between one section of potential recipients and another.[26]

What is the proper distinction between genuine rights and spurious socio-economic or welfare rights? The answer lies in terms of scarcity and its impact on the two different sorts of rights. In its most extreme formulation, the argument is that traditional rights such as the right to life or to freedom of speech are essentially negative and, as such, cost less in terms of resources. The right to life is not a positive right to resources, but the negative right not to be killed; the right to freedom of expression is not a right of access to the media or other resources, but a right to be free from the coercion of others.

The duties which correspond to these rights are essentially negative. We respect these rights when we abstain from coercion, violence, and interference. As such, at least ideally, these rights can be respected in a wholly costless way because respecting them entails *abstaining* from action. In the real world, however, such rights are not costless in terms of securing their protection. People do coerce, hinder, and interfere and these actions have to be prevented by the state through committing its resources such as police forces, courts, prisons, etc. Of course, the range of resources required to protect civil and political rights is on a vastly smaller scale than those which would be necessary through the provision of hospitals, schools, welfare, etc., to secure open-ended social and economic rights. Nevertheless, this undermines the earlier argument that there is a categorical or logical difference between the two sorts of rights and turns the difference into more one of degree than of kind. However, the critics of social and economic rights such as Rose and Peters, Powell and Cranston, still argue that the difference is a significant one.[27]

So, for example, Rose and Peters argue that 'the language of rights is the language of obligation, but the language of benefits is

54

the language of bargaining'. On this view, constitutional rights are categorical and can be met without excessive state expenditure; welfare rights are not – they are open ended and, when linked to political bargaining and pressure groups, will inexorably push up the level of state expenditure. Once linked to the idea of rights, these expenditures will be very difficult to restrict or divert.

Hence citizenship should be defined as equality in civil and political rights, not in socio-economic rights. In addition, any attempt to equalize social and economic resources would in its turn have an effect upon civil and political liberties, as the argument about the direction of labour cited earlier shows:

> What we, who prefer a free market economy, oblige ourselves to remember is that any attempt to relieve the difficulties of human existence by destroying freedom of choice under stable rules, destroys the humanity of law.[28]

Again the moral basis for public expenditure in terms of the citizenship argument is rejected except in so far as the state secures a basic minimum rather than seeks equality and welfare rights. The best hope that citizens should have of increasing their resources is through the free market, not through attempts via state expenditure to equalize resources.

THE MARKET AND THE CRITIQUE OF REDISTRIBUTION

This is the negative side of the welfare case. It is now important to pursue the positive argument in favour of the market as the best means of securing an advance in living standards. The argument here is the so-called echelon advance or trickle-down effect which has been integral to defences of the market since Adam Smith. This argument is central to justifying the view held by conservative capitalists when they argue, as in a Selsdon Group Manifesto:

> The basic principle upon which Conservative policies should rest is that what the public wants should be provided by the market and paid for by the people as consumers rather than taxpayers. The function of the government should not be to provide services, but to maintain the framework within which markets operate.[29]

It is essential to this programme to show that most 'services' are not a response to moral imperatives such as freedom, justice, equality, rights, or citizenship. Second, and as important, the conservative case requires a reasoned defence of the market order, and this is what conservative capitalists have tried to do by drawing upon the classical liberal tradition and its modern defenders, Hayek and Friedman.

There are perhaps three elements to the positive case for the market. The first has already been mentioned – the trickle-down effect in regard to living standards.[30] The second is consumer choice. The third is more a political defence of the market and is concerned with planning and the political implications of a planned as opposed to a free-market economy.

The first is perhaps the least theoretical part of the case. It also relates to the critique of equality and the conservative view about low rates of taxation which have already been discussed. It is that, in a free market, people's living standards rise more quickly than they do under any other alternative planned or semi-planned economy. What the rich consume today will trickle down to the rest of society and that this is the effective means of raising living standards and eliminating poverty. However, it does require inequality in two respects, first for the rich and second for the entrepreneur. Rich people will seek outlets for their wealth; the economy will seek to satisfy their demands for luxury goods; these luxury goods become standardized and trickle down to the rest of the population over time.

To take two of Hayek's own examples, air travel was once a preserve of the rich, as were refrigerators. Indeed, had it not been for the demand for these commodities from the rich, they would hardly have entered the market-place at all and would have remained for the private use of inventors. Because the rich had the economic resources to make an effective demand for such goods, factories producing refrigerators and aircraft were built. From this beginning, what were luxury goods became available to wider and wider groups of people.[31] Without this initial inequality, the goods would not have become available to all or most of the people in society, with consequent rises in standards of living – foreign holidays, air travel, which helps economic growth, frozen and chilled foods, and all the consequential growth in employment and convenience for consumers.

Inequality is also important for the entrepreneur because putting money into new products with no guarantee of success is clearly a risky business. If the rewards of success had been taxed away under an egalitarian scheme for state expenditure, then these successes would never have been achieved. Why should entrepreneurs have to take the risk?

The market in its constant adjustment to changing demands is a world of uncertainty. It is the entrepreneur who identifies a demand and subject to competition and within the law, in the hope of profit seeks to satisfy it . . . without entrepreneurs the system will not work. . . . But there will not be successful entrepreneurs unless there are both substantial rewards for success and sanctions against failure.[32]

The rich and the entrepreneurs are consequently essential to a successful market economy. Conservatives argue in favour of an enterprise culture in which the rewards of success are regarded as necessary conditions for economic growth to be of benefit to all. These rewards should not be subject to the politics of envy and egalitarian countermeasures.

The second argument is about consumer choice. Here the political argument is straightforward, that the market reacts better than a planned economy to consumer choice in giving individuals what they want. The defender of the market will argue that there are rarely shortages of ordinary consumer goods and that this is because the market responds more effectively to these demands than the public sector of a state such as Britain does. To take a case present in political discussion at the moment, does the public-sector educational system at the moment give children the sort of education, training, and discipline which their parents would choose? This has led to a demand to try to introduce a kind of surrogate for the market into the state educational system through vouchers so that parents would be able to exert more control over the education of their children. For the moment this has been rejected as impractical, but this has not satisfied many supporters of market-based conservatism.

The other side of the argument has been a forthright rejection of the case mounted most clearly by critics of capitalism, such as Galbraith, who have argued that the market does not meet self-generated demands but in fact manipulates demands through advertising so that consumer sovereignty is a myth. Thus Galbraith argues in *The New Industrial State*:

> The initiative in deciding what is to be produced comes not from the sovereign consumer who, through the market, issues the instructions that bend the productive mechanism to his ultimate will. Rather it comes from the great producing organization which reaches forward to control the markets that it is presumed to serve and, beyond, to bend the customer to its needs.[33]

This argument (and other versions of it) has been very influential in calling into question the thesis of consumer sovereignty. Counter-arguments are mounted to the Galbraithian critique and the answer is couched in terms of three propositions. The first is that if large-scale companies, including multinationals, are so immune to the market and are in such control of generating demand for their products, why is it that there have been some spectacular failures – Rolls-Royce, Lockheed, BIA? Market forces caused the collapse of these businesses – why would this have been so if Galbraith's thesis is correct? The second argument is that many products put on sale in the market with lavish advertising actually fail. Between one-third and a half of all the products put on the market actually fail. Surely most are introduced with advertising to influence demand. Why should this be so? Sir Keith Joseph cites the Ford Edsel car as the most spectacular example of this feature of the market.[34]

Finally, if Galbraith's thesis, which Joseph regards as the 'conventional wisdom', is true, why should it be the case, as it clearly is, that most firms do market research before production and advertising. It appears therefore that the companies which do this both respect consumer preference and see this as a necessary condition for consequent supervision and advertising. For all of these reasons therefore the conservative defender of the market is prepared to accept the thesis of consumer sovereignty. Bureaucracies and state agencies, by contrast, are not responsive to the market because their members have a separate set of institutional interests to pursue, other than those of the consumer.

The final argument is about the inefficiency of centrally planned economies and the threat to democratic values which they embody. The argument is an old one between socialists and classical liberals.

[margin note: This, surely, argues the case that manufacturers dont consult the buyer]

The key arguments were put in the 1930s by Mises, Menger, and Hayek in laying the basis for modern market-based conservatism. The arguments are epistemological and moral. The epistemological argument concerns the type of knowledge used by economic agents in pursuit of their goals. Hayek and the Austrian school generally argue that a good deal of this knowledge is highly specific to individuals and the circumstances in which they find themselves. In a sense it is tacit knowledge which cannot easily be put into propositions. It is a matter of knowing *how* rather than knowing *that*. Many people make use of this sort of knowledge when they choose one product rather than another; entrepreneurs use it when they conjecture about demand. It is a matter of hunch and intuition in highly specific and particular circumstances.

Although the knowledge is not theoretical or propositional, it is vital to the efficient and effective pursuit of economic goals. It is a type of dispersed knowledge which could never be available to a central planner – not just for technical reasons, for example, that computers are not powerful enough, but for reasons of principle: the knowledge itself is dispersed and specific. Because this knowledge is not available to the planner, planning will be less efficient than the market, and in particular the price mechanism, in co-ordinating individual demands on the economy arising out of the specific circumstances of individuals to which a central plan cannot be responsive. So planning the economy, even in the modest fashion attempted by post-war British and, to a lesser extent, American governments is bound to be more inefficient than the free market.

The second objection is moral and this in turn has two aspects. The first is that planning in some sense presupposes moral agreement. Otherwise there could be no priorities in the plans set up, whether by politicians, bureaucrats, or interest groups. It may work in wartime, but the circumstances of war are quite different from peacetime in that the need to defeat the enemy overrides every other sort of disagreement. In peacetime pluralism reasserts itself and it is unlikely that in these circumstances sufficient agreement could be attained in order to secure anything like a long-term plan. There is, *pace* President Carter, no moral equivalent to war to galvanize society.

This critique does not merely apply to overall attempts at planning. It also applies to specific areas in which the government seeks to assert a view of the public interest in the economy, for example, in the field of incomes and prices policy. In Britain particular scorn was expressed by market-based conservatives for Prime Minister Heath's attempts in the latter part of his premiership to produce a specific policy for prices and incomes through the Price Commission and the Pay Board. They thought it was ludicrous to assume that there were objective answers to the question of relative rates of pay to be found independently of individual evaluations in the market. The same attitude is taken toward 'comparable worth' in the United States where job evaluation studies are used as a basis for establishing an 'objective' scale of worth for given occupations, so that male- and female-dominated occupations may be brought into parity.

All of these arguments are therefore attempts to shift the agenda of politics from the public-state to the market-private sphere, and in subsequent chapters we shall see how far American and British politics have been affected by these ideas. However, before doing that, it is necessary to consider three further aspects of the critique of social democracy and liberal capitalism: the role of bureaucracy, the stalemate produced by 'interest-group liberalism', and the impact upon government itself of the welfare-state mentality.

BUREAUCRACY

The critique of bureaucracy mounted by conservative capitalists is concerned with several things: the character of bureaucracy as a producer interest group with goals and purposes distinct from the purpose of the enterprise being undertaken; the lack of response to consumer demands; and, finally, the role of bureaucratic discretion in relation to the rule of law, particularly in circumstances in which illusory or spurious claims to social justice arise.

The first aspect of the critique is heavily dependent upon the analysis of bureaucracies produced by the public-choice school of political analysis. The key books in this genre are Niskanen's *Bureaucracy: Servant or Master? Lessons from America* and *Bureaucracy and Representative Government*[35] which disputes the account of bureaucracy found in Hegel's *The Philosophy of Right*, that the bureaucracy is the universal class whose interests are the same as those of the state – seeking the public good and implementing it. Niskanen's view, popularized by the Institute of Economic Affairs, challenges the 'public servant' view of the civil service, largely by applying an analysis of rational maximizing behaviour drawn from public choice and economic theory to the behaviour of bureaucracies. In this view, civil servants and public officials seek their own advantage by maximizing agency budgets as a means of obtaining greater prestige, job opportunities, regrading, and more power. In the view of the public-choice school, civil servants are able to do this largely because they are not responsive to market mechanisms. If we compare the behaviour of a firm operating in a market, we can see that governmental agencies do not have to reveal the cost of a unit of output at different levels of production. This means, in effect, that bureaucracies have a monopoly of information about the costs and benefits of what they are doing. Elected politicians find it very difficult to challenge this monopoly in an effective way. When cutbacks occur, bureaucrats are able to use their information and the control that comes with it to counter-attack by the 'bleeding stump' strategy mentioned earlier in the chapter.

The only strategies available to deal with this are: to reduce the amount of money available for the civil service by imposing cash limits on it; to seek greater competition between agencies, a strategy with obvious limitations; to introduce external-change agents to maximize efficiency and to reduce waste; and finally either to contract out civil-service responsibilities to the private sector or, more radically, to privatize them completely. All of these have been tried by both governments. In Britain, we have seen since 1979 a reduction of manpower; MINIS (Management Information System for Ministers) models of management efficiency applied particularly at the Department of the Environment and the Ministry of Defence; the introduction of a special unit, the Rayner team, to seek economies and root out waste; and the privatization of bureaucratic responsibilities.[36]

The second element of the critique of bureaucracy is more theoretical. Once government takes on the role of distributing national resources to industry or to groups of individuals in pursuit of social justice, then in the nature of things there cannot be wholly general rules which can govern the distribution of these resources. The administration of such policies must lead to a very great deal of administrative discretion. As John Gray argues, defending this view:

> It would also entail according to governmental authorities a
> span of discretionary power over the lives of citizens which

would be intolerable even if it were not likely to be abused in the service of private interests.[37]

Take the two examples which Gray gives to illustrate the point. If we have a state system of medicine, but have no clear and agreed idea of the nature of medical needs and the relative weight and urgency of particular needs, then the claims of need cannot be easily ranked against one another according to general rules. The consequence of this in Gray's view is that:

> Bureaucratic authorities charged with distributing medical care according to need will inevitably act unpredictably, and arbitrarily from the standpoint of their patients for want of any overarching standard governing choice between such incommensurable needs.[38]

Similar arguments apply to housing policy, which is Hayek's own example: those who live in publicly provided houses will find that their lives will be infected 'with uncertainty and dependency on unforeseeable bureaucratic interventions.'[39] An example of this would be local bureaucratic-political control of council houses where dependency is created on local council housing departments which will find it difficult to deal in a rule-governed way with people whose housing needs are radically different. This is *not* because of malfeasance on the part of bureaucrats; it is inevitable when decisions have to depend on individualized circumstances. In this situation the radical solution is to seek the highest degree of privatization of the public housing stock possible, and this, of course, is what the British government did with its policy of privatizing council housing by offering them for sale to tenants at very favourable rates. In the sphere of health the solution would be similar although in Britain virtually impossible to achieve.

The important point from the conservative perspective is that this would reduce the scope for administrative and bureaucratic discretion and reinstate in a strict sense the rule of law as understood in classical liberalism. Once the state gets into the business of subsidization, intervention in the economy, or large-scale welfare provision, the rule of law is undermined because then the aim of government is to produce particular results. The administration connected with such policies must be to some degree arbitrary and discretionary.[40]

INTEREST-GROUP LIBERALISM

The first part of the argument about bureaucracy, that it over-supplies in its own interests, is to treat bureaucracy as just another interest group in society. As we saw in the argument about social justice earlier in the chapter, the understanding of interest groups is a central feature of conservative arguments, and it is to a wider elaboration of this thesis that we must now turn.

There are various aspects to the critique of interest groups in social democratic societies such as Britain and the United States, but the most important for our purposes concern three things: the theory of interest groups developed by conservative thinkers such as Hayek, the effect of interest groups on party competition, and the phenomenon described by Theodore Lowi and Samuel Beer as pluralist stagnation. Taken together these various features of interest-group politics are the target of a vigorous critique of British and American politics in the period of the post-war consensus.

Interest-group politics has been a central feature of the way in which political scientists in western countries have sought to conceptualize the major features of Western European societies. Pluralists have tended to reject normative theories of participatory democracy as naïve and unrealistic in modern, complex, large-scale societies and have seen direct participatory democracy as applicable, if at all, to small-scale societies such as the Greek *polis* or the Swiss *canton*. In their view, democratic politics is about the accommodation of rival interest groups, no one of which has countervailing power over the rest. The state, or the government, is not able to govern without regard to interest groups in the activities of which the major interests in society are thought to be represented. At the same time, as interest groups thus constrain government, no single interest group can outweigh all the others, and it is in the competition between interest groups that, as Robert Dahl has argued, democracy resides. Interest groups wax and wane. If the interests are important enough, they will command attention. In the work of classical pluralist thinkers, such as Dahl and Kornhauser, the actions of interest groups are a bulwark against domination by individuals. In belonging to interest groups of various sorts, citizens develop a sense of corporate identity. They develop information and contacts as well as cohesion. In this way as Hegel first predicted, *contra* Rousseau, the membership of inter-

63

mediate association is vital to the growth of civic sensibility. It cannot be developed by isolated individuals acting alone. If inter-mediate groups are not strong, then there is the possibility of the development of a mass society the members of which will be prey to totalitarianism and centralized political mobilization.

In this sense therefore interest groups are a central defence against the development of totalitarianism. Because pluralists see these groups as autonomous and in competition with one another, and because any individual is likely to be a member of more than one group, a plurality of groups will be maintained and this will sustain a wide variety of interests and values which will be important to a democratic society. Democracy then is not so much about individual participation in politics as about pluralistic compe-tition between interest groups. As Dahl puts the point:

> Independent organizations are highly desirable in a democracy, at least in a large scale democracy, whenever democratic processes are employed on a scale as large as the nation state, autonomous organizations are bound to come into existence. They are more, however, than a direct consequence of democratizing the nation state. They are also necessary to the functioning of the democratic process itself, to minimizing government coercion to political liberty and human well being.[41]

However, this picture is rejected by individualist conservative critics of interest groups on the ground that the consequences of interest-group pressure is destructive of social stability. The reason is concerned again with the role of government going beyond the provision of basic public goods such as defence and law and order. In so far as government goes beyond these functions and seeks social justice through welfare and social security, going beyond a minimum, or providing subsidies, or seeking political allocation of resources through planning, or the shape of production by regional policies and so forth, government will encourage the growth of more and more interest groups relating to those sorts of government provisions, services, and subsidies.

Then a rather destructive form of interest-group competition will arise. The demands of interest groups in these contexts are insatiable just because in the case of things their welfare, health, and education demands are in principle open ended. Furthermore, the demands of various groups are incompatible. Given a limited amount of public expenditure, an increase in resources for one group is likely to be at the cost of some other group. Either that or the pressure to meet the needs of the most important groups will place an impersonal pressure on public expenditure which will make people worse off in the long run. Samuel Brittan has provided an elegant example of how he sees this thesis working. Given that the only resources which governments have are drawn from taxation or, to put it another way, from our fellow citizens, he argues:

Each party to the bargain is likely to be given some concession which is only mildly damaging to the rest of the community. One group may receive an injection of public money to finance a wage increase unavailable in the market; another large section will receive rent controls and subsidies; and another large group 'mortgage concessions' leading to overinvestment in dwellings. But the harm done by the sum total of these restrictive practices and special deals is very far from mild. Each of us suffers from the concession to special groups to which we do not belong. We would all be better off in the not so long term if we could achieve the only horse-trading worth doing, i.e. an agreement by every group to relinquish its special privileges on the understanding that other groups did the same.[42]

Once these concessions have been granted by government, they are very difficult to withdraw. A state which confined its scope to the provision of a narrow range of public goods and a minimum level of welfare provision would not be so susceptible to interest-group pressure. In the view of traditionalist as well as individualist conservative critics the problem is exacerbated in Britain. The Labour Party is seen by them as the embodiment of a set of interest-group pressures in the form of the trades unions, the first significant organized pressure groups to have a central constitutional role in a ruling party.

The problem is further exacerbated in a political system characterized by a party-based electoral system in which the limits of government are not antecedently fixed, for example, by a constitution or Bill of Rights. Given that government is in the business of providing goods, services, resources, subsidies, pay, welfare, education, health, etc., it becomes very difficult for parties, in competition with one another for votes, to be outbid in the range

65

of interest groups which it promises to satisfy if elected to power. Hence, once government takes on the role of providing the range of services indicated, it is very difficult for political parties not to turn electoral politics into a necessarily unprincipled auction in which benefits are promised to different sorts of pressure groups.[43] In the view of many critics this process reached its zenith in the 1983 British election and in the 1984 American presidential election when, in their view, both the Labour Party manifesto and the candidacy of Walter Mondale for president consisted of little more than a list of promises to a coalition of interest groups without any great thought about how the range of promises hung together and the overall coherence of the programme. In Britain this led in a hilarious case to the Labour Party's having to explain why it sought to ban fox-hunting – by and large not a sport supported by Labour voters – and not angling which is a popular working-class sport, but which in the view of critics is no less cruel. A trivial example no doubt, but one which in the view of critics clearly represents the defects of interest-group politics.

In the view of critics such as Sir Keith Joseph the pattern of the post-war settlement and the inexorable rise of interest groups has led to the middle ground moving in a leftward direction as the government has taken on more responsibilities. This 'ratchet effect' has made it seem, so it appeared in the mid-1970s, that the Conservative Party had to be inextricably committed to a leftward movement in society as the result of all the factors discussed above. Only a determined move to 'roll back the frontiers of the state' and to try to divest the state of at least some of its over-extended role could lead to a mitigation of interest-group pressure. The same observation was made of the Republican Party by Milton Friedman.

In the view of critics such as Hayek and observers such as Beer,[44] the growth of interest-group politics living in a symbiotic relationship with the growth of government has been a central institutional factor in stagflation. The combination of high unemployment and high inflation, against all the assumptions of Keynesian economics, was attributed to the influence of interest-group pressures on the supply side of the economy. Take, for example, the issue, which Beer cites, of trade and industry spending by central government. By 1970 the British government was spending a billion pounds per year, 6 per cent, of all central government expenditure on subsidy to private industry, but it seemed equally clear that by the mid-70s this colossal amount of money had done very little to modernize British industry and a good part of the reason for this could be found in interest-group pressure.

The argument here is very indebted to public-choice theorists such as Buchanan and Tullock. In their view interest-group pressures mean that governments allocate resources not in terms of principle or widespread moral agreement in society, because this is not available for reasons which were discussed earlier, but in response to the political power and clout of interest groups. This is the point made in a discursive way by Brittan in the above quotation, but in the view of the public-choice theorists this poses central problems for democracy. The reasoning here is as follows. The gains made by interest groups, or distributive coalitions as Olson calls them, are highly concentrated in the members of such groups, and the possibility of obtaining such concessions helps to mobilize support for such interest groups and to account for the political pressures which they are able to exert. However, the costs of such concessions are widely dispersed in society among taxpayers and voters. The gains are palpable and immediate; the costs are dispersed and marginal. The costs of each concession to the dispersed and fragmented citizenry are small, the gains to the interest groups are large and immediate. Hence, it is very difficult to mobilize citizens against interest groups which are so concentrated.

However, although the costs to each taxpayer for each interest-group concession are small, the incremental costs are very large, particularly because they inhibit economic growth, innovation, and change. Interest-groups become entrenched over time and indeed can come to exist in a symbiotic relationship with governmental agencies when these are the agents of resource allocation and subsidy. We can take two frequently cited examples. In the United States it is argued that the Interstate Transport Commission, far from being a neutral regulatory agency acting in the public interest, has in fact become the spokesman for the American railroads; in Britain it is argued that the Ministry of Agriculture has become the representative of farming interests. If this point is conjoined with the same theorists' approach to bureaucracy which we discussed earlier, it can be seen to be a powerful analytical theory. If an interest group increases its resources to its members by a price rise, a subsidy, or a tax concession, then this will not only increase the resources available to that group, it will also produce inefficiency and rigidity for two reasons. In the first place it will encourage further resources into the area where the concession has been gained and, since the concession has been made for political rather than market reasons, this will result in further inefficiencies. Second, again because the interest-group concessions have been made for political rather than market reasons, they will prove difficult to withdraw in the light of changing economic circumstances.

Mancur Olson argues in *The Rise and Decline of Nations* that interest-group politics of this sort produces social rigidities which affect the supply side of the economy and which produce stagnation. He applies this analysis to the pattern of economic development in some OECD countries and argues that one element in the superior economic performance of Germany and Japan, compared with Britain and some regions in the United States, is the result of the fact that the Second World War broke down interest-group rigidities in such countries. It has often been argued that the war was paradoxically beneficial to Germany and Japan because industrial regeneration, when it occurred, meant that they re-equipped with the latest technology. Olson argues that, while this may be true, the breakdown of interest-group rigidities was also very important. As we shall see later in the book, in Britain the so-called growth of corporatism in the post-war world gave an institutional and therefore even more rigid role for interest groups such as the Confederation of British Industry and the Trades Union Congress, particularly the latter in the period 1974–9 with the social contract between unions and the Labour government.

The solution to the problem is seen as twofold. The first is, as Brittan argues, to induce interest groups simultaneously to give up special interests. This is a Hobbesian problem for which there is no clear solution. It is obviously easier after a war when rigidities have broken down, but it is difficult to achieve in normal conditions. Indeed David Stockman's *The Triumph of Politics* is a plaintive account of how someone who thought that it was possible received a political education from Congress. The second task is for government. It is not surprising therefore that a good deal of the work of the public-choice theorists has been in the area of trying to think up new constitutional restraints on government to limit its power in this field – a labour which is more salient in the United States with a written constitution than it is in Britain.

The lesson to be drawn from all of this in the view of conservative critics is that the very extension of the role of government has in fact weakened it. In order to mobilize legitimacy and consent, government has to appease major interest groups which are not constrained by either long-term considerations or a concern for the public good. Because government has extended its responsibilities, interest groups have moved in on these more extreme responsibilities in a competitive way, leading to economically dangerous levels of public spending.

This kind of diagnosis lay behind the sort of argument popular in the mid-70s about ungovernability. As Professor Anthony King elegantly put the point: 'The reach of British government exceeds its grasp; and its grasp . . . is being enfeebled just at the moment when its reach is being extended.'[45]

The traditionalist argument for the first proposition is clear. The individualist conservative argument for the second is also latent in what has gone before, namely that government in extending its responsibilities has become enmeshed in open-ended commitments which are electorally important in the fields of welfare, social security, health, and education. Indeed government seems to have a widely assumed responsibility to take care of a range of unforeseen consequences, even in the wholly private sector – King's own example of this is the fact that the British government felt constrained to step in to deal with the consequences of the collapse of the Court Line, a wholly private holiday firm which went bankrupt. Some market-based conservatives criticized the US government loans to Lockheed and Chrysler on the same basis (though both are now profitable firms). The only solution is to try to narrow the framework of government and the sphere of its responsibilities. As King says:

> Academic political scientists have traditionally been concerned to improve the performance of government. Perhaps over the next few years they should be more concerned with how the number of tasks that government has come to be expected to perform can be reduced.[46]

This plea is echoed in Mrs Thatcher's statement:

> There is now an imperative need to stop the growth of government and to re-establish urgently just what the functions of government are. It is a bitter irony that as government has

aspired to do more and more it has become unable to discharge these priorities and its obligations to ensure that we have military stability and reasonable security at home and abroad. Thereafter, it can consider the other functions where it has a traditional but not necessarily a monopoly role . . . My first call, therefore, is for a defined role for government. There should be a demarcation between the public and private sectors in that both can contribute productivity to the 'mixed economy'.[47]

A critique of the post-war role and responsibilities of government therefore lies at the very heart of the conservative-capitalist case in Britain and the United States.

THE DILEMMA OF DEPENDENCY

Even if a way could be found to make government provision of welfare efficient and non-disruptive to the economy, some conservatives argue that it is counter productive because welfare creates dependency among its clientele. The issue of dependency, however, plays differently as between individualist and traditionalist conservatives and constitutes something of a dilemma for the ideology of conservative capitalism.

Dependency theorists, such as Lawrence Mead in his book, *Beyond Entitlement*, and Charles Murray in *Losing Ground*, argue that economic growth may be a necessary condition for improving the position of the poor, but it is not a sufficient one.[48] Poverty is not just a matter of the possession of resources, it is also a question of the cultural attitudes and dispositions of many poor people. Under the welfare state the poor have grown increasingly reliant upon the state and lost their sense of initiative. The work ethic has been weakened. Many poor people have lost their sense of obligation to their family and to the wider community.

The same arguments have appeared recently in Britain in the speeches of John Moore, the Secretary of State for Social Services, and in a symposium sponsored by the Centre for Policy Studies that was addressed by Mead, Murray, and Richard Nathan, all of whom are in the forefront of the dependency movement in the United States. Posed in terms of welfare and dependency, these issues have a close bearing on Mrs Thatcher's interest in Victorian values which she sees as centring on the qualities of self-reliance and independence.

So strong is this view in the United States now that the American Enterprise Institute (AEI) has recently published *A Community of Self-Reliance: The New Consensus on Family and Welfare*, a study that its distinguished authors regard as the statement of a generally agreed perspective on dependency. They start from the point that poverty is as much rooted in personal behaviour as in lack of resources, and that these forms of behaviour have been encouraged by the rather indiscriminate form of modern welfare:

> some observers have come to see existing welfare policy as toxic; they believe that it is damaging to the very poor it intends to help. Even if welfare policy has not caused the widespread behavioural dependency that has now become so highly visible, at the very least existing public policies have done little to remedy the situation.[49]

Welfare's separation of clients from the world of work leads to an abandonment of the values necessary to paid employment and, indeed, family life as well. Existing welfare policies may encourage the break-up of families by making the cost of separation easier to bear, by not requiring the fathers of illegitimate children to support their upkeep, and by mitigating the costs of promiscuity and fecklessness.

The American Enterprise Institute report concludes that:

> Many of the poor need order in their surroundings and in their lives; they need the intellectual and moral skills that enable them to escape from poverty and to live as full and independent citizens. Low income is comparatively easy to remedy; to overcome behavioral dependency requires much more human, complex and difficult engagement.[50]

It is argued that successful behaviour to stay out of poverty is not mysterious and includes completing education; getting married and staying married; staying employed, even if at a level of income and conditions below one's absolute aim.

Money income does not define poverty in this view; character is as important. The AEI report comments that 'the most disturbing element among a fraction of the contemporary poor is an inability to seize opportunity even when it is available and while others

71

around them are seizing it.' This emphasis upon character, internal morale, and personal control as a central aspect of poverty is not at all new. It was a central feature of the approach of the Charity Organization Society in Britain in the nineteeth-century[51] as well as the 'settlement houses' in the United States. In this view, resource provision had to be discriminating and discretionary in order to encourage the development of personal habits conducive to survival in a competitive society.

In both Britain and the United States the emphasis in this approach is upon the family and the centrality of the role of the father in maintaining it. The objective is to encourage men to have a greater sense of family responsibility towards their own offspring and to provide a role model for them so that there can be a break in the generational cycle of dependency and deprivation. The point is made graphically by conservative commentator George Gilder:

> In the welfare culture money becomes not something earned by men through hard work, but a right conferred on women by the state. Protest and complaint replace diligence and discipline as the sources of pay. Boys grow up seeking support from women, while they find manhood in the macho circles of the street and the bar or in the irresponsible fathering of random children.[52]

Gilder's assessment fits into a broader conservative critique of feminism that lays part of the blame for the feminization of poverty to attitudinal shifts about gender roles.

Both the AEI report and such conservative spokesmen as Michael Heseltine[53] in Britain suggest that part of the solution is to bring welfare recipients into the workforce by threatening them with a loss of benefits. 'Workfare' programmes reinstate the nineteenth-century notion of requiring work in exchange for welfare. A variation on this approach known as 'learnfare' makes the continuance of benefits conditional on dependent school-age clients' remaining enrolled in classes.

Against the charge that this demonstrates a lack of compassion, the defence is that inducing a condition of dependency is not a compassionate act either. Workfare may be harsh in the short run, but it can break the cycle of despair. Furthermore, there is the philosophical point that, if benefits are conferred without reciprocity, that is without discharging a concomitant obligation, then this will undermine the basic dignity of recipients and set them apart from the citizenry generally.

This last point goes to the heart of Lawrence Mead's argument that the rights guaranteed in a democratic society imply a corresponding obligation to live in terms of the dominant values of the society within which the individual rights are granted. After all, the very existence of rights depends upon that society and its values; why should not the obligations equally require a recognition of social values? Since democracy rests upon the capacity to make choices, and rights are accorded to protect this capacity, why should public policy on welfare undermine the very capacities on which democratic citizenship depends?

These arguments are powerful, if it is assumed that the problem of dependency is as it is presented by conservative capitalists. There is room for argument here. Frances Fox Piven and Richard Cloward in their book, *The Mean Season: The Attack Upon Welfare*,[54] dispute the statistical basis for assuming that the problem of dependency is widespread and argue that the real problem is lack of the sort of opportunity that rewards the character traits Gilder and others are concerned about. Nevertheless, the conservative-capitalist critique of dependency picks up on the resentment that working people feel toward those who receive public benefits.

It is worth noting, however, that the tension between individualist and traditionalist versions of conservatism poses a dilemma on the question of dependency. We noted earlier that individualist conservatives reject conceptions of social justice as a basis for public policy because there is no consensus possible about issues such as merit, desert, or need. such claims are inherently subjective. The market is best suited to accommodating this reality since it allows for individual valuations of the worth of each person's claims and efforts. The state, on the other hand, cannot secure social justice precisely because of this diversity of moral valuations.

But the dependency argument assumes something different: that there is indeed a desirable set of values relating to human character that define individual virtue in a capitalist society. The proposal of the American Enterprise Institute and others who accept this analysis is that these should be the basis for public policy on welfare.

In order to avoid incoherence, conservatives must be able to explain how it is that one set of values concerned with individual virtue can be the concern of the state, while another, relating to the proper level of resources for an individual, cannot be. There is a further dimension to the argument and it concerns the capacity of the state. The state is presented by Hayek and Friedman as lacking the capacity to involve itself with distributive questions because of the complex, fragmented, dispersed, and largely tacit knowledge that is required. The market is thought to be the institution that responds most efficiently to this aspect of the human condition. For Friedman, the state's only role with respect to welfare would be to provide subsistence resources through a 'negative income tax'.

Yet the Workfare/Learnfare policies assume that the state has a role in seeking to develop individual virtues in welfare recipients. Certainly a state which gears its policies to the maintenance of certain virtues will be a long way from the limited government prefigured by Adam Smith and his individualist conservative followers. It is not a path that would attract the advocates of a neutral stance regarding economic behaviour as well as social and personal behaviour understood in a wider context.

Conservative capitalists who accept dependency theory do seem to imply that we have some kind of insight into what forms moral dispositions when it comes to questions of welfare, but that such knowledge of moral concerns is totally unavailable to democratic governments as they address issues of redistribution, need, and desert more generally. Dependency theory leads straight to traditionalist paternalism and the idea that 'Victorian values' can form the basis for state policy, a reversal of *laissez-faire* in the most sensitive areas of human conduct.

There is as well the problem of hypocrisy. While the poor are to be regulated to induce moral behaviour by the terms of dependency theory, the rich are given licence to be indulgent by the terms of free enterprise and *laissez-faire*. There remains the criticism that dependency-based policies amount to the class-based imposition of values upon the poor that are merely a pretence on the part of the rich – the central criticism of the Victorian moral order.

We will see in the next chapter how this and other tensions within conservative capitalism were manifest in the process of implementation of policy prescriptions. We will explore the basis of the split within conservative capitalism between its older traditionalist establishment and the newer forces of market-based individualist conservatism. To the extent that a fresh conception of conservatism was laid before the public, the grounds for political success were prepared. That this individualist version of conservativism justified policies of monetary and fiscal restraint on broader philosophical grounds meant that the new political formation could move forward on a broad front. To the extent that underlying philosophical differences remained among conservatives, however, there was the basis for serious policy disputes at crucial moments in the policy-making process. It is important to establish the conceptual basis for these differences at the outset.

Chapter Four

TRADITIONALISTS AND INDIVIDUALISTS: CONFLICT IN THE MOVEMENT

Throughout their histories, the Conservative Party in Britain and the Republican Party in the United States have contained traditionalists and individualists, those who believe in using authoritative institutions to secure social and economic ends, and those who preferred to see the operation of the market wherever and whenever possible.[1] What made it possible for Reagan and Thatcher to offer a fresh alternative to the post-war consensus was their ability to advance the individualist cause while alternately resisting and accommodating the rear guard action of the traditionalist establishment. The initiatives taken on both sides of the Atlantic were greatly affected by internal dissension within conservative ranks.

The terminological paradox is that conservatism, a movement originally rooted in an attack on rationalism and individualism and suspicious of capitalism's development in various respects, is now seen as the primary defender of the capitalist market society. In the course of the analysis we will see that this is not so much a transformation as the development of a rival inclination. Conservative capitalism is a hybrid of these rival tendencies. The competition between them has, at times, endangered the programmes of both the Reagan and Thatcher governments.

While there is division within conservative capitalism on major questions concerning the role of the state, both tendencies begin from a sense of the limits of human nature and an acceptance of inequality. Where classical liberals see the rational individual capable of contracting with others for the mutual improvement of the human condition, the conservative sees a spiritual, fallible, limited, semi-rational personality whose behaviour cannot be improved by reason alone. Rather than using the state to move such creatures toward procedural equality and abstract justice, the conservative concern is to provide the appropriate environment for the nurturing of the particular strengths of each personality.[2]

In an influential article on the nature of modern conservatism, Samuel Huntington argues that conservatism takes three political forms: as the programme of the aristocracy, as an autonomous theory emphasizing 'justice, order, balance, and moderation', and as a situational response to threats against established institutions. Underlying each of these, however, is the assumption of inequality – whether in blatant form as aristocratic self-interest, or more subtly as the justification for a version of order that emphasizes the role of institutionalized élites.[3]

From this analysis of the inequality that characterizes the human condition, which is what unites conservatives of all kinds, flow divergent streams of thought about what the role of the state should be.[4] As the discussion of policy will reveal, the *traditionalist* stream has two sources: classical natural-law doctrine and the 'organic society' conceptions of Edmund Burke. The belief in a natural order is as old as philosophy, and the political form given to this belief in the middle ages embraces a version of hierarchy that is congenial to those who accept divisions of society on the basis of class or of religious commitment. For Burke society is an interdependent web of relations of obligation and authority based on custom and faith. Rationalism is suspect; too much freedom is an invitation to licence; and egalitarianism is a threat to civilization.

The individualist stream, by contrast, follows from the nine-teenth-century utilitarianism of the Manchester liberals, as recast by Ludwig Von Mises, with emendations by Friedrich Hayek, and Milton Friedman, various libertarian theoreticians, and the 'public choice' school of modern political economists. The central point is a belief in individual initiative; the use of governmental power to improve an individual's competitive position is immoral.[5] The only role for law lies in protecting the freedom of individual choice from encroachment by others. The individualist conservative version of 'equal opportunity' is passive, emphasizing the absence of obstacles, rather than the presence of requisites for individual competition.

More specifically, these differences between individualist conservatives and traditionalists may be seen in several dimensions of principle and policy: attitudes toward individualism, the role of the élite, and the limits of rationality. In the remaining sections of this chapter, we will examine and illustrate each disagreement over principle as a way of making clear the differential in the policy implications of individualist market-based conservatism and traditionalist conservatism. Policy conflicts inherent in these differences will emerge in more detail in their historical and political context in the chapters on the implementation of conservative capitalism.

INDIVIDUALISM AND INSTITUTIONALISM

Individualism is the guiding value of classical liberal political thought. Modern conservatives who borrow from this tradition, however, discard the nuances. The ideal of individual freedom is unencumbered by any of John Locke's concern for equity in the distribution of scarce goods, or of John Stuart Mill's understanding that the individual pursuit of pleasure must be disciplined by a regard for the social consequences of others making the same choice in the same case. While classical liberals placed individual liberty at the top of their scale of values, there was always at least a secondary regard to the welfare of the community. Not so in the individualist conservative adaptation. Community is but the consequence of individual choices made for whatever reason, and the only limit allowed is protection from coercion.

Individualist conservatives defend themselves against charges of indifference to community welfare by arguing that the voluntary actions of free persons are the only true basis of community. To the extent that the community expresses a moral dimension of human life, it can only come about through free choice. Structural constraints, apart from the restriction of force, cannot a true community make.

Traditional conservatives approach the question of individual freedom quite differently. It is excesses arising from personal licence and permissiveness that are at the root of social and political evil. Traditionalists would like to control these excesses, but they undertake the task fully mindful of the imperfection of the instruments available. Individual leaders can't be fully trusted. Mass democracies are as capable of tyranny as of moderate action. The most rational schemes of law will inevitably overlook human frailty and the vagaries of law enforcement. Well-founded institutions are the best guarantee against these excesses and dangers.

Traditionalists argue that, by providing for a plurality of traditional institutions, each dealing with an important sphere of life, the 'ensemble of forces' in society can act in some sort of harmony for the preservation of order and, just possibly, the advancement of civilization. Institutions such as the family, the church, craft unions, corporations, charitable trusts, and the government all have their distinctive characteristics. However, each should be characterized by genuine authority rather than simply the exercise of power. The distinction is described by Robert Nisbet:

> Power I conceive as something external and based upon force. Authority, on the other hand, is rooted in the statuses, functions, and allegiances which are the components of any association. . . . Authority, like power, is a form of constraint, but, unlike power, it is based ultimately upon the consent of those under it; that is, it is conditional.[6]

While there is an opening to democracy in this conception of authority, traditionalists are wary of simple majoritarianism. Rather than constructing institutions from the bottom up through scrupulous attention to voter's desires, traditionalists prefer to concentrate on the role of leadership in assuring that institutions are 'closely united to objectives and functions which command the response and talents of members'.[7] Authority should be accountable to experience and tradition as much as to momentary majorities.

Individualist conservatives, on the other hand, see traditional institutions as the problem, not the solution. In Britain, the revolt of the party traditionalists against the enthusiasts of the market approach became sufficiently widespread for a splinter group of thirty MPs, named Conservative Centre Forward, to be briefly formed in May of 1985 to challenge Thatcher's policies in Parliament. The movement was led by Francis Pym, prominent spokesman for moderate 'centrist' Toryism and former Cabinet member. Pym juxtaposes the doctrine of *laissez-faire* with Marxism as the extremes of British politics – placing traditionalist Toryism in the middle.[8]

The disaffection of traditionalists in the Commons during Thatcher's second term was part of a pattern that found another traditional institution, the Church of England, becoming openly critical of Thatcher's economic policies. A report issued in December 1985 by the Archbishop of Canterbury denounced Thatcher's economic policies for increasing the gap between rich and poor, and for failing to consider the moral issues behind economic policy.[9]

Traditionalist movements in Great Britain, similar to the American moral majority, advocate bolstering the family, disciplining sexual behaviour, and advancing the agenda of the church. That these initiatives have taken second place to economic and international priorities has resulted in some clear expressions of dissatisfaction with Thatcher – as with Reagan – on the part of moral traditionalists.[10]

In the United States the moralist agenda generates similar contradictions with the *laissez-faire* thrust of administration policy. Despite much lip service by the administration, there remains no prohibition of abortion, an issue that clearly divides individualists from traditionalists, nor has there been progress at the national level on authorizing school prayer. Television continues to be largely uncensored and the Reagan administration's own report on pornography has yet to yield serious legislative results. It remains difficult to argue for regulation of the market in pornography, while deploring regulation that affects the environment, job safety, nuclear power, and transportation, among other policy areas.

The larger issues of the split between individualist and traditional conservatives is reflected a division in the ranks of Republican voters in the United States. A survey by Norman Ornstein reveals a sharp difference between 'enterprisers' and 'moralists'. The former are described as affluent, white, pro-business and anti-government, and moderate on social issues; the latter as middle-aged, middle-income, southern, and conservative on social issues and foreign policy. They occupy roughly equal segments of the Republican voters.[11] Appeals to both tendencies bolstered the political success of conservative capitalism, but the policy conflicts between them remain, as we shall see, largely unresolved.

THE ROLE OF GOVERNMENT

The question of the scope of the social mandate of government is at the core of individualist and traditionalist differences. The credibility of traditionalist conceptions of authority and class rests upon the public perception that these differentiations function in the best interest of the whole society. In so far as government is involved in maintaining these distinctions, the legitimacy of government itself is at stake. Yet market-based approaches to policy strip away the symbolic environment of institutional authority, advance individual self-interest as the only dependable motive, and celebrate the competition that results. Whatever this may do to energize economic activity, it encourages the view that government is the reverse of the people's protector. Government becomes the enemy. It is perceived as a source of unfair advantage for the clientele of powerful interests. As Milton and Rose Friedman remark in *Free to Choose*:

> There is, as it were, an invisible hand in politics that operates in precisely the opposite direction to Adam Smith's invisible hand. Individuals who intend only to promote the *general interest* are led by the invisible political hand to promote a *special interest* that they had no intention to promote.[12]

Friedman here endorses the central tenet of libertarian beliefs about government as a mask for powerful interests.

Traditionalists, by contrast, argue for an active role on the part of institutions, led by government, to moderate human weaknesses by attending to the needs of various strata of the population. As Robert Behrens has observed in characterizing the approach of Prime Minister Heath, it was the mission of conservatives to use

> political skills to create a fresh balance between different elements and doctrines in society when their imbalance threatened social harmony. . . . In times of undue individualism the party might defend the state, yet in times of state authority and socialism, it would champion the individual. Confronted with the question: 'What will you conserve?' the [traditionalist] response was an unabashed, 'That depends.'[13]

In the United States, the struggle over the proper role of government is played out in Congress between Republicans and Democrats, and, at least as consequentially in terms of Reagan's agenda, within the Republican Senatorial and Congressional ranks. The splits reflect in part the rearguard battle of liberal capitalism against its conservative rival, as well as the normal considerations of constituency politics. Yet there is also an ideological component to

81

the fight as the Republican 'moderates' have drawn their justificatory rhetoric from traditionalist conceptions of the role of government, while the protagonists are the partisans of *laissez-faire*.

This helps to explain why there was complicity between both Democrats and Republicans in the pre-Reagan era on using government means to extend programmes benefiting the poor beyond the basic safety net. As David Stockman points out:

> Between 1956 and 1977, Congress passed thirteen major acts expanding or liberalizing the social insurance programs. These included creation of the disability programme in 1956, Medicare in 1965, big benefit increases in the early 1970s, and automatic indexing of Social Security in 1972. Over two decades an average of *80 per cent* of House Republicans and *90 per cent* of Senate Republicans voted for these expansions.[14]

In fact, the poverty programmes grew far faster in the Nixon–Ford years than in either the Kennedy–Johnson or the Carter administrations. The Republican Congressional delegation that participated in this growth acquired seniority in the Reagan years and was able, as we shall see in Part 2, to blunt his structural initiatives to a substantial degree.[15]

The intent of individualist conservative initiatives is, among other things, to devalue the very role that traditionalists reserve for government: maintaining the balance of interests and forces in society that, left unchecked, might rend the social fabric and lead to the anarchy of personal aggrandizement.

THE ROLE OF ÉLITES

Individualist conservatives have a curiously contradictory attitude toward the role of élites in society. While espousing a radical conception of individual freedom, they are also the first to celebrate the achievement and entitlement of the talented and the exceptional. In self-consciously choosing to promote a market-based society with huge inequalities, Friedman and Hayek are making way for an extremely powerful élite – all in the name of individual freedom.

Yet individualist conservatives characteristically regard traditional élites as without legitimacy. Just as Adam Smith's doctrine of *laissez-faire* was an attack upon the self-serving policies of a short-sighted aristocracy, so modern individualist conservatives often regard customary élites as impediments to the exercise of creativity. The market is seen to be the best arena for the emergence of talents and abilities. Consequently individualist conservatives prefer precisely the kind of élite that has been excluded from the traditional aristocracy: the businessman, the victorious competitor, and the successful self-interested entrepreneur.

Traditionalists have a different view. While the rigours of commercial activity may foster the finer qualities, the market is an institution too responsive to mass taste, too vulnerable to materialism, and too expressive of chance and good fortune for it to be a fully reliable proving ground for the formation of character. The *arriviste* is hero to the individualist conservative, boor to the traditionalist.

The association with élitism has, of course, been the historic albatross of traditional conservatism. In part, the charge of blind class bias is not justified if the theory of conservatism is consulted – rather than the practice. An élite properly shaped by experience, breeding, and constant discipline is the goal of conservative institutionalism. Exemplars may be found in any honourable walk of life, not just at the top.

At the same time, traditional conservatives historically have been suspicious of mass democracy. In an indirect fashion, pro-market ideology is an intellectual co-conspirator in the rise of democratic attitudes and even of egalitarian practices in the workplace – a development deeply threatening to traditional élites.

Ralph Miliband, writing in 1978, identified a process termed 'de-subordination' in British life:

> De-subordination means that people who find themselves in subordinate positions, and notably the people who work in factories, mines, offices, shops, schools, hospitals and so on do what they can to mitigate, resist and transform the conditions of their subordination. This process occurs where subordination is most evident and felt, namely at the 'point of production' and at the workplace in general; but also wherever else a condition of subordination exists, for instance as it is experienced by women in the home, and outside.[16]

Both Miliband and Samuel Beer, who notes a similar phenomenon as a 'decline of deference', observe that this has contributed to the downfall of the 'civic culture.'[17] While both argue that this development is the product of democratic reformism in the political sector, it is also the case that the consumerism of the market-place leads to a democracy of expectations, a faith in mobility, and an appetite for gratification that is unsettling to the established order and to its mission of instilling the virtues of self-discipline that make the 'civilized life' possible.[18] The disintegration of family structure, for example, is often attributed to the pressures of the market psychology.[19]

Through their advocacy of the market, individualist conservatives are party to populist political initiatives to 'return power to the people'. Their role as carriers of the democratic creed is significant, although it is quite distinct from the 'romantics' of the left and their community-based conception of direct democracy.[20] However, the combination of libertarian and romantic tendencies has made the movement toward democracy all the more powerful – and ultimately all the more threatening to traditionalist values. This combination has some conservative intellectuals worried. Escalating levels of aspiration and expectation have created a 'rising tide of entitlement' that threatens the western way of life in the eyes of some members of the establishment.[21]

Traditionalists have a proprietary interest in the civic culture which, though it has elements of liberal rationalism in its British version, heavily favours the prescriptive role of the upper classes. There is even an element of *noblesse obligue* to the welfare state that is not lost on its critics. Milton Friedman complains of 'the affinity between aristocracy and socialism' arguing that the British welfare state and even the American New Deal 'owes more to the Tory principles of the nineteenth century than to the ideas of Karl Marx and Friedrich Engels.'[22]

In contemporary British politics, the complaints of individualist conservatives about traditionalist foot-dragging on Thatcher's programme have resulted in open hostilities. Sir John Hoskyns, a partisan of the new conservatism and former head of the Prime Minister's Downing Street Policy Unit, accuses the traditional élite of 'a proprietorial feeling towards the country as a whole, almost as if it were an estate of which they were the benevolent owners.'[23] More seriously, Sir Keith Joseph's attempt to reduce grants to university students nearly threatened the continuance of the Conservative government's majority in Parliament.[24] To strike at the funding of education was to threaten the most revered institutional basis for conveying British civilization and culture, as well as to reduce the chances of mobility for the non-élites among Mrs Thatcher's electoral coalition.

In the American experience the role of the élitist establishment is less visible than in Britain, but of its potency there is no doubt. Apart from the prominence of aristocratic associations, the essential difference between the American and British élites is that the American élite is its business leadership. In Britain the traditional élite is more broadly representative of the military, the arts, the rural gentry, and the professions.[25] For this reason, there is in the United States less cause for controversy between market-based conservatives and the scions of traditionalism. Yet there are two factors that widen the breach: regional differences and the nature of the peculiarly American set of institutions that carry on élitist values and customs.

It was the traditionalist Eastern establishment that Reagan had to beat in order to make his way to the White House. He did it by rallying the political forces of the 'sunbelt' states of the southwest around an appeal to patriotism, populism, and free markets. Yet the crudity of this doctrinal appeal ran counter to the sensitivities of that network of foundations, 'think' tanks, media baronies, and intellectual coteries supported by the 'old' money of the eastern establishment. The political form of this resistance was the candidacy of George Bush, nominally a Texan, but in fact the scion of a politically prominent Connecticut family. In the heat of the campaign, Bush denounced Reagan's supply-side programme as 'voodoo economics'. Bush, who had headed the Central Intelligence Agency and served as Ambassador to the United Nations and to China, was schooled in the tradition of the Ivy League, and thoroughly versed in the nuances of the foreign-policy establishment. It was this establishment air that helped defeat him in two races for the Senate. Reagan's decision to invite him to join the ticket as vice-presidential candidate in 1980 was classic politics and an acknowledgement that the foremost cleavage within the Republican Party was between its Eastern establishmentarian wing and its western *laissez-faire* populists.

One leader of the movement toward a populist, market-based conservatism is Richard Viguerie. His assessment of the establishment embraces the collusion between both Democrats and Republicans at the élite level:

On most issues, there's not a dime's worth of difference between the élites of the two major parties. The élitist leaders of both parties support busing [for school integration] or accept it without much protest; they oppose school prayer, support high levels of spending on welfare programs, and oppose tax cuts. They want Congress to appropriate more money for the International Monetary Fund and for foreign aid, which bails out the big banks because the money in turn is used to pay the interest on loans from the Chase Manhattan Bank and other international banks. They oppose tuition tax credits and support trade with communist countries.[26]

As we shall see, the élite Viguerie complains of is clearly involved in hobbling a number of Reagan's libertarian policy initiatives.

In Britain the trade unions, through the Trades Union Congress (TUC), and employers' organization, latterly the Confederation of British Industries (CBI), were given an increasingly central role in economic policy-making by governments of all sorts. Any consensus between government, the CBI, and the TUC General Council is of necessity a consensus between élites. Keith Middlemas in his important book, *Politics in Industrial Society*, wrote about the development of 'corporate bias' in British politics.[27] Since the First World War, government has been led to treat more directly with these dominant economic-interest groups, resulting in the downgrading of Parliament and democratic processes.

In general therefore the argument against the corporate bias was that it made incomes policy, for example, more dependent on non-state agencies such as unions, bringing more of social and economic life across the political threshold. This turned what could be seen as sharp economic and industrial disagreement into a political struggle. The legitimacy of government itself was put at stake, as in 1974 and 1979. When it worked as it did in the 1960s for quite long periods, it did so only by increasing inflationary pressures by exerting influence on government for more public expenditure on welfare etc., from the union side, or subsidy on the employers' side. Given the importance of inflation and its connection with pressure groups, particularly those which had crossed the political threshold, it was central to the strategy of the market-based conservatives that government should eschew such arrangements and should seek, so far as possible, to depoliticize economic and social relationships.

RATIONALITY: THE LIMITS OF DOCTRINE

Aside from the conflicts over the role of the élite, individualists and traditionalists differ on the role of reason in human affairs. Burkean conservatism was founded in a revolt against the rationalist assumptions of Lockean classical liberalism. While both kinds of conservatives would place strong limits on the reach of the social contract, the individualists have their own version of the rationalist faith: a doctrinaire belief in the market-place as the ultimate social institution. The market-place as a cipher for self-interest in the making of choices is the centre-piece of a whole architecture of social-choice theory. It is precisely the doctrinaire claims of the defenders of *laissez-faire* for the rationality of the market-place that traditionalists distrust.

Robert Behrens argues that rationalism doesn't really divide conservatives from non-conservatives today since both versions of conservatism have more than a sufficiency of doctrine.[28] However, there appears to be something qualitatively different in the subjective pragmatism of the traditionalists when compared with the objective-sounding economism of the individualist conservatives. Elaborate claims are made about the power of the unrestrained market to mete out justice. The unfettered market is to remove the blight of underdevelopment, solve the problem of welfare dependency, lead to more disciplined personal behaviour, and stimulate the modernization of industry.[29]

Many of these goals are included in the traditionalist programme; the problem is that the market has its own logic and it is independent of élite judgement and control. There is no inherent protection of the values of 'theocentric humanism' or of the customary mores and preferences that form the core of traditionalist belief.[30] As Arthur Aughey points out, 'There is no necessary correlation between an economic system based on free enterprise and market relations and a cohesive community. Conservatism presupposes a community, one nation, exhibiting "differences" but not to the extent of irreconcilable conflict. Society must be conscious of itself as a whole, it must have a common sense of identity.'[31]

Part of the difficulty of implementing a rationalist doctrine in complex governmental structures is that the results are often internally contradictory. The Reagan administration's credo dictated a devolution of federal responsibilities to state and local governments.

This was to serve the populist aim of returning power to the people, as well as the market argument that such local authorities would compete to reduce social services in the effort to attract new investment. To the extent that the initiative was implemented, what resulted was an increase in confusing and contradictory forms of state regulation and service financing, and, very probably, a less efficient environment for economic growth.[32]

In Britain, the controversy over centre-local relations took similarly peculiar twists. Promises of devolution were quickly subordinated to the need for tight control from the centre over local social spending in order to serve the fiscal entailments of monetarism.[33] In both countries, the pattern appears to be that populist preferences for localism generally lose out to the imposition of class-based policy preferences from the top.[34]

One of Thatcher's closest calls in Parliament came in the summer of 1985 over the issue of raising the salaries of top government executives. The logic of the market-place dictated that the best talent could not be had without substantial increases. A regard for the restraint shown in the pay policy for teachers, nurses, and lower-level civil servants, as well as the condition of the country generally, led forty-eight Conservative MPs to defect. One Tory from the West Country remarked that the Government should behave 'with a little more sensitivity, a little more humility, and a little less arrogance'.[35]

Thatcher's increasingly severe troubles in the House of Lords provide further illustrations of these tensions. In surveying ten major defeats that forced the Government to modify its positions in the period 1979–84, Donald Shell points out that Conservative peers:

> seem reluctant to acquiesce in the new ideological conservatism; instinctively they prefer the cautious approach to change which sees the need to make exceptions when new policies are invoked, and which is sensitive in a paternalistic way to the delicate social fabric Mrs Thatcher seems ready to destroy.[36]

However divergent the logic of the market and the preferences for order of traditionalists might be, there has been an attempt by the theoreticians of contemporary conservatism to resolve the contradictions. The general argument is that the market is not without its ordering properties. It is a demonstrably effective means of spreading the ownership of property to a wider class of citizens who can then form the core of a stable social structure.[37] Yet the materialism and the self-indulgence the market encourages are troublesome for traditionalists, as is the evangelical zeal with which the market is promoted as an institution having the key to all social wisdom.

In a larger sense, the rationalist mentality of corporate managerialists among the individualists is at odds with traditionalist romanticism. Sheldon Wolin observes that the new individualist conservative view:

> conceives the world as a domain to be rationalized into orderly processes which will produce desired results according to a calculus of efficiency. Its mode of action is 'rational decision-making'; its ethic is enshrined in cost-benefit analysis; its politics is administration. The romantic conservative, who yearns for Georgian manors, Gothic gardens, and Chartresque piety, has need of a special insensibility if he is to plead for a *status quo* so devoid of sentiment, tradition, and mystery to ally himself with those whose profession requires that the world be objectified and abstracted of its human and historical idiosyncrasies before the decision-makers can make sense of it.[38]

While some individualist conservatives would not so easily embrace these implications of their devotion to the market, it is nevertheless the case that the market delivers power into the hands of those who can master the application of utilitarian techniques of management and innovation. It is, in the end, a rival temperament to the traditionalist sensibility.[39]

CONCLUSION

Armed with new economic doctrines that made anti-statism appear to be the key to prosperity, individualist conservatives wrested from the traditionalist party establishments in both countries the means of gaining power through an appeal to the electorate based on disgust with government and a rising faith in the market-place. As we will see in Part 2, when it came time to make good on these criticisms by developing policies to deal with the real world, it was predictable that the consequences would not always be what the theoreticians had in mind.

It was also predictable, given the splits in the conservative-capitalist movement, that there would be considerable waffling. We will see how these innovations and contradictions were played out in certain key dimensions of policy.

This analysis, set against the larger background of the political fortunes of Reagan and Thatcher, will form the basis for our concluding reflections in Part 3 on possible responses from the left.

Part Two

IMPLEMENTATION AND APPRAISAL

Chapter Five

THE RISE OF CONSERVATIVE CAPITALISM IN THE UNITED STATES

The story of the emergence of conservative capitalism in the United States can be told largely in terms of the political accomplishments of one man: Ronald Reagan. While he rode the currents of a movement that was deeply involved in American political history, he is the person who brought it all together in a politically workable form. After brief attention to the ideological background from which Reagan emerged, we will focus on his long campaign to stir an American revolt against liberal capitalist policies. Through this prism we will see the major intellectual currents merge into a stream of energy that overwhelmed politics-as-usual and altered the basis of the rivalry between the two major political parties.

The conservative-capitalist movement has broad significance for the whole range of governmental policy; we will focus here on domestic issues and, within that, income-security policy and related structural issues that comprise the core of the conservative revolt against the politics of liberal capitalism. By way of contrasting the treatment of rich and poor during the Reagan administration, there will be a brief discussion of policies toward corporate mergers and takeovers. We will examine as well the internal tensions within the movement between its two disparate tendencies: traditionalism and the individualist perspective of market-based conservatives.

While the American conservative-capitalist movement drew strength from the writings of intellectuals such as Friedrich Hayek and Milton Friedman, there was a level of ideological combat that was closer to the everyday preoccupations of average citizens. A coterie of journalists and commentators under the leadership of William F. Buckley and his associates at the *National Review* served as the means of transmitting ideas for those who became the activists and leaders of the conservative resurgence. They took the critique of liberal-capitalist institutions and policies and gave it political potency in the form of symbols and slogans that made the connection between theory and practice in eliciting support for conservative goals.

For much of the post-war period, conservative advocacy was directed primarily toward foreign policy and the development of a militantly anti-communist posture. Rejecting bipartisanship as it had been nurtured by Senator Arthur Vandenberg and other members of the traditional Republican establishment, the younger conservatives made common cause with Senator Joseph McCarthy and the 'China Lobby' that wanted to roll back the Chinese Revolution through the encouragement of an armed and aggressive Republic of China based in Taiwan. These foreign-policy questions and the ways in which they interacted with the double critique of liberal capitalism and conservative traditionalism are beyond the scope of this book. However, it is important to note that the disasters that befell the anti-Communist cause with the discrediting of Senator McCarthy, the decline in popularity of the Vietnam War, and the disgrace of President Nixon, whose career was born in the fervour of 1950s anti-Communism, all contributed to a turn toward the domestic scene on the part of Buckley and his conservative compatriots. While the foreign policy dimension of conservative capitalism continues to have great impact as evidenced by the distancing of the administration from the United Nations, the militance of American policy toward Communist overtures in the Third World, and the vast military build-up justified by references to the 'evil empire', we will concentrate on the domestic sphere where the discontinuity of major policies caused by a resurgent conservatism can be most clearly seen.

The setting of the stage for the emergence of Ronald Reagan really took place in the 1964 election campaign. In that year, conservative Republicans out-organized and out-manoeuvred the party establishment and nominated Senator Barry Goldwater to oppose Lyndon Johnson for the Presidency. Goldwater's economic adviser was Milton Friedman. The themes of that campaign were quite simple: an attack upon big government and a confrontational attitude toward communism. Johnson, whose prior record in the Senate revealed him to be a conservative on military issues, had little trouble with the latter and, indeed, a militant anti-communism was

94

the hallmark of his foreign policy. But the attack on big government did not hit home with the voters perhaps because the efforts made under Kennedy's New Frontier and the putative 'War on Poverty' were in their early stages.

As the Goldwater campaign stumbled toward a major defeat, his speechwriters came up with a stem-winding appeal to conservative values designed as a fund-raising device. Goldwater demurred at the rhetorical style and suggested that someone skilled in the art be found to give the speech. Thus Ronald Reagan, brought in for the occasion before an invited studio audience, made his famous televised appeal and raised $5 million for the campaign. He also staked his claim to national prominence in conservative circles.

Paradoxically, it was the pursuit of a conservative foreign policy that divided Lyndon Johnson and his Vice-President, Hubert Humphrey, from a major segment of the Democratic Party and led to the split that enabled Richard Nixon to win in 1968. Reagan had also been a candidate for the nomination in 1968, but with victory in sight and the memory of the Goldwater debacle still too fresh, the Republican Party turned to Nixon as the 'moderate' candidate instead.

Yet Reagan had acquired a formidable political base and was, as Governor of California, succeeding in taking the initiative on behalf of conservative policies in the very place where liberal and radical ideologies had reached the highest stages of development. Reagan continued to cultivate the right, but the tide turned against the Republicans after Nixon's resignation and Ford's succession to the office. Reagan wasn't quite strong enough to take the nomination away from the new incumbent. Ford's ill-fated campaign of 1976 was overcome by the sentiment for new leadership and Jimmy Carter succeeded in capturing the Presidency, albeit without a fresh mandate based on any clear sense of where reform liberalism should take the nation.

By 1980, the Democratic Party and its leader, President Jimmy Carter, were mired in a seeming confusion over domestic policy compounded by the Iran hostage crisis. With the economy reeling from the effects of the oil crisis and the federal government in disarray over the relative priority of domestic and military spending, the image of Ronald Reagan as a leader with a plan for restoring America's greatness came into focus for more and more Americans. His election was in some ways the mirror image of Franklin Roosevelt's triumph over the discredited policies and administration of Herbert Hoover in 1932. There were similar sallies against the impotence of the incumbent regime and analagous appeals to the promise of a new ideology that would sweep away the errors of the old system, and to the track record of a Governor of a populous state who appeared to have coped with a contemporary crisis. It is not surprising that there was, as well, the same sense of a mandate for new leadership. The mandate was made to seem all the clearer by the absence of a coherent programme by the Democrats and the losses to their Congressional ranks of pillars of the liberal establishment engineered in substantial part by the National Conservative Political Action Committee.

Once installed in power, the influence of George Bush and that of other traditionalists was quickly subordinated thanks to the zeal of the individualist conservative element in the Reagan coterie and the President's willingness to embark upon an adventurous course of action predicated on the sort of critique of liberal capitalist institutions discussed in chapter 4. What followed was an astonishing episode in American politics with clear precedent only in the famous 'Hundred Days' of the Roosevelt Administration. The formulation of the budget in the spring of 1981 set out a new model of federal governance derived directly from market-based conservative ideology. It was that budget and its complement of 'New Federalism' policies that set the framework for the whole of the Reagan administration's domestic programme. The opposition of the traditionalists and moderates in the Republican Party, muted at first, became more and more significant as the true fiscal and human costs of the Reagan proposals became clearer.

RONALD REAGAN AND INCOME SECURITY POLICY

The crux of the domestic struggle was over the scope and justification of a safety net for the poor and the disadvantaged. In a society characterized by intense competition and with little in the way of a class history that would support an attitude of *noblesse oblige*, the question of what the government should do about the poor has long been answered by a patchwork of responses at myriad levels of authority in the federal system. Two great policy initiatives, the New Deal in the 1930s and the Great Society of the 1960s, attempted to rationalize this system by moving the issue to a national level. It was this direction of policy that individualist conservatives set out to reverse. The key issue was income security. Those who believed in unbridled *laissez-faire* questioned the fundamental premises of government assistance to those whose incomes fell below the poverty line.

Nothing was so characteristic of liberal capitalism as its attempts to meet the problem of poverty through government programmes. Ambivalent about the direct approach of providing actual employment or a guaranteed income, the New Deal and the Great Society, partly as a nod to conservative scepticism, concentrated instead on indirect forms of assistance through the 'helping professions': social workers, teachers, health professionals, and community assistance agencies. While the New Deal focused on national means of addressing these problems, the Great Society attempted to mix national initiatives and funding with various forms of local involvement and control. In fascinating struggles with state and local governmental units, some of these programmes were funded from Washington directly to neighbourhood-based organizations. What was begun as political creativity in the Great Society became for conservatives a target for charges of building up bureaucracy, fostering inefficiency, encouraging personal irresponsibility, and undermining established authority. In these senses, the critique of the Great Society appealed to both individualist and traditionalist Republicans, though, as we shall see, the policy responses generated by the rise of Ronald Reagan caused considerable strain between the two tendencies.

A brief history of Ronald Reagan's association with welfare policy provides essential insights into the conflicts that have shaped income-security policy. The ideological history of what came to be called the New Federalist Program really begins with the California Welfare Reform Act of 1971. The centre-piece of Ronald Reagan's governorship, it was a response to rapidly growing welfare rolls and to pressure from federal welfare administrators to raise Californian Aid to Families with Dependent Children (AFDC) payments to reflect cost-of-living increases.[1] Essentially, the approach was to tighten eligibility, impose a one-year residence requirement [later struck down], simplify the administration of the law, and raise the benefit levels to those remaining on the rolls.

The California Welfare Reform Act was associated with a turn-around of substantial proportions in the caseload. Some analysts attributed the turn-around to an improving economy, increased use of abortion services, satiation of the eligible population, and the stringent new regulations enforced pursuant to the law by Robert Carleson, then Reagan's Welfare Director.[2] The Welfare Reform Act was, in any event, a success by all the criteria of politics.

The importance of the act for our purposes is that it was conceived by Reagan and Carleson as their libertarian alternative to the Nixon administration's Family Assistance Plan (FAP), a guaranteed-minimum-income proposal. FAP represented the culmination of a campaign to get traditional conservatives into a coalition with reform liberals that would place welfare on a national footing along with Social Security as a part of the nation's basic safety net.[3] The connection to California politics was present from the beginning as the person responsible for developing the proposal was a former moderate Republican state legislator, John Veneman, who had fought hard in 1967 against Governor Reagan's proposal that Medicaid benefits be reduced.

Daniel Patrick Moynihan, a prime mover within the Nixon administration for the proposal, reports that Nixon's receptivity to income security came directly out of a concern for the threat, readily apparent in 1969, to the dissolution of traditional authority in America.[4] Moynihan, in fact, played upon Nixon's interest in Disraeli to acquaint him with traditional conservative perspectives on the uses of social policy as a means of national unification.[5]

Perhaps the earliest traditional conservative to propose a minimum income in the United States was Senator Robert Taft of Ohio, the standard bearer of the post-Second-World-War conservative establishment.[6] President Nixon followed in this vein when he presented the Family Assistance Plan (FAP) as part of a domestic programme he entitled, ironically, the 'New Federalism'. While the governors of other states, faced with similar increases in welfare roles, lobbied for federalization of welfare in a manner similar to FAP, Reagan opened the path to an alternative state-based approach. His success made him a leader among individualist conservatives and those traditionalists who feared the rise of a 'welfare ethic'. Both Governor Reagan and Welfare Director Carleson testified against FAP before Congress. Reagan was politically the nation's most potent critic of the proposal, and had a great deal to do with its defeat.[7] The Nixon White House worried that Reagan could use the issue to pose a threat to Nixon's renomination in 1972.[8] As the campaign began, James Reichley reports that Nixon refused to compromise with the liberal Democrats in the Senate who were sceptical of FAP's low benefit levels, thus killing its chances, because he felt that more could be gained politically by attacking a similar proposal made by George McGovern in the course of the Democratic primaries.[9]

In any event, when FAP came to a vote in the Senate in the Democratic version proposed by Senator Ribicoff, it failed 52 to 34. It was indicative of future struggles over the principle of national minimums that, among the Republican Senators that Reichley categorizes as 'Fundamentalists' and 'Stalwarts', the vote to kill it was 22 to 5. These are the Republicans who draw their economic philosophy from the libertarian side of conservatism. Among the 'Moderates' and 'Progressives' who take a more traditionalist view of the functions of the state, the vote was 10 to 2 in favour.[10] Republican opposition, combined with Democratic suspicions about the adequacy of benefit levels, as well as the distribution of political credit, given the Republican patrimony of the plan, sufficed to kill what would have been the most consequential change in income-security policy since the advent of Social Security.

The result for Reagan was a much stronger hand as leader of a national conservative movement – a strength derived directly from his involvement in the welfare policy area and his opposition to FAP in particular.[11] As welfare became a symbol for all that was presumed wrong with government, Reagan could assume the mantles of both prophet and redeemer.

There was also an unsuccessful attempt to revive a form of FAP in the Ford administration as a negative income tax. The concept of the negative income tax was originated by Milton Friedman in 1943 and was intended to replace all other subsidies for the poor with a single subsistence-level payment. Friedman's argument was that government programmes, particularly those that employed the bureaucracy to provide direction and counselling were inherently wasteful and inefficient. He regarded the straightforward transfer of cash through the taxing mechanism as less objectionable.[12] As proposed, the negative income tax was the bare bones form of FAP. The adviser who had the most telling effect in dissuading Ford from advancing the plan was another California conservative, Martin Anderson, a trenchant critic of government spending, who would return to the White House as one of the architects of President Reagan's 1981 spending cuts in programmes for the poor.[13]

For these reasons of political history, conservatives came to see welfare policy as an issue associated with questions of federalism, and Ronald Reagan as the policy leader. The issue again became a factor in presidential politics in 1976 when an ill-conceived proposal to turn welfare over to the states (similar to the New Federalism) derailed Reagan's campaign for the nomination.[14]

THE IMPLEMENTATION OF CONSERVATIVE CAPITALISM

The struggle over income security was at the core of the ideological initiatives of the Reagan years. The budgetary recisions and cuts in 1981 and the consolidation of numerous programmes into block grants in the autumn of that year were the dramatic openers in a campaign to reverse the growth of social spending. The specific question as to whether the states or the federal government should finance welfare was the pivotal structural issue of President Reagan's New Federalism proposal, introduced in his State of the Union message in January of 1982. The New Federalism programme was originally envisioned as a sweeping change in the structure of federal relations involving drastically different budgetary priorities, the shifting of categorical aid programmes into block grants, large reductions in federal regulatory activity, the return of revenue sources to the states, and the establishment of enterprise zones to aid economic development.[15] When fully implemented, the New Federalism was to rival the New Deal and the Great Society as revolutions in the federal system.

Like its two predecessors, this revolution was driven by ideo-logical conviction and powered by the perception of widespread support for change.[16] Yet the revolution was never quite completed. It consisted of domestic budget cuts and programme consolidations rather than the fundamental structural reorganization envisioned in the original New Federalism proposal. Whether the New Federalist agenda is completed depends on clearing the hurdle of true struc-tural change. Whether that final hurdle can be cleared depends in part on whether the ideological thrust that has energized the move-ment can be sustained in view of internal conflicts between traditionalists and individualists, as well as between adherents of liberal capitalism and conservative capitalism.

It was indicative for the future of income-security policy that Reagan's California Welfare Reform Act was explicitly an alternative to federalization of Aid to Families with Dependent Children (AFDC). When Reagan became President and proposed his New Federalism, it was the trade-off of AFDC to the states that was to be the centre-piece of the structural revolution in federal relations. Individualist conservatives believed that competition between states to lower welfare tax loads in order to position themselves for economic development would, by the logic of the market, accomplish the policy goal of reducing the availability of welfare. The tax savings would stimulate job-producing investment, thus lowering unemployment and welfare dependence simultaneously.

THE NEW FEDERALISM: WORKING TOWARD STRUCTURAL CHANGE

But, when it came time to implement the Reagan programme, the issue of income security proved to be the focus of some important differences within the administration. A lot has been written about the split within the White House staff during the first term between the 'hard-liners', generally typified by Edwin Meese, and the 'pragmatists' identified with James Baker. There are indications, however, that the New Federalism programme was affected by a split that was ideological as much as temperamental. The issue in this split was precisely the matter of federalization of AFDC. The nature of the split reflects classic tensions between individualist and traditionalist strains of conservatism. Two key actors in the New Federalism initiative illustrate these ideological tensions: Robert Carleson and David Stockman.

Robert Carleson, formerly the President's Assistant for Human Resources and Executive Secretary of the Cabinet Council on Human Resources, appears at all the crucial stages of the New Federalism debate, including the more controversial Reagan administration initiatives in Social Security reform, housing policy, foodstamp programmes, urban enterprise zones and Medicaid.[17] More than any other figure on the staff, he invoked the classic themes of libertarianism: 'Income earned belongs individually to the people who earn it. It does not belong to the state, nor does it belong by right to any other segment of the population.' Welfare should be provided only to those who 'because of advanced age or permanent and total disability, are unable to support themselves'. All others should be required to work in compensation for their benefits if they aren't excluded entirely, including the mothers of children.[18]

What Carleson (and libertarians generally) do not deal with is inequality of opportunity. Liberals, by contrast, argue that inequality of opportunity creates deprivations that must be addressed by government. George McGovern, the Democratic presidential candidate in 1972, makes the point in responding to an article, cited above, and written by Robert Carleson on 'Social responsibility'. McGovern comments, 'Regrettably, it [Carleson's] is a philosophy rooted in the Horatio Alger fiction that achievement is but a matter of will; it is scornful of all that science tells us about the physical, psychological, environmental, economic, and social factors that can inhibit the realization of human potential.'[19] McGovern's list of opportunity factors is substantial and it covers the programmatic agenda of liberal capitalism. Senator McGovern was defeated for re-election in 1980, the year of Reagan's presidential victory and of the defeat of numerous liberals targeted by the National Conservative Political Action Committee in the US Senate and the House of Representatives.

Both Carleson and Stockman reject McGovern's analysis of the problem. For Carleson, the question of who has a right to what is answered, as we have seen, by determining who has produced the income. There is no conception of social interdependence, no accounting for social scientific research on opportunity factors, and no consideration of the cost of inequality as an assessment against income in the form of taxes for social spending. David Stockman rejects efforts of the kind McGovern envisions as simply the recurrence of utopianism against the realities of original sin. Following upon his reading of Reinhold Niebuhr, Stockman's view was that 'The institutions of society cannot perfect [man]; the defects of any particular social and economic order did not corrupt him.'[20] An activist role for government, as envisioned in the liberal capitalist programme, fails on either rationale to do anything other than introduce a new opportunity for corruption. Stockman's memoir of his role in the Reagan administration is, in large part, a moralistic diatribe against the venality of politicians who do as their constituents ask without regard to what he conceives to be 'principle'.

While both reject liberalism, the tension between individualist and traditionalist tendencies within the administration sheds considerable light on the fate of the New Federalism initiative. What differentiates Stockman from Carleson is that the former Director of the Office of Management and the Budget argued the case for the New Federalism budgetary reforms as the precondition to making effective policy – policy which would include means-tested national health care and 'universal income maintenance'. Robert Carleson, by contrast, favoured devolution of AFDC and had doubts about the federalization of Medicaid.[21] Stockman had argued that the categorical aid programmes drained away money and political energy that should be going into an overall rationalization of federal responsibilities. Budget reductions, programme consolidations, and devolution of the categoricals were needed to control the federal budget. However, Stockman sees a distinction between these strategies, on the one hand, and the need for certain national minimums in the areas of health and income security on the other. The federal level should concern itself with 'foreign policy, the social insurance systems we run nationwide – Social Security, Medicare, and means-tested entitlements – that embody all those fundamental commitments that have been made'.[22]

Stockman's position accords with the traditional conservative argument that society has a commitment to its dependent citizens which must be met as a matter of obligation. Programmes that attempted to alter the distribution of advantages in the market-place, however, were subject to the Budget Director's cuts and/or devolution to the states.[23] The intent was to 'attack weak claims, not weak clients'.[24]

The Reagan budget deficits meant that any effort to rationalize entitlements at the federal level would require cutting back drastically on benefits to those whose claims were, in any way, weak. Stockman learned that weak claims and weak constituencies are not the same thing, and political realities are more significant than fiscal realities. An affordable federalized Medicaid would exclude many marginal recipients covered under current state programmes – and that was politically unacceptable, just as the full assumption of Medicaid costs was fiscally impossible in view of the deficits. In fact, there is good reason to believe that this dilemma undermined the New Federalism negotiations in the spring of 1982. Richard Williamson, the President's agent in the negotiations, in a retrospective analysis remarked that footdragging by 'certain administration officials, whose enthusiasm for the New Federalism initiative had dissipated', was responsible for the failure to complete the Medicaid-for-AFDC swap. He locates the problem in the Office of Management and the Budget and attributes it to a 'senior OMB official'.[25] The matter of income security was, in any event, the issue of principle that could not be resolved between the governors, both Republican and Democratic, and the Reagan White House.

These differences on the crucial question of federalization of AFDC are symptomatic of differences on a wider scale of issues. John Kessel, in measuring policy preferences displayed in interviews with Reagan White House staff members, found divisions into 'unalloyed conservatives', who think national defence is the only legitimate federal activity, 'domestic conservatives', who favour some new domestic programme initiatives, and 'lenient conservatives'. The differences among these groups are not great, but it is interesting that Carleson appears among the 'unalloyed conservatives', and Stockman in the 'domestic conservative' category.[26] Stockman reports similar splits between James Baker, then Chief of Staff, who defended traditionalist priorities, and thoroughgoing libertarians such as Donald Regan, former Secretary of the Treasury and Baker's successor as Chief of Staff.

In his memoir Stockman variously describes himself as an 'intellectual conservative' and a 'social idealist' who thought supply-side economics, along with a rationalization of means-tested entitlements, could genuinely help the poor – he was intent on using libertarian means for traditionalist ends. As it happened, the fork in the road was reached early in the administration when Stockman realized that 'the safety net was no longer compatible with the President's fiscal policy'. Stockman then became the architect of a series of public relations manœuvres, while battling to force the issue of fiscal responsibility behind the scenes, albeit unsuccessfully. The vast increases in the military budget effectively ended the 'Reagan Revolution', in so far as it was associated with fiscal prudence. No acceptable levels of cuts in social spending could restore it. Any kind of rationalization of federal-state responsibilities for income security along the lines Stockman had earlier proposed was completely out of the question. The consequence was a vastly increased debt.[27]

As for President Reagan, he has referred to his philosophy as 'libertarian', yet his positions reflect a mix of individualist and traditionalist values.[28] The President's economic policies seem to be individualist, while his social positions are traditionalist. Economic solutions revolve around privatization, while social policy moves toward government-enforced prayer, censorship, and drug-testing. The crosscut comes in the area of governmental programmes for the poor. The safety net is recognized, though degovermentalization of social responsibility is encouraged.[29] While a libertarian would oppose the federalization of Medicaid and AFDC, and a traditionalist might federalize both in barebones form, the New Federalism proposed a swap of one for the other at the federal level.

Whatever their effect on the implementation of the New Federalism, these ideological differences among individualist and traditional conservatives have been less apparent than the tactical flexibility of the Reagan administration in advancing its programme. The result has been the creation of a form of New Federalism expressed in budgetary priorities, the apparent denationalization of regulatory functions, tax-reduction and tax-shifting from the federal to the state and local levels, and the consolidation of numerous social-welfare programmes into block grants. The effect has been to give the appearance of considerable advances on the individualist conservative agenda; however, the forces of resistance both within the Republican Party and among the opposition party have become increasingly powerful.

THE STALEMATE OF CONSERVATIVE-CAPITALIST POLICIES

The halcyon days of 1981–82 were the highpoint of President Reagan's success in imposing a conservative-capitalist agenda on the nation's politics. His ability drastically to reorganize the budgetary priorities as well as the tax structure in those two pivotal years was demonstrated to a degree few would have predicted. However, the key structural reforms eluded him with the collapse of the New Federalism negotiations in the spring of 1982.

The indicators of lost impetus for the Reagan revolution are to be found in Congressional voting patterns. The time-tested measures of Congressional strength are the 'party unity' score and the 'conservative coalition' score. The first measures the degree of cohesion in voting by each party in each house of the legislature; the second measures the frequency and cohesion of block voting by Republicans in combination with conservative southern Democrats. The low point of party unity for Democrats was 1981 (69 per cent), with scores of 78 per cent and 79 per cent for the first two years of the second term. The year 1981 also provided the high point of Republican unity in Congress (76 per cent), while in subsequent years it has reached a low of 71 per cent.[30]

Meanwhile the potent combination of conservative Democrats and Republicans that passed the President's programme, despite a Democratic majority in the House, was likewise at its strongest in 1981. The coalition was operative on 21 per cent of the votes and was victorious in the House of Representatives on 88 per cent of those votes, and in the Senate on 95 per cent of the conservative-coalition votes. After that year, the appearance of the coalition was less frequent (14–18 per cent) and its winning percentage dropped to an average of 77 per cent in the House and 92 per cent in the Senate.[31] These variations in voting strength are the margin of control in American domestic politics. The President, after 1982, did not have the power to dictate new departures in policy, nor to complete the agenda he had begun with such dramatic effect only a year earlier. For these reasons, 1981–82 remain the benchmark years for measuring the policy intentions of the conservative-capitalist movement. The deterioration of this initiative is evidence of the strength of liberal-capitalist forces as well as the counter tendencies within the conservative movement on social-equity issues.

The remainder of the Reagan Presidency has been characterized by a consistent pattern. Proposals for budget cuts and phase-outs for domestic programmes continue to emanate from the White House, but at a much slower pace. The structural agenda remains stalemated. Most recently the administration has been forced to retreat on welfare reform.[32]

Other parts of the domestic policy-making system have asserted themselves as Reagan's mandate began to pale. Subsequent tax changes have redressed partially the bias in his first tax cut toward the rich at the expense of the poor and middle class. The major overhaul of the tax system completed in 1986 was 'revenue neutral' and did not include a major element of the Reagan tax proposal that the deductibility of state income taxes be eliminated. This provision would have carried forward the ideological intent of the New Federalism by means of the tax code. It would have placed states with higher income taxes (and social-service levels) at an even greater disadvantage in the competition for industries and investment. By allowing the deduction of state income taxes, there is at least some compensation in the federal tax system for those states that make an effort to deal with social services in a progressive manner.

The military build-up has continued at a rate exceeding inflation and has drained off whatever revenue might have been available for new initiatives in dealing with poverty in the United States. However, even the rate of growth of military expenditure has been slowed as Congress has ever more persistently asserted itself in reducing the military budget proposed by the President and increasing domestic expenditures.

The invigoration of the states as originators of policy has proceeded as much in reaction to the abdication of federal-policy responsibility, particularly in regulatory activities, as in an effort to accommodate the new budgetary priorities. States have lost huge amounts of federal revenue and, as a result, have had to cut back on many services to the disadvantaged that were once mandated by federal programmes.

The Reagan administration has had more success in implementing departures from traditional policies in an area where less is required by way of Congressional co-operation. The illustrative area is anti-trust policy to which we now turn.

ANTI-TRUST POLICY: THE FREE MARKET AND OLIGOPOLY

While welfare policy requires positive legislative action by government, anti-trust policy is essentially tied to enforcement by the executive branch through the Justice Department and, less directly, the Federal Trade Commission. In this policy area the Reagan administration has moved more effectively and in a consistent direction suggested by the canons of *laissez-faire* doctrine.

Anti-trust policy involves a major tenet of the free-market faith. The remedy for monopoly is thought to be competition. Save in the most extreme cases, the assumption is that monopolies, by driving up prices, will call into the market-place rival producers who will introduce fresh competition.[33] While the Reagan administration has not embraced monopolization, it has promoted policies designed to facilitate corporate mergers. Corporate-financed seminars on the teachings of the conservative 'Chicago School' of economists have advanced the proposition that mergers are good for the economy.[34] The argument is that whatever inefficiencies may accrue to the increasing size of large corporations and conglomerates, these will be corrected by the pressure of competition. The political consequences of the combinations of economic power that are thus created are not part of this specialized assessment.

While a good deal of the traditionalist establishment owes its wealth to the activities of the 'Robber Barons' of the last century, an attitude of moderation has been institutionalized among major sectors of the eastern establishment. Continuity and stability have been cultivated at some cost to innovation and expansion for its own sake. The Reagan forces were determined to change this arguing in part from notions of economy of scale and in part out of a lack of other solutions to the growing competitive position of foreign-based oligopolies.

Ronald Reagan came into office as a vocal critic of major anti-trust actions taken by the Justice Department under his predecessor. During his administration, cases involving major food producers, AT&T, and IBM were either settled out of court, dropped, or dismissed by the Justice Department and the Federal Trade Commission.[35] 'Bigness is not necessarily badness', declared Attorney-General Edwin Meese.[36] Meanwhile opposition in Congress was weakened by conservative victories and a perceived shift in the tide of opinion.

From 1981 to 1986 the annual number of mergers increased by nearly 40 per cent and the value of those mergers, where figures were disclosed, increased by 120 per cent.[37] Corporate takeovers have swept the economy and the premiums paid for takeovers have consumed funds that might otherwise have been used for productivity improvements. Average premiums paid for takeovers two decades ago were in the range of 25 per cent. With the advent of the Reagan administration, average premiums jumped to 50 per cent and there were cases where individual premiums were more than 100 per cent.[38]

The guidelines under which corporate mergers would be restrained by the Justice Department were revised in 1986 for the first time since 1968. The emphasis in the index that measures the legitimacy of mergers was switched from the *number* of firms controlling a majority share of the market to the *size of market share* of dominant firms among those holding a major share. This index helps avoid monopoly, which even the most thoroughgoing libertarian would favour, but does nothing about oligopoly which was the focus of the previous index.[39] In fact, the Justice Department has argued before the US Supreme Court that anti-trust rules should be relaxed to allow companies to engage in a 'conspiracy in restraint of trade' by collusion between its own internal divisions.[40]

The enormous concentrations of power that flow from this attitude toward the structure of the economy seemed not to concern the administration, nor has there been any reservation expressed about the role of paper values derived from mergers in inflating the stock market. The financial rewards to those who reap the dividends are very great. However several authorities in the field worry about the political power of the new combinations. Others doubt that the advertised advantages in international trade will materialize. The drastic decline in the trading position of the United States in the last few years would seem to argue that these doubts should not be dismissed. One expert notes that in 1980, 'we [US industries] spent more on mergers and acquisitions than we did on basic research and development,' and the trend has only increased since.[41]

This brief comment on anti-trust policy is intended as a means of illustrating the divergent impact of market-based conservative policies on the poor and the rich. While income-security programmes are targeted for reduction, policies allowing ever greater combinations of wealth and power at the top are pursued vigorously. In the next chapter we will see how the distributive characteristics of the system have changed during this same period of time.

FUTURE PROSPECTS FOR CONSERVATIVE CAPITALISM

While it is accurate to say that the structural changes in the level and financing of income-security programmes sought by the Reagan administration have not been achieved, the net effect of their budgetary policies has built in a set of priorities that may well be irreversible for the foreseeable future. The consequences of the massive military build-up entail future commitments of revenue that cannot be dismissed by a new administration, assuming there were the will to restore a more liberal set of priorities. The hand-maiden of the military build-up, the interest on the enormously expanded debt, is an even less malleable factor.[42] Consequently the long-term reversal of the share of income devoted to assistance to the poor that could not be accomplished by structural change has been accomplished in large part, and paradoxically, by the fiscal entailments of the military build-up and the huge increase of the deficit and its servicing requirements.[43] The result, while it may serve the predilections of some market-based conservatives for the way poverty is dealt with, can hardly be reassuring for those who are also concerned about the long-term health of the economy – or, indeed, for the size of government in relation to the rest of the economy.

David Stockman, in a classic traditionalist attack upon the perils of democracy, lays the blame for the fiscal disaster squarely upon Ronald Reagan:

> The baleful outcomes now being recorded are attributable to a new and far more profound disturbance in the equilibrium of American government. By means of flagrant agitation and excitement of a democratic electorate's most singular vulnerability – resentment of the taxation its collective demands for public expenditures compel – Ronald Reagan has transformed the nation's institutionalized budgetary process into an extraordinary *fiscal plebiscite*.
>
> Rather than helping to broker and manage the federal government's annual trillion-dollar lottery of giving and taking among its multitudinous constituencies, he has deployed his vast popularity and communications skills toward a single end: arousing, mobilizing, and concentrating the ordinary citizenry into an overpowering block vote against necessary taxation.[44]

For this reason, the entirety of the programme that Hayek and Friedman would have government follow in managing its relation-ship to the rest of the economy has not been put in place in the United States. William Niskanen, an intellectual architect of conservative capitalism, remarked in October of 1987, 'We have a bigger government, with higher spending. We've slowed regulation down, but we haven't reversed it. In other words, there was no Reagan revolution.'[45] That is not, however, to say that Reagan's programme has been without major impact, only that a conclusive reversal of the New Deal has not taken place.

Individualist conservatives who see that the build-up of government through military programmes is a threat to their principles will not regard the Reagan revolution as anything to be proud of. The part of the programme that has been accomplished is a reduction in the kinds and amounts of assistance to the poor, and the liberalization of policy on corporate mergers.

Those traditional conservatives who believe in some provision for the poor, as well as liberal capitalists who believe that government should provide at least indirect assistance toward equality of economic opportunity, will have reason to examine the distributive impact of the Reagan policies enacted thus far. As the effects of these moves on the position of the poor, in particular, become evident, the ideological initiative behind the structural-reform agenda of the New Federalism can be tested and evaluated. Did the Reagan programme lead to freedom for all – or economic bondage for some and increasing wealth for élites? Is it really an initiative on behalf of fairness, genuine economic growth, and increasing opportunity? Or is the impact of Reagan's conservative-capitalist revolution merely the strengthening of the position of the dominant economic classes? These are the questions we now take up in turning to the impact of conservative capitalism in the United States.

Chapter Six

THE IMPACT OF
CONSERVATIVE CAPITALISM
IN THE UNITED STATES

Policies derived from the tenets of conservative capitalism have already altered greatly the equation of 'who gets what, when, and how?' The issue of inequality and its implications for the opportunity structure is the point of collision between liberal and social democratic versions of capitalism on the one hand, and conservative capitalism, in either its individualist or traditionalist variant on the other. Consequently an evaluation of the prospects of conservative capitalism must take account of the economic impacts of the policies so far enacted. There are general indicators that these policies have worsened the pattern of inequality in American society. This evidence suggests that, while some individualist conservative goals have been achieved, traditionalist fears of social disarray have been reinforced. The economic gains that have been made are not based upon sustainable growth in the non-military economy, nor have they been shared equitably by all levels of society. The gains owe at least as much to deficit spending as to 'supply-side' economics, and the effect of the latter has been to disadvantage the poor.

As we saw in the previous chapter, the watershed of policy change occurred early in President Reagan's first term of office. As a key to the policy thrust of the conservative-capitalist movement, an analysis of the impact of the budget cuts and tax changes of that period serves very well. The impact of those initiatives can then be traced through to changes in income distribution, patterns of employment and unemployment, the redistribution of government income transfers and tax 'expenditures', changes in the workforce, the size of the deficit, and the political environment for future initiatives. A review of these elements of the impact of conservative-capitalist policies will enable us to assess some of the effects on the overall balance between government and the marketplace.

BUDGET CUTS AND TAX CHANGES

Substantial cuts to income-security programmes were a notable feature of the first Reagan budget. As Richard Nathan pointed out, 'These cuts fell most heavily on one group, the so-called working poor, made up primarily of female heads of household and their children living on a combination of earned income and welfare.'[1] Budget cuts and programme changes in the safety-net programmes alone meant that the federal-government expenditure per capita for poor people fell from about $1,700 in 1980 to $1,575 in 1983, a 7.3 per cent decrease. The President claimed that total spending on the poor went up in his administration, but that was the effect of the recession on the size of entitlement populations.[2]

While the cuts were substantial, they were considerably less than those originally proposed by the Reagan administration. In its first major budget initiative the administration proposed cutting 'human capital' programmes by nearly 40 per cent. Congress agreed to cuts averaging 23 per cent.[3] Aid to Families with Dependent Children (AFDC) was slated to increase by 9.8 per cent; a cut of 28.6 per cent was proposed by the Reagan administration; and Congress enacted a 14.3 per cent decrease. Food stamps were targeted for a 51.3 per cent cut; Congress accepted a 13.8 per cent reduction. The most dramatic example was the Women, Infants and Children programme; a proposed cut of 63.6 per cent became, in the hands of Congress, a 9.1 per cent increase.[4]

Because the changes were made in the midst of a recession, they had a particularly burdensome impact on the poor. In a strong economy, it was estimated that the independent effect of the Omnibus Budget Reconciliation Act (OBRA) welfare-programme changes would have increased the poverty level by 2 per cent (557,000 people of whom 300,000 are children).[5] By advancing the proposal in a period of deep recession, the impact was additive. According to one study, the OBRA changes plus the recession increased the projected poverty population by 7.6 per cent as compared with a 5.7 per cent increase attributable to the recession alone.[6]

The cuts impacted particularly upon the working poor. The

Reagan administration made a deliberate effort to force those with marginal welfare eligibility to choose work over welfare, though the choice could go the other way. One result has been a continuing increase in the feminization of poverty. More than one-fifth of the families in the United States are raised by a single parent (up from one-ninth in 1970). As one study pointed out, 'Cuts in AFDC, food stamps, Medicaid, childcare, and job training programs are not cuts that affect different groups in society. They all affect poor women simultaneously, creating terrible hardship.'[7]

Various alterations in the tax laws resulting from the Reagan administration's overall tax cut were particularly hard on the poor. The federal tax burden for a poverty-level family of four changed from a $134 refund in 1978 to a $285 payment in 1982, and a $383 payment in 1985.[8] Prior to these changes, the tax threshold was substantially above the poverty line, and after them it fell to more than 10 per cent below the poverty line. Had the tax law not been changed again, the threshold would have reached 20 per cent below the poverty line in 1988.[9] The tax burden was increased by the additional impact of rises in state and local taxes to compensate for federal-revenue reductions. The distribution of the Reagan tax cut was sharply unequal in its effect on dollars retained by the taxpayer. The tax cuts added amounts ranging from nearly nothing for the less-than-$10,000-a-year bracket to about $1,500 for those in the $20,000–$40,000 bracket, and to more than $8,000 for those with incomes larger than $80,000.[10]

INCOME REDISTRIBUTION

While it can be argued that the New Federalism initiatives should be distinguished from changes in tax policy, the fact is that, for purposes of analysing shifts in the opportunity structure, they were both part of the revolution in federal relations that Reagan envisioned upon taking office. The most significant impact, for the purposes of the ideological debate, was to make more unequal the distribution of income.

According to 1984 Census Bureau data, the bottom 40 per cent of the population lost ground since 1980 with respect to the top 40 per cent in annual median income (−$477, +$1769).[11] A staff report of the Joint Economic Committee (November 1985) finds that the real income of families has been especially hard hit: the lowest quintile lost 23.8 per cent in mean income from 1979–84. Losses to the three middle quintiles were 14 per cent, 10.5 per cent, and 3.2 per cent, with a gain to the top quintile of 1.5 per cent.[12]

The losses in median family income began to be reversed in 1982 and it had risen 10.7 per cent by 1986 – very likely as a result of the stimulus of federal deficit spending. However, the 1986 income distribution figures revealed that the income share of the top 20 per cent increased to 46.1 per cent, the highest recorded by the Census Bureau since 1947. The share going to the middle 60 per cent declined to 50.2 per cent from 52.7 per cent in 1980, and the share to the bottom quintile went down from 4.1 per cent to 3.8 per cent.[13] Distributive consequences attach directly to the tax changes, attacks on unions, and other economic manipulations associated with supply-side economics, as well as to the payments made to finance the federal deficit.

These shifts bear out the direction of the projections generated on the basis of modelling reported by Palmer and Sawhill in August 1984. According to the Urban Institute's simulations of the impact of Reagan's policies, the lowest quintile was to lose 7.6 per cent of its income and the top quintile stood to gain 8.7 per cent. While some redistribution would have taken place because of the recession, the Reagan policy increased the inequality of the redistribution. When measured against the Urban Institute alternative (more conventional) policy model, the Reagan policies added 1.6 percentage points to the gain of the top quintile; and increased the loss of the bottom quintile by an additional 4.1 per cent.[14]

These pessimistic predictions of the consequences of Reagan's policies for the poor were available from very nearly the outset of his administration. The most recent data indicates that the lowest fifth have seen their real income decline by 32.3 per cent in the period from 1973–85, while the top fifth have slightly improved their share. There is no question that, wholly apart from the recession in the late seventies, Reagan's policies have disadvantaged the poor.[15]

The overall poverty rate rose sharply from 13 per cent in 1980 to 15.3 per cent in 1983, and then declined to 14.4 per cent in 1984 and 13.6 per cent in 1986. However the rate, even after three years of economic recovery, remains well above the 11–12 per cent poverty rate of the seventies. There were more poor people in 1986 (32.4 million) than there were when President Johnson declared the War on Poverty. In 1986 dollars, a family of four was deemed to be in poverty if it had a cash income of less than $11,203.

As Sheldon Danziger, Director of the University of Wisconsin Center for Research on Poverty, points out, 'A decade of progress against poverty was wiped out in four years (1979–1983).' There was a 49.4 per cent increase in the number of people living in poverty from 1979 to 1984. In assessing studies of the four factors responsible for this increase – demographics, increased inequality of earnings, the recession, and changes in transfer programmes – Danziger concludes that 'spending cuts and unemployment were about equally responsible for the rise in poverty.'[16]

The increasing numbers of homeless and impoverished people living on the streets of major cities has been graphic testimony to the result. In twenty-four of twenty-five large cities surveyed by the US Conference of Mayors, there were an increased number of homeless people in 1986 over 1985. The report pointed out that housing assistance had decreased from $31 billion in 1981 to less than $10 billion in 1986. The same survey reported that the number of poor people increased in two out of three cities, and decreased in only two cities.[17]

The principal culprits seem to be unemployment, a decline in real wages, and uneven distributive effects of such economic recovery as there has been. As the US Conference of Mayors report notes, 'nearly nine out of ten of the cities said the recovery has not helped the hungry, the homeless or other low-income people in their city'.[18] Supply-side economics hasn't solved these problems, and the fiscal changes of the New Federalism have cut the benefits of dependent citizens, thus aggravating their plight.

THE REDISTRIBUTION OF GOVERNMENT TRANSFERS AND TAX EXPENDITURES

Some critics have pointed out that the poverty rates reported by the Census Bureau do not include the value of in-kind transfers such as food stamps, subsidized school lunches, public housing, Medicare and Medicaid. When these are added in to the calculation for the 1982 poverty rate, for example, the rate drops to between 6.4 per cent and 9.8 per cent depending on the valuation of benefits.[19] However, this simply proves the point that these subsidies are vital to the reduction of poverty. It is cuts in these programmes that threaten the progress made against poverty in the 1970s. The housing subsidy alone has been cut from $27 billion to $9.9 billion.[20] In addition, the person who originated the poverty measure argues that inaccurate adjustments over the intervening years have resulted in understating the poverty rate by 20 per cent.[21]

The debate over the effect of transfers to the poor has to be placed in the larger perspective of transfers generally and what are now termed tax 'expenditures'. Tax expenditures are defined as 'revenue losses resulting from special or selective tax relief'. Economist Wallace Peterson, in a study of transfers and tax expenditures before and after the Reagan policy initiatives, points out that transfers to income-assistance programmes were cut by 3.8 per cent, while transfers to income-neutral social-insurance programmes increased by 17.2 per cent and to interest payable to individuals by 44.4 per cent.

Simultaneously the ratio of income on which taxes were paid to income excused from taxation (tax expenditures) grew from 54.9 per cent in 1980 to 84.4 per cent in 1983. For corporations, the ratio grew in the same three years from 63.1 per cent to 108.2 per cent! After the Reagan tax cut took effect, more corporate income was excluded from taxation than included.[22]

Who received the benefit of the income redistributed through tax expenditures? We can approximate an answer to the question by establishing income groups and constructing a ratio between the percentage of *tax returns filed* and the percentage of tax expenditures received by each group. We have also constructed a second ratio that indicates the relationship of the amount of taxes paid to the tax expenditures received in each income group. The first ratio shows how the distributive effects work in terms of the numbers of taxpayers in each income category. The second ratio shows how expenditures are returned in relationship to the amount of taxes paid.

The first ratio, that between the numbers of taxpayers in each income group and the share of total tax expenditures received illustrates the disproportionate political strength of the rich. They receive a far larger share of the benefit of tax expenditures per capita than do the poor (a ratio of 21:1 contrasted with .1:1 for the poor). In terms of a dollar return on their tax payments, the poor get about $2 back for every $1 they pay, while the rich come out about even. But the price is paid by the near poor and the middle-

Table 6.1 Who benefits from tax 'expenditures' (1983)

Income	A Tax returns filed	B Taxes paid	C Tax expenditures received	Ratio of C:A	Ratio of C:B
$	%	%	%		
0–999 (poor)	36.9	2.2	4.5	0.1:1	2.0:1
10,000–19,999 (near poor)	26.0	13.9	10.2	0.4:1	0.7:1
20,000–49,999 (middle-class)	32.7	51.1	45.5	1.4:1	0.9:1
50,000–99,999 (affluent)	3.7	18.3	25.1	6.8:1	1.4:1
100,000+ (rich)	0.7	14.6	14.7	21.0:1	1.0:1

Source: Ratios computed from data reported in Wallace Peterson (1985) 'The US "welfare state" and the counterrevolution', *Journal of Economic Issues*, 19(3), September: table 9, p. 623, based on US Treasury Reports compiled for former Senator Walter Mondale and US Representative Henry Reuss

income groups who, unlike the affluent, the rich, and the poor, receive less than they pay. This form of governmental redistribution of income has been increasing rapidly. The ratio between taxes raised and tax expended through various loopholes remained at about 31 per cent throughout the 1970s. By 1983, as a result of the Reagan initiatives, it jumped to 48 per cent. Consequently increasing the amount of tax expenditures has helped the extremes at the expense of the middle and has returned a much larger per-capita advantage to the rich than to the poor. Other tax changes, as we saw earlier, meant that the poor were further disadvantaged by lowering the threshold of taxable income.

The most recent study of the distributive effects of tax changes found that the poorest decile will pay almost 20 per cent more of their income in taxes, and the richest decile about 10 per cent less in 1987, than in 1977. The tax burden for the population as a whole remained constant in this period.[23]

Claims by the Reagan administration that government 'social' spending is a welfare giveaway to the poor are simply false. When the whole picture of assistance programmes, transfers, and tax expenditures is computed, the government acts as the redistributor of up to one dollar out of every three of personal income, according to Peterson's calculations based on government data, and by far the disproportionate share goes to the rich. If subsidies to income groups via the military budget and other forms of government spending on goods and services were added into the calculation, the results would be even more skewed toward the upper-income groups.

Consequently the real picture of income redistribution in the Reagan years is that the already disproportionately low per-capita return to the poor has been reduced, while the return to the rich has been increased substantially – and all this within an expanding governmental sector of the economy. The rhetorical justification for these cuts to the poor has depended upon conservative symbolic appeals to values of thrift, hard work, and a rejection of governmental assistance. However, if, as the rhetoric also claims, government redistribution is unearned income, the total effect of the Reagan years has been to move the rich further away from productive work at the expense of the poor and, to some degree, the middle class.

These have been the costs of Reagan's policy initiatives, but the costs were to be justified by a return to health of the general economy and, by extension to its bottom sectors, an improvement in the position of the poor. The favoured maxim of the Reagan administration was: 'A rising tide lifts all boats.' It is time to see how, in fact, the distribution of 'boats' – in the form of jobs – has changed during the Reagan Presidency.

CHANGES IN THE WORKFORCE

The advertised advantage of supply-side economics was to be the creation of jobs. The unadvertised advantage of its governmental policy correlates, including the New Federalism, was to be an increasingly numerous and tractable labour force. Reduced social programmes would force the poor to choose low-paid labour over dependency on government hand-outs. The union movement would be stripped of its governmental protection and faced with the stark pressures of international competition.

The labour force has become more tractable, but the creation of jobs did not proceed at the rate promised. Furthermore, the kinds of jobs that were created were largely low-paying service jobs dependent on an economy artificially expanded by deficit spending. The net effect is the downward mobility of those least able to compete: from industrial job to minimum-wage service job or no job; from subsistence-level governmental benefits to sub-marginal benefits, or no benefits at all.

The distributive characteristics of the unemployment problem reveal the significant ideological dimensions. Rudy Oswald, the Research Director for the American Federation of Labor – Congress of Industrial Organizations (AFL-CIO), points out that in 1986 nearly 6 million of the 8.4 million unemployed had 'no unemployment benefits of any kind'. Furthermore, government statistics report that there are 1.2 million 'discouraged workers' who have given up looking for jobs, and 5.4 million who work at part-time jobs in the absence of full-time employment. The unemployment rate for blacks is typically more than double that for whites.[24] The ideologically-based initiatives of the administration have done little to assist those who have been the most affected by under-employment and unemployment. On the contrary, administration policies, as we have seen, have created further hardship for these groups.[25]

There is also the problem of re-employment for those who have lost their jobs due to plant closings and relocations. A study by the Congressional Office of Technology Assessment reports that only 60 per cent of those who lost their jobs for these reasons in the period 1979–84 found re-employment. Of those, 45 per cent took pay cuts – the majority of them at levels less than 80 per cent of their former wages. The impact fell disproportionately on middle-aged white workers in blue-collar occupations. It should be added that this is a group that formed the backbone of the Democratic coalition ever since the New Deal.[26] In fact, half of the jobs created from 1979 to 1985 paid less than the poverty-level income.[27]

The reason for these poor results is that, according to Bureau of Labor Statistics studies, virtually all of the jobs added to the economy from 1982 to 1986 were in the relatively low-paid service sector.[28] In fact, 97 per cent of net employment gains for white men since 1979 have been in the low-wage stratum (as opposed to fewer than one out of four at that level in the 1973–79 period).[29] Manufacturing jobs are being exported. The balance of trade in the manufacturing sector moved from a surplus of $13 billion in 1980 to a deficit of $113 billion in 1985. Finally, in early 1988, a dramatic devaluation of the dollar has improved employment in manufacturing.

As is the case with the oceans, the tide that rises in one place recedes in another. The Reagan policies haven't created the kind of real sustainable growth that provides, as in the post-Second-

World-War period, rising prosperity and decreasing inequality across all sectors of the income distribution.[30] Supply-side economics has failed to produce real gains for those hardest hit by the inequalities of a market economy. What has been accomplished is the reinforcement of an underclass of marginalized individuals who experience frequent periods of unemployment. Increasingly these are minorities living in urban areas. Richard Nathan who directed several studies of the impact of the Reagan cuts for the Brookings Institution, and who served as Director of the Office of Management and the Budget in the Nixon administration, stated recently that, 'Urban problems are getting worse at precisely the time the nation is doing less about them,' and that the increasing concentration of poor people in the cities is 'the real urban problem'.[31]

The Reagan administration has stressed the fact that a great deal of the increase in poverty is occurring among households headed by single women. The implication is that it is poverty by choice – a choice that was encouraged by the structure of Great Society poverty programmes and one which is morally wrong.[32] This has been one of the justifications for cutting benefits for the working poor to force an exit from dependency.

Given the employment situation, the choice is no more than a dilemma: reduced benefits or marginal jobs, neither of which provide livable circumstances for raising children.[33] The mother who chooses the exit from dependency for the marginal job gains a few dollars and her children lose her presence in the home, often with no real substitute since child-care programmes are low on the list of Reagan priorities. Add the Reagan administration's retreat on equal employment opportunity and affirmative action, and the likelihood that the marginal job will lead to something better diminishes.[34] The mother who decides to stay home with the children under reduced AFDC, food stamps, and medical assistance, struggles with a harsh burden. Add Workfare to the bargain, and even the benefit of a parent in the home is lost. However these realities may impact upon the behaviour of the parent, the children have to live with increasingly difficult circumstances.

THE FISCAL CONSEQUENCES

Despite the cuts in domestic programmes affecting the poor, the federal budget has continued to rise. The failure to break the deadlock over domestic v. military spending has meant that the federal budget has steadily escalated. The early years of the Reagan administration saw an increase in the percentage of the GNP that went to government from an average of 32.1 per cent in the 1970s to an average of 37.2 per cent under Reagan.[35] Fiscal year 1986 brought the first trillion-dollar federal budget.

Revenues, owing to tax cuts, have not kept pace. The result is, of course, the mushrooming federal deficit. The outstanding debt rose by 146 per cent from 1980 to June of 1986 and now amounts to over $2 trillion – $220 billion of it attributable to fiscal year 1986 alone. The Reagan administration has now presided over an expansion of the deficit by a greater amount that all of his predecessors put together.

Apart from the increasing burden this puts upon the working population of the nation, the distributive consequences of the deficit attach primarily to the impact of interest payments. The interest on the debt has grown from $80.4 billion in fiscal year 1980 to an estimated $196 billion in fiscal year 1986. As a percentage of the GNP, it grew even faster than the military budget. In addition, the average maturity of the debt has increased from three years nine months at the end of fiscal year 1980 to five years as of mid-1986. This increases the interest load substantially and stretches out the period over which the debt could be repaid, were there the will to do so.[36]

Interest on the debt amounts to a highly regressive tax on the population. The top 1 per cent of the population held approximately half of all the stocks and bonds in 1976, the last year for which there is reliable data. We may assume the same tiny proportion of the population continues to be the principal beneficiaries of interest payments on the debt.[37] While the President lays the blame for the deficit at the door of Congress because of its preference for domestic spending over military, it is the military budget that accounts for the lion's share of the growth in federal outlays. Entitlements as a percentage of the total budget have decreased by 1 per cent, while non-defence discretionary spending has decreased by 8 per cent. Military spending has increased from 23 per cent in 1981 to 28 per cent of the budget in 1987, and interest on the debt from 10 per cent to 14 per cent.[38]

Efforts to control the debt, as in the Gramm-Rudman-Hollings legislation, have focused on a balanced reduction between military and domestic categories. The only other pathways out of fiscal disaster on the domestic side seem to be either a devolution of income-security programmes to the states, or the institution of means-tests for major entitlements such as Medicare and the taxation of Social Security benefits so as to recoup revenue from well-heeled recipients. Individualist conservatives prefer the course of devolution; traditionalists would favour means tested entitlements in a rationalized system. Equally as important, the former would likely be opposed by traditionalists, and the latter by individualists. Consequently there is no policy consensus with the conservative-capitalist movement.

In addition, the political realities are that neither strategy can command sufficient support to overcome obvious sources of opposition. Devolving substantial responsibilities to the states without substantial quid pro quos is, as was discovered in the New Federalism negotiations, to brook the bipartisan opposition of the nation's governors. Alternatively, to institute means tests for major entitlements is to undo the political coalition that made their enactment possible in the first place. The tacit bargain in the creation of Social Security was that the rich could be persuaded to pay disproportionately to subsidize the poor only if the rich could collect on the same basis as everyone else. That same bargain makes Medicare possible. Less explicitly, a host of middle- and upper-class subsidies appear to be the political trade-off for such low-income assistance as is available from the federal government.

As David Stockman reports in a book appropriately titled, *The Triumph of Politics*, there is no way to persuade Congressmen whose re-election depends on the clientele of these various subsidies that such consequential shifts are in their interest. Stockman's assertions on this point are curious in that he claims to have discovered these political realities only in consequence of a bitter learning experience as Budget Director from 1980–85. Had he known better, he intimates, the deficit-inducing policies of his tenure would not have been initiated.[39] Yet in 1975, five years before Reagan's election, in an article entitled, 'The social pork barrel', Stockman previewed the thesis of his later apology and pointed out that, over time, conservatives as well as liberals become supporters of social spending. His 1975 article contains a prophetic remark, 'Should some bespectacled budget analyst in the Executive Office Building propose that the [social] program be reduced or eliminated, the retreat [from Conservative opposition] will be shown to have come full circle, as a chorus of reputedly conservative Congressmen gravely intone: "I'm four square for cutting the swollen federal budget, but this is the wrong program at the wrong time in the wrong place." '[40] As it happens, Stockman wound up cutting benefits to the poor without obtaining either a rationalization of income-security programmes to the federal level, or obtaining significant cuts in middle-class subsidies. As William Greider summarized it in reporting his famous interviews with Stockman:

> To reject weak claims from powerful clients – that was the intellectual credo that allowed him [Stockman] to hack away so confidently at wasteful social programs, believing that he was being equally tough-minded on the wasteful business subsidies. Now, as the final balance was being struck, he was forced to concede in private that the claim of equity in shrinking the government was significantly compromised if not obliterated.[41]

Stockman was willing, however, to consider tax increases as a way out of the impasse – a tendency that drew rebukes from libertarian hard-liners such as Donald Regan, formerly Treasury Secretary and Chief of Staff in the White House.[42]

If the will to change was not present in Congress, neither has it been present in the Reagan White House, according to Stockman's account. Stockman remarks, 'The $800 billion worth of deficits were the result of the spending he [Reagan] didn't want to cut.'[43] Whether the reluctance was compassion, political prudence, or the lack of consensus within conservative ranks can't be definitively established. However, a truly united conservative movement with a single programme would have made such resolve easier to come by. As it was, Stockman claims: 'The fact was, there wasn't a semblance of a Reagan ideological coalition in the Congress to support the [fiscal] revolution.'[44]

Consequently, Reagan's fiscal initiatives have so far led only to deadlock on the domestic front, vast increases in military expenditures, and tax policies that have resulted in horrendous deficits. The tax reform recently enacted will only redistribute the burden somewhat more equitably; the proposals are designed to be 'revenue neutral'. Meanwhile the deficit is, according to observers such as Leonard Silk of *The New York Times*, 'at the root of the nation's dependence on foreign capital, the overvalued dollar, the record trade deficit, and the struggles to re-establish order to the budget and the national economy'.[45] This judgement is widely shared among the nation's economists.[46]

The trade deficit for the United States has reached historic proportions. After becoming the world's largest debtor nation in 1985, the trade deficit doubled in 1986. At the time of writing, a decline in the value of the dollar has improved the picture slightly, but the overall problem of disadvantageous terms of trade remains. The policy choices appear to be either to allow further erosion in the income of working families, or to find a way to get additional production out of the population by investing in technology and human resources in a more efficient fashion. The second course of action seems to be excluded by virtue of ideological constraints on the role that government is supposed to play in a *laissez-faire* system. To the extent that investments have been made through the defence budget, the effect is to produce non-consumable goods and services that add nothing to the real basis of the economy. These investments tie up resources and add to inflationary pressures in periods of economic improvement. It is the threat of inflation that is used to decry the economic impact of increasing social spending for the poor when, in fact, defence spending has at least as great an effect. We will return to this matter in chapter 11.

For the present, it can clearly be seen that the net effect of Reagan administration policies on the structure of the job market has been to decrease unemployment, largely through the effect of massive increases in defence spending, while replacing many manufacturing jobs in the non-military economy with lower-paid service jobs.

POLITICAL IMPACT

The continuing high levels of poverty place the justification of further New Federalist initiatives in doubt. While individualist conservatives may be reassured by the rhetoric of anti-statism that envelopes Reagan's policy proposals, traditional conservatives in Congress, the corporate world, and the churches have evidenced signs of restlessness over the increasingly difficult position of the poor.[47]

Republican Senator Robert Dole, in response to concerns about the image of the Republican Party as the 'rich man's party', has proposed balancing low-end cuts with high-end tax increases: 'If you're going to do equity on the low end, you have to do equity on the high end.'[48] Commenting on the growth of a 'permanent and growing under-class,' the Chairman of American Can Company recently remarked:

> We will need to reaffirm the role of government in helping the poor and the dispossessed. We will need to put aside, once and for all, the notion that poverty, hunger, and homelessness are problems for everyone but government. We will need to make clear once again that government is the one social institution in this country that is best able to help the poor and dispossessed.[49]

Concern in traditionalist circles continues to increase. The bishops of the US Roman Catholic Church, not previously noted for their liberalism in American politics, endorsed by a vote on 225 to 9 a pastoral letter on the economy that said, 'That so many people are poor in a nation as rich as ours is a social and moral scandal that we cannot ignore.' The letter went on to point out that while economic growth 'is an important and necessary condition for the reduction of unemployment, it is not sufficient in and of itself,' and called for greater governmental efforts to assist the poor.[50] The letter, drafted under the chairmanship of Archbishop Rembert Weakland of Milwaukee, prompted a rebuke by conservative columnist William F. Buckley entitled, 'A prayer for Weakland's failure,' that essayed the *laissez-faire* line on solving the problems of the poor.

Higher levels of poverty reinforce an endemic problem in US society: racism. The United States remains a society sharply segregated economically by race. The Census Bureau in the first systematic study of wealth distribution (as distinct from income distribution) in more than twenty years found massive differences between the wealth of white families and that of black and Hispanic families. The average ratio of assets was 12 to 1 for whites over blacks, and 8 to 1 for whites over Hispanics.[51]

The racial consequences further illustrate the divisive impact of the Reagan programme. The devastation of the black family and the feminization of poverty generally have placed increasing numbers of children below the poverty line. The 1987 poverty rate for black children was a whopping 45.6 per cent.

The social consequences of poverty and inequality are everywhere to be seen. Rates of imprisonment continue to climb and the United States now has more than a half million people in jail. The prison population grew 8.4 per cent in 1985 alone and is up 68 per cent since 1977.[52] It is the highest rate of imprisonment in the Western industrialized world. The United States has, for some time, had more private police than public police. Fears for personal safety have become a daily preoccupation for more and more people.

The President attempted to defend the fairness of his administration's policies toward the poor in a series of assertions in 1981 and 1982 that were contradicted by the facts. He pointed out that overall federal spending has in fact increased, and that this shows his administration is not harming the poor – however, he forgot to mention that the military budget accounts for the increase; assistance to the poor has been cut. The President suggested that increases in direct benefit payments from 27 cents of every federal dollar in the Kennedy years to 43 cents in the Reagan years indicates that compassion has not been dispensed with – but forgot to say that most of the current subsidy programmes were created after Kennedy's death by progressive Democrats.[53]

President Reagan pointed out that food-stamp assistance expanded 16,000 per cent in fifteen years – overlooking the fact that in the base year, 1968, food stamps were an experimental programme in a few hundred counties, not a national programme. The President claimed that the supplemental food programme for women, infants, and children had not been cut, but rather combined with another programme and expanded – leading to a retraction after it was discovered that the programme had been combined and cut by 25 per cent. He claimed not to have cut Social Security but did by ending student benefits for children of deceased or disabled workers.[54]

A more realistic assessment of the initiatives of the first term must be that what was accomplished is a form of 'de facto new federalism'.[55] Substantial changes in priorities did take place in the first term, particularly in areas affecting the poor. The priority given to military spending has been pursued relentlessly, and in the face of mounting opposition from Democrats and Republicans alike, right through to the proposal for the 1988 budget. Some concessions have had to be made on domestic spending, but only with the greatest reluctance.

However, the foundations for a permanent structural change were not secured in the first term, nor have they been since. As one observer put it, 'no clear winner (the federal government or state and local government) emerged' from the first-term efforts at 'separating the functions of the federal government and the states into neat spheres'.[56] The Reagan budget for fiscal year 1985 actually proposed a modest increase in federal assistance to state and local governments.[57]

There are pressures from within conservative-capitalist ranks that could even reverse the decentralizing structural tendency of the New Federalism. On social issues there was a significant new departure in federal policy with the imposition of federal highway-assistance sanctions for those states that refused to conform to the 21-year-old drinking age.[58] The nationalization of authority over an issue that is traditionally within the purview of the states is paralleled in proposals for other areas such as cable television, public-employee pensions, and banking regulation, among others.[59] Were Reagan's initiatives on abortion followed, a similar structural result would obtain. When it comes to mandating restrictions on individual social behaviour in particular, traditionalists give notions of decentralization short shrift.

Apart from social issues, it isn't at all clear that deregulation will necessarily enliven the springs of commerce. In fact, it can have the reverse effect. Partly for these reasons, Reagan's programme of deregulation got off to a much touted beginning, only to fizzle in the face of implementation difficulties and cross-cutting priorities.[60] The principal problem was, according to Timothy Conlan, that 'deregulating the private sector can easily conflict with deregulating states and localities.'[61] The more the federal government loosens the reins on private industry, the more the states pick up the slack and complicate business's problems with a welter of conflicting restraints.

In a response to this phenomenon that violates the whole premise of the New Federalism, the Reagan administration has supported a stringent federal law that would override state authority in the area of consumer-product-liability regulation. The legislation would pre-empt state law-making power through a novel and precedent-setting expansion of federal authority over liability determinations.[62]

The drive toward a comprehensive New Federalism is stalled in good part because of profound political and ideological disagreements within President Reagan's own ranks, as well as the resistance the programme has encountered at all levels of the governing system. The nation's governors issued a report in February of 1986 characterizing Reagan's approach to federalism as a 'one way street' with responsibility flowing to the states unaccompanied by dollars, and calling for tax increases and defence cuts as an alternative approach to deficits.[63]

While the separation of ideological motivation from political prudence can never be entirely clear, we can shed additional light on the role of ideology by comparing the Reagan administration with the government of Prime Minister Margaret Thatcher to see if the same fault lines appear within the British version of conservative capitalism. If it becomes apparent that the conservative-capitalist movement lacks the unity of conviction that would make a true structural reform possible, then it becomes more likely that tides of time and political chance may well work their way unaffected by any long-term change in the system. On the other hand, it may well be that the parliamentary system, with the government in command of a working majority, will facilitate the implementation of a programme despite substantial reservations – reservations that in the American arrangement of 'checks and balances' between the three branches of government acquire institutional standing in the forms we have seen in this and the preceding chapter. In that event, the divisive potential of the market-based conservative's programme will very likely be realized to a much greater degree in Britain than in the United States – a prospect that clearly worries analysts of British public opinion.[64]

CONCLUSION

Of course the Democratic Party and the Labour Party have both suffered similar internal clashes between left and right tendencies. The New Deal's greatest political liability was the perception that it was socialist in character – this tied domestic policy to potent symbolic and substantive issues in foreign policy. After Roosevelt's initial success with the New Deal, it took Democratic presidents who had established their conservative credentials in foreign policy, i.e. Truman, Kennedy, and Johnson, to advance the domestic agenda of greater governmental activism. The New Deal consensus fell apart in the presidency of Jimmy Carter, whose credentials in foreign policy were, if not tarnished by a softness on communism, certainly damaged by an image of ineffectiveness.

The Labour Party's internal splits have been much more consequential for the staying power of its programme. The left has been too strong for the Labour Party simply to dismiss. Efforts to straddle the factions in the Wilson period produced little more than a confusion of policy. Attempts to resolve the split on the left yielded part of the voter disaffection that made Thatcher's triumph possible. The search for models of governmental activism has not produced a clear and appealing programme for the Labour Party, nor for the contemporary Democratic Party. We will return to these issues in the conclusion. However, it is important to realize that internally divided movements have their limits, and that both liberal capitalism and conservative capitalism share that problem.

We have focused on issues of federalism because they were at the heart of the New Deal and were to be at the heart of the Reagan 'Revolution'. Consequently these issues are, on one level, a barometer of the political fortunes of conservative capitalism. At the same time, it must be said that defederalization and devolution have, on the merits, supporters among liberals and some varieties of socialists. Populists of the left have always favoured placing authority close to home.

In fact, an unintended consequence of the New Federalism may be that states have regained their status as the incubators of progressivism, a title lost to the federal government in the heyday of the Great Society. The historic pattern of policy innovations emerging from such laboratory states as California, New York, and Wisconsin may return. States have been expanding their revenues faster than the federal government has been cutting its assistance – resulting in a net fiscal gain at the state level. The percentage of the federal budget devoted to state and local governmental assistance declined from 14.0 per cent when Reagan became President to an estimated 11.2 per cent in fiscal year 1985. Meanwhile federal revenue as a source of state funds shrank from 31.7 per cent in 1980 to 23.7 per cent in 1984.[65]

In policy areas such as comparable worth, states have provided the leadership rather than the federal government.[66] While states may be able to assert progressive-style creativity in some areas of policy, however, they cannot, acting separately, solve the fundamental structural problems of welfare and the provision of jobs for the unemployed. John Herbers, a long time observer of federalism, reports that the result has been the reversal of the trend toward more inter-regional uniformity of income levels: 'in the 1980s, a new kind of disparity emerged, a crazy-quilt pattern of the haves and have-nots.'[67]

What conservative capitalism has amounted to in the United States is a movement that has lacked the cohesiveness to mount a true structural revolution. It has, instead, led to series of policy initiatives that have worsened inequality, while not achieving a permanent basis for economic growth and development. Indeed, the impact on the poor and vulnerable elements of the middle class, such as middle-aged blue-collar workers, has been devastating. Individualist conservatives have yet to prove their case; traditionalists have good reasons to consider their scepticism well founded.[68] The impasse of conservative capitalism creates new opportunities for the left – a theme we will return to in the final chapters after surveying developments in Great Britain.

Chapter Seven

THE RISE OF CONSERVATIVE CAPITALISM IN BRITAIN

We offered a complete change in direction – from one in which the state became totally dominant in peoples' lives and penetrated almost every aspect of life to a life where the state did do certain things, but without displacing personal responsibility. I think we have altered the balance between the person and the state in a favourable way.

(Margaret Thatcher, *The Times*, 5 May 1983)

In 1976, by which time free-market ideas were becoming more dominant in the Conservative Party, Conservative governments had been in power for seventeen of thirty-one post-war years, 1951–64 and 1970–4. Many of the leading figures in the renaissance of conservative capitalism in Britain such as Mrs Thatcher, Nigel Lawson, and Sir Keith Joseph, successively Industry Secretary and Education Secretary in two Thatcher governments, have argued very strongly against the effects of the social democratic consensus and the range of ideas which underpinned it. The period of the mid-1970s when Mrs Thatcher succeeded Mr Heath as leader of the Conservative Party was a turning point in post-war politics.[1]

The story of how this turning-point was reached is in substantial part a matter of understanding how the social democratic consensus was developed and then dismantled in view of a particular assessment of its failures. This assessment was advanced in a determined and intellectually coherent fashion by Mrs Thatcher and the intellectuals and politicians who supported her successful drive for the premiership. The consensus itself originated in an analysis of the 'lessons' of the Second World War and of the Depression before it, as well as of the ultimate weaknesses of the Keynesian approach to governmental policy. Against this background of perceived failure, a restatement of the market-based approach to incentives and inter-sectoral relations was successfully asserted. Each element of this analysis bears closer examination.

THE GROWTH OF THE STATE

At its most fundamental level the consensus concerned the role of the state in modern society. The role of the state had been expanding over a long period in British political history, but the two world wars, and in particular the Second World War, strengthened and consolidated this development.

One plausible measure of the growth of government is the percentage of GNP devoted to public expenditure and the figures for this show how dramatic the growth of government in the United Kingdom has been. At the end of the eighteenth century total government expenditure constituted only just above 10 per cent of the GNP. By 1890 the percentage had declined to below 10 per cent, but by 1920 at the end of the Great War it had gone up to 26 per cent. By 1940, at the very height of the Second World War, public expenditure was 60 per cent of the GNP; in 1960, 41 per cent; in 1970, 47 per cent, and in 1979, 52 per cent. So judged by the resources commanded by the political- as opposed to the private-market sphere, there can be clearly discerned the growth of incremental statism. The growth has been most marked since the Second World War.[2]

Other indices tell the same sort of story. In 1851 only 2.4 per cent of the workforce was employed in the public sector (including defence). In 1921 the figure was 10 per cent; by 1951 14.5 per cent; by 1971 19.8 per cent, and by 1976 22.7 per cent of the workforce (5.79 out of 25.5 million of the working population). The growth of public expenditures and the growth of public-sector unemployment is therefore a centrally important political fact.

Within this expenditure, welfare, along with economic and environmental services, has shown the very largest increases. In 1890 defence accounted for 26.7 per cent of total public expenditures and the other services for 35.7 per cent; in 1979 defence amounted to 10.7 per cent of public expenditures; the other services for 80.7 per cent. As a percentage of GNP, defence has increased from 2.4

per cent in 1890 to 5.5 per cent in 1979, and the other services from 3.2 to 41.8 per cent during the same period.

The growth of the role of state and in particular of state welfare, educational services, and the provision for the unemployment benefit has thus been a marked feature of the twentieth century. When the Thatcher government came into power in 1979, the state controlled 52 per cent of GNP, employed 22 per cent of the workforce in the UK and presided over a welfare budget which had expanded inexorably and dramatically compared with defence.[3]

WAR AND THE RISE OF THE STATE

Many conservative critics of these developments have argued that experience of war was crucial in this development. A. J. P. Taylor, in his classic *English History 1914–45*, has evoked the contrast between the role of government before and after the Great War particularly well:

Until August 1914 a sensible, law-abiding Englishman could pass through life and hardly notice the existence of the state, beyond the post office and the policeman. He could live where he liked and as he liked. He had no official number or identity card. He could travel abroad or leave this country for ever without a passport or any sort of official permission. He could exchange his money for any other currency without restriction or limit. . . . The Englishman paid taxes on a modest scale: nearly 200 million pounds in 1913–1914, less than 8 per cent of the national income. The state intervened against eating adulterated food or contracting certain infectious diseases. It imposed safety rules in factories and prevented women and adult males in some industries from working excessive hours. The state saw to it that children received education up to the age of 13.

Since 1 January 1909, it provided a meagre pension for the needy over the age of 70. Since 1911, it helped to insure certain classes of workers against sickness and unemployment. . . . Still, broadly speaking, the state acted only to help those who could not help themselves. It left the adult citizen alone. All this was changed by the impact of the Great War. The state established a hold over its citizens which, though relaxed in peacetime, was never to be removed and which in the Second World War was again to increase. The history of the English state and of the English people merged for the first time.[4]

Both wars contributed to the reshaping of British society, but nowhere more so than in the field of government and politics. In both wars there was a major militarization of society which led to government's being able to organize society and the major interest groups and classes within it in pursuit of an unquestioned common goal.

This mobilization of society and economic activity seemed to show in political terms that the doubts of classical liberals about the desirability of state intervention and their strictures on its beneficial effects were misplaced. The proof of the pudding is in the eating, and during two world wars government in Britain seemed to have demonstrated competence in managing and planning national resources. It effectively mobilized society and its major interests around common goals which rendered very marginal the influence of classical liberals who were quite dubious about state intervention.

This confidence in the competence of state power influenced wartime politicians and civil servants, many of whom assumed high office after the war, and subsequently coloured their attitudes. Certainly the experience of the Second World War and its impact on the post-war years is seen by many free-market conservative critics of the post-war settlement as being fundamental and crucial to leading British society in the wrong direction. Sir Keith Joseph points the contrast in the following way:

> Until recently government was expected to confine its role to setting the framework within which people would be free to pursue their own mixture of self-interest and altruism. . . . The Second World War brought about a swing of the pendulum in which it came to be believed that government could do almost everything for everybody without infringing freedom or opportunity.[5]

This is an important theme and it is worth quoting Sir Keith again:

> [The war] not only increased the actual role of the state, but also increased belief in the efficiency, indeed the virtual omnicompetence of state intervention. The closing victorious years of the Second World War were euphoric . . . wars are

times of full employment, of national purpose, of an expanded role for government. It was only natural that the socialist-Keynesian theses on the capacity of government to solve social and economic problems should find the climate congenial.[6]

Nigel Lawson in his lecture, *The New Conservatism* argues as follows:

This, for a whole generation was Britain's finest hour: it was also a time when the state was seen to arrogate to itself in a cause whose rightness was not open to question, all the apparatus of central planning and the direction of labour.[7]

The fact that this degree of development of state power was in fact in both world wars aligned with victory and a resurrection of national pride also explains why the growth of governmental power was seen in a *positive* rather than a *negative* light, and one which cast a long shadow into the post-war world. It seemed in Britain that victory had been attained by planning and by co-ordination, whereas in defeated countries the opposite, and in the view of free-market conservatives, a more appropriate lesson was learned. Commenting on the growth of state power, Nigel Lawson argues as follows:

The Federal Republic of Germany provides the perfect counterpoint to this. But there it was not associated with the benevolent despotism of a Churchill, but with the evil tyranny of a Hitler. As a consequence the economic lesson the German people learned from the war was the evil of state power rather than the benevolence of state power; the German trade union movement was imbued with the hostility to state intervention (which had been used to suppress free trades unionism altogether) in contrast to the British trade union movement's delusion that its objects can most effectively be secured through the agency of state interventon; and even the social democrats were driven to embrace the principles and practice of the market economy.[8]

Victory in war contributed to the legitimacy of the form of government power used to attain the victory and this was a persuasive influence on post-war politics. So wartime experiences consolidated and legitimized the growth of government.

These arguments about the impact of war on modern political

economy are far from being merely impressionistic or anecdotal. They have, on the contrary, received considerable academic attention particularly by Peacock and Wiseman in their book *The Growth of Public Expenditure in the United Kingdom*.[9] Others followed the Hayekian argument, outlined in *The Road to Serfdom*, that government co-ordination is necessary and indeed possible in wartime conditions because there is an overriding goal, namely defeat of the enemy, and all the activities of society can be made subservient to this overall aim. However, there is in peacetime no equivalent of this: individual goals and preferences are varied and government both cannot and should not seek to co-ordinate production and consumption plans in peacetime. Frequently in the post-war years politicians have talked about various problems, notably poverty and the energy crisis, as the moral equivalent to war in setting an overriding goal for society. The argument of the free marketeer is that there is in peacetime no moral equivalent to war which would justify and indeed enable government to play the co-ordinating and collectivist role that it plays in war. Peacock and Wiseman's arguments are more detailed and are in fact formulated in terms of a hypothesis – what they call the displacement hypothesis. Because of the over-riding and agreed goal of defeating the enemy and the necessary collectivization of society to meet this, governments are able to exceed what were previously regarded as tolerable levels of taxation. Ideas of what are tolerable levels of taxation are fundamentally changed and because of the sense of solidarity which prevails during war and its aftermath, this displacement is not reversed in the immediate post-war period. This is exactly what happened in the post-1945 period. The Beveridge Report, *Full Employment and a Free Society*, was produced in 1944 at the height of the collectivization of British society and set the tone of the post-war political settlement. This rise is not merely compared to the aftermath of the First and Second World Wars. Between 1800 and 1814 when the government was involved in the Napoleonic conflict government spending as a proportion of GNP rose from 12 per cent in 1790 to 29 per cent in 1814, but it did eventually fall back to 10 per cent in 1900. However, income tax, introduced as a special wartime measure, persisted. The difference with the twentieth-century experience is partly explained with the capacity of government to co-ordinate activities and perhaps also the difference in the degree of public mobilization for the war effort. Of course no one would argue that this is in any sense a total explanation of the growth in the role of government. To understand the Conservative approach to these issues, reference will have to be made to those discussed in chapters 2 and 3 but, nevertheless, there is a range of considerations which Conservative defenders of the free-market have been keen to emphasize in the British context.

THE LESSONS OF THE DEPRESSION

Also very important in drawing what free-market conservatives in Britain regard as the wrong conclusion from the wartime period was the contrast with the 1930s. Many post-war political leaders, perhaps most notably Harold Macmillan, Prime Minister 1957–63, but also R. A. Butler, Chancellor of the Exchequer in the first post-war Conservative government, and also to some extent Sir Anthony Eden, Prime Minister 1955–7, drew upon their experiences in the 1930s. They saw these years as a period of *laissez-faire* capitalism which resulted in a deep period of recession and unemployment. Macmillan, particularly during this period, was very critical of what he saw as the government's failure to intervene in a positive way to plan economic performance. In a series of articles, speeches, pamphlets, interventions in parliamentary debates, and in his books, *Reconstruction* (1933), *Planning for Employment* (1935), *The Next Five Years* (1935), and *The Middle Way* (1938), Macmillan and his associates argued for a revised form of conservatism which would wean the party away from the *laissez-faire* policies of classical liberalism.

The aim was not to supplant capitalism, but rather to use the state to provide the best framework of planning within which private enterprise could act without the massive costs which it had produced in the 1930s. For example, he argued in favour of the public control of certain key industries such as fuel and transport. The state should assist industrial rationalization and mergers to create economies of scale and companies of a size large enough to compete effectively in world markets where larger companies particularly in the United States and Germany were operating. National Industrial Councils should be created to plan for each major sector of the economy to ensure that output did not exceed demand for products. State action could also help to ensure greater efficiency and co-ordination in purchasing raw materials for industry, in marketing, and in research and development. State regional policies should be developed which would ensure that investment was directed to deprived areas. In 1935 he argued in the Commons that 'we shall have to take great power in the hands of the State to direct in what localities and areas fresh industrial development will be allowed'. In addition, there should be a role for the state in industrial disputes and this would in turn be supplemented by a minimum wage and a social security level which would be guaranteed by law.

All of this would obviously require a reform of central government to make it possible to carry out this task. In *The Middle Way*, Macmillan discusses various reforms in the government machine that would add up to what he calls 'planned capitalism'. He saw this approach as vital to the maintenance of the capitalist system, if its own anarchical and irrational tendencies, so clearly revealed in the 1930s, were not to deliver the country into a form of state socialism. *The Middle Way* therefore has to be a middle way between *laissez-faire* capitalism and state socialism. Macmillan saw this as central to the conservative tradition of *One Nation* paternalism popularized by Disraeli – the free market could not create one nation, and state power had to be used to secure the economic basis for national unity.

Macmillan's ideas were given a great fillip by the development of Keynes' ideas, and in a 1936 speech in the Commons he clearly showed his adherence to Keynesian ideas. Although these were purely theoretical ideas in the 1930s, the experience of the next war served to lay to rest the idea that government did not have the capacity to do these things.

After the election defeat in 1945, the Conservative Party, particularly under the guidance of the Conservative Research Department, set about formulating policies which reflected the desire to avoid a return to the 1930s. The Conservative Party was attempting to move away from its association with a failed *laissez-faire* philosophy. In the *Industrial Charter* of 1946, largely inspired by R. A. Butler, there was an insistence that government must play a major role in the economy in the interests of full employment, economic efficiency, and social security.

Unemployment and social security are very important to this development. During the period of wartime coalition government, the government had come to accept the responsibility for securing full employment and, with its acceptance of the Beveridge Report on social security, it had accepted the duty of government to provide for the basic welfare needs of citizens.

In addition, Butler had piloted through the Commons the reforming Education Act of 1944. Given these basic functions, government had to play a fundamental role in economic management of the economy. The maintenance of high levels of employment came to be seen as the fundamental economic duty of government, and Keynesian techniques appeared to show the mechanisms whereby this could be achieved. In this manner, the Conservative Party sought a way out of its ideological past commitments and practices. Even the word 'planning' was embraced. For example, in a supplementary pamphlet on the *Industrial Charter*, Butler argued:

> The term 'planning' is a new word for a coherent and positive policy. The conception of strong Government policy in economic matters is, I believe, at the very centre of the Conservative tradition. We have never been a party of *laissez-faire* . . . Conservatives were planning before the word entered the vocabulary of political jargon.[10]

This approach culminated during the Macmillan premiership in the founding of the National Economic Development Council (NEDC), an initiative prefigured in a Commons speech by Selwyn Lloyd, the Chancellor of the Exchequer, in a debate in the Commons on 25 July 1961. NEDC, which still survives, was charged with drawing up long-term plans for the economy.[11]

So after the war the Conservative Party accepted the need for state intervention in economic affairs in a planned and not merely piecemeal way, a high level of public expenditure, full employment as a direct goal of government policy, and the whole range of social services inaugurated by the 1945–51 Labour government. They also accepted Keynesian techniques of economic management, the public ownership of key industries – steel was the only significant nationalized industry denationalized in the 1951–64 period, and, in certain circumstances, an incomes policy in the early 1960s and from 1972 to 1974. Crucial to this was the experience of war and the apparent capacity of government demonstrated during that period, together with the need to rethink conservative policy in the light of the experience of the 1930s.

In the same way as we saw leading market-based conservatives such as Nigel Lawson and Sir Keith Joseph argue that the wrong lessons were learned about the role of the state during the war, so too they argue that mistaken inferences were drawn about the 1930s. Indeed, they see that part of the problem of the 1930s was a misguided intervention by government in the economy in the light of world economic chaos. They reject the characterization of the period after the fall of the Labour government in 1931 as one of *laissez-faire*. In fact they see state intervention, particularly from the mid-1920s in the monetary field, as to some extent a confirmation of their own monetarist assumptions.

For example, in Sir Keith Joseph's view, the major blow inflicted on the British economy was the government decision, after five years of deflation, to return the pound to the unrealistically high value of $4.86 to the pound sterling, followed by a short-sighted intervention in the money markets by the Treasury and the monetary authorities. In his view, as an act of government policy, the exchange rate was set 10 per cent too high. It was this more than anything else which accounted for the susceptibility of the British economy to the Wall Street crash.[12]

In the 1930s quite a lot of this damage was undone by the National Government (Conservative in all but name) which, in Sir Keith's view, wisely abstained from economic intervention and corrected the overvaluing of the pound sterling when it went off the gold standard in 1931. This led to expanded growth and employment, and a rise in home ownership. So in a sense it was misplaced government intervention in the economy rather than *laissez-faire* which caused the problem of the 1930s. This has been misrepresented by socialists and Keynesians who believe, against the facts in Joseph's view, that the experience of economic management in the 1920s and 1930s actually confirms some features of the monetarist alternative to Keynesianism.[13] This mistaken analysis of the 1930s was important to making employment the central economic objective, accepted by the Coalition Government in 1944, rather than the control of inflation and a policy of 'sound money'.

This effort to re-evaluate the experience of the 1930s is an attempt to exorcize a ghost in the Conservative past which played a major, and in their view disastrous, role in changing the direction of conservatism in a more interventionist, pro-planning, pro-Keynesian way. A sense of guilt for the 1930s was an important factor in the change of conservative attitudes:

We found it hard to avoid the feeling that somehow the lean and tight-lipped mufflered men of the 1930s dole queue were at least partly our fault. . . . It was as though we were trying to make amends to the unemployed of a generation back by exaggerating unemployment in our own time.[14]

KEYNES AND THE CONSERVATIVES

Of course, many of these aspects of post-war conservatism with its ideas of planned capitalism would have been purely theoretical had they not been allied to Keynesian ideas about how in detail the capitalist economy could be managed in order to secure the goals of higher employment and public welfare. The Keynesian consensus dominated economic thinking in both the professional and public arenas until the early 1970s.

Despite the revisionist views of Nigel Lawson and Sir Keith Joseph about the 1930s, it appeared to many that the depression of the early 1930s showed the bankruptcy of *laissez-faire* and the need for the state to play a role of greater responsibility in the economy. Keynes' ideas set out in his *Treatise on Money* (1930) and the *General Theory* (1936) served to show a way forward in demonstrating how the state could play a part in macro-economic management which would stop well short of socializing the economy. If government could indeed play this role successfully, with it would go new responsibilities and, in particular, responsibility for full employment.

Keynes was not a believer in economic planning in the more direct sense of government having detailed policies about prices and wages, rather he assumed that demand management and the fiscal and monetary policies outlined above would be sufficient. Nevertheless a more direct approach to planning the economy could be seen as a natural consequence of Keynes' ideas and here again in the view of subsequent critics of Keynesian if not of Keynes, the war was a crucial factor.[15] It did seem as though government was able to play an effective role in the more direct management of the economy in terms of prices and incomes. It also seemed that there were clearly ways in which the experiences of the 1930s could be avoided in the post-war world.

Of course, what was meant by planning did vary across the political spectrum. For some within the Labour Party, before and after the war, planning meant detailed physical planning of the economy to ensure that certain communal goals such as social justice could be achieved. In the Liberal Party, the original ideological home of *laissez-faire* and free trade, Lloyd George's *Yellow Book* contained large elements of planning, as did many conservative initiatives in the policy formulation area as we have seen. By 1954 Angus Maude and Enoch Powell, the latter an early apostle of free-market conservatism, were able to argue:

> From this apparent ability of the state to abolish unemployment at will and to induce an immense increase in production of those things which were needed, many people concluded that post-war reconstruction and national prosperity in peace-time could be achieved by the state with equal efficiency.[16]

There were, of course, dissenting voices. F. A. Hayek published his *Road to Serfdom*, a diatribe against planning, in 1944 with the revealing dedication to 'The socialists of all Parties'. Sir Arnold Plant, Lionel Robbins, and others largely concurred. But these thinkers were effectively marginalized and, as Powell and Maude reluctantly make clear, there was a consensus emerging in favour of government management of the economy. While it stopped well short of the sort of planning adopted by many socialists, it still went beyond the demand management envisaged by Keynes, and the alternative was seen by many to be a return to the ineffective *laissez-faire* policies of the 1930s.

Thus the experience of war, the desire to escape from at least the perceived politics of the 1930s, and the Keynesian opportunity led to the transformation of conservative attitudes to public policy in the post-war period in Britain. When the first post-war Conservative government came to power in Britain in 1951, it accepted the broad lines of post-war politics and policy as exemplified by the Labour government of Clement Atlee. It did not seek any fundamental changes in the general pattern of the settlement, accepting the nationalization of coal, gas, electricity, the railways, the Bank of England, the National Health Service, and Social Security legislation. It did denationalize steel and abolish rationing, but the latter was a relic of the war and was unlikely to last long, whichever government dominated in the 1950s.

Indeed, the policies of the Conservative Party and the outgoing Labour government seemed so similar to many that the term

'Butskellism', invented by the *Economist*, combining the names of R. A. Butler, the Conservative Chancellor from 1951, and Hugh Gaitskell, the Labour Chancellor of 1950–1, became something of a catchword to describe the policies of the 1950s. This term is no doubt misleading and certainly does an injustice to Hugh Gaitskell who was a radical egalitarian, but nevertheless does capture something about the public, journalistic, and academic perceptions of the period. It also fits quite well in the British context to the 'end of ideology' thesis about western societies developed by Daniel Bell in the 1960s.

Certainly, from the left, it seemed as though the change in both conservative doctrine and practice were so complete that Anthony Crosland, the main theorist of British social democracy, was able to argue in his epochal *The Future of Socialism*,[17] that Britain was no longer a capitalist society. Crosland argued that the divorce between ownership and control in business and industry had meant that the issue of who owned British industry was much less fundamental than the question of the managerial accountability of those who had effective control of corporations and took investment and marketing decisions. The growth of democracy meant that political demands for social expenditure on education, health, and welfare was irreversible, and that no government could use unemployment as an instrument of policy. The balance of power on the shop floor shifted away from owners and managers in the direction of trade unions. The availability of Keynesian techniques now made state intervention a fact of life to which even conservatives had accommodated themselves in the post-war world.

Although there were still strong differences between the parties in foreign policy, in domestic policy, particularly in terms of whether state welfare was to be seen as an instrument of egalitarian redistribution, and about the nature of the education system, the main parameters of politics were nevertheless accepted in Crosland's view largely because of democratic pressure and were irreversible. This meant in his view, and this reflected the perception of many, that the extremes in politics both of *laissez-faire* and of Marxism were now marginal. Marxism was no longer an adequate characterization of modern society which Crosland saw as statist and post-capitalist, embodying a fundamental shift in power away from the owners of capital. *Laissez-faire* capitalism was outmoded because the techniques of economic management were in place and what was needed was the political will and competence to use them. In his view both the left and the right in politics had to operate within this fundamentally changed pattern of politics and distribution of power.

THE DECLINE OF KEYNESIANISM

On this kind of analysis a continued and incremental level of economic growth was important for both sides of the political spectrum: on the right to maintain public expenditure and to meet new needs as well as to meet rising expectations of living standards; and on the left in order to finance egalitarian social policies so that greater equality could be secured, using the fiscal dividend of growth to maintain the absolute position of the better off and to improve the relative position of the worst off. This would avoid the social tensions which would be generated by an attempt at a *direct* redistribution of income and wealth to benefit the worst-off members of society.

Given the importance of economic growth on both sides of the political spectrum, a good deal of political argument was in fact not so much about overall goals, but about the technical means necessary to secure growth within a broadly Keynesian consensus. Throughout the 1950s and 1960s orthodox Keynesian techniques were followed in budgetary policy to secure growth and high employment, agreed as a fundamental duty in the 1944 *Employment Policy* White Paper. This meant that, when unemployment was seen as too high, taxes were cut and government capital expenditure was increased. However, this did lead to a stop–go cycle, as it came to be called, when governments, operating orthodox Keynesian policies, found themselves in exchange-rate crises as happened in 1957, 1960, and 1973 under Conservative governments, and in 1964 and 1966 under Labour governments. These exchange-rate crises led government to reverse its policies, raising both taxes and interest rates in order to preserve a fixed parity for the pound. A good deal of political debate was focused on how to break out of the stop–go cycle and to secure sustained growth, high levels of employment, and an acceptable level of inflation. The debate was about the type and degree of government intervention, not whether government should intervene at all. Many initiatives were taken to break out of the stop–go cycle. There was the dash for growth in 1963–4, inaugurated by the Conservative Chancellor Reginald Maudling and the increase in the money supply during the Heath administration.[18] There was the attempt at an incomes policy – mooted in the Macmillan period (the National Incomes Commission was set up in July 1962) and carried forward by the Wilson government in the Board for Prices and Incomes, and continued by Heath in 1972–4, in an attempt to control the inflationary consequences of 'go' phases of the cycle. These devices, plus devaluation, were all ways in which government sought to intervene in order to break out of the stop–go cycle, but there was still the broad consensus that, first of all, government had an active role to play in the economy to secure steady growth and employment. Broadly speaking, this meant inflating if unemployment is high, and deflating in a balance-of-payments crisis.

However, by 1974–5 this policy was looking pretty threadbare in the light of the OPEC oil-price rise because in these circumstances unemployment rose, as did balance-of-payments deficits (because of higher energy bills), and inflation was rising to record post-war levels. This nexus of problems, which came to be known as stagflation, did not seem to be amenable to orthodox Keynesian remedies. In Britain, after the Heath government fell, it was the Labour government which first faced the full scale of the dilemma and a new approach had to be found. The first elements of this new approach were to be found in the Healey budget of 1975 when he refused to reflate or stimulate demand, despite growing unemployment, which would have been the orthodox Keynesian answer. By the time of the Labour Party Conference in 1976, the Prime Minister made his now famous remarks which seemed to herald the collapse of the Keynesian consensus:

> We used to think that you could spend your way out of a recession and increase employment by cutting taxes and boosting spending. I tell you in all candour that the option no longer exists and that in so far as it ever did exist it only worked by inflicting a bigger dose of inflation into the system.[19]

This speech was followed by the approach to the International Monetary Fund to secure a loan in the light of the collapse of sterling on the world markets, a loan which required in its letter of intent[20] a commitment to reduce the budget deficit and the level of government borrowing. This marked the end of the intellectual hegemony of Keynesian economic thinking. Of course, it would

146

be a mistake to think that the Labour government abandoned Keynesianism altogether. It did keep other elements of what had come to be seen as Keynesianism – incomes policy, regional aid, subsidies, and the like and thus combined elements of Keynesianism with monetarism. Nevertheless, these developments marked a watershed in post-war politics because, if the economic basis of post-war assumptions about politics was destroyed, then there would have to be a rethink of the role and the limits of government in changed circumstances.

In the late 1970s it was only the monetarists, or more broadly the market-based conservatives associated with or sympathetic to the Conservative Party with its new leader, Margaret Thatcher, who appeared to have a coherent programme. They proposed an answer to both the technical problems within the economy, which had triggered the collapse of the Keynesian consensus, as well as to the broader questions of the role of government and the directions of public policy which went historically with Keynesian theory.

The decline of the 'Keynesian consensus' also put into doubt the rest of the 'social democratic consensus' in Britain in the post-war world, as leading conservative capitalists have themselves recognized. It is therefore of vital importance to draw from that the more overtly political implications about the role of the state, the level of public expenditure, and the place of welfare in modern society.

INCENTIVES AND INTERSECTORAL RELATIONS

The Thatcher group rejected the idea that governments could balance their budgets by increasing taxation, even though monetarism strictly speaking could allow this as a solution to the problem. The reasoning here turns upon claims about incentives for individuals and profitability for companies. Given that the long-term aim is to secure real economic growth within a framework of monetary stability, it is argued that individuals will only work effectively and efficiently if they have an incentive to do so. Taxation levels are already too high for this without increasing them further to finance government-induced budget defects. In addition, the accumulation of personal wealth is important in providing the basis for entrepreneurial activity without which innovation and growth cannot be achieved. Finally, it is argued that high levels of tax on companies,

147

for example, through corporation tax in Britain, have a deleterious effect upon company profitability and investment in new plant and technology. Overall the government has sought, in pursuit of their policies, to reduce personal taxation, with a target of 25 per cent of taxable income, from the level of 33 per cent which they inherited; to reduce higher rates of taxation from 83 per cent to 40 per cent and to take measures to increase the profitability of companies. To do this would be to attempt to reverse what Sir Keith Joseph has called 'socialist attitudes to wealth creation' which have 'since the war been put most sustainedly into action'.

It is central in the conservative-capitalist approach to taxation that high levels of personal and corporate taxation should not be used to finance a budget deficit in order to meet government spending commitments and indeed, in present circumstances, cannot do so without further sharp declines in the work incentive and the profitability of private enterprise on which ultimately all government spending rests. Mrs Thatcher and Sir Keith Joseph and the other leading lights of the free-market counter-revolution within British conservatism assumed that it was the result of the ratchet effect of socialist and collectivist assumptions which have dominated British politics since the war. It is important in this context to note that within public expenditure in the British situation is to be included not just expenditure on welfare, education, law and order, defence and social security, but also expenditure on nationalized industries, state subsidies to private industry, expenditure on regional aid, and the state contribution to the budgets of local authorities. What matters in the market-based conservative view is the intersectoral relationship between the public and private, the state and market, the subsidized and unsubsidized sector of the economy, and the economic consequences of the intersectoral balance.[21] If all of these dimensions of state expenditure are included, along with public-sector pension supplements and undisclosed deficits, then the state sector in 1974, according to the *Blue Book on National Income and Expenditure*, accounted for two-thirds of GDP and the private sector for one-third. It is against this background that the arguments deployed by conservatives in favour of cutting back the state sector have to be considered. The arguments are as follows.

First, a steadily increasing state sector, particularly with the built-in momentum which has decreased the private sector from three-fifths to one-third between the mid-1950s and 1974, has had the effect of reducing the tax base outside the sector of personal taxation. A decline in the number of businesses and the amount of real resources generated within them reduces the level of revenue coming to government. Given the size of the public sector and the political impossibility of financing that expenditure out of personal taxation, even if that was desirable, it follows that the growth of the state sector is inherently inflationary, given the monetarist view of inflation. Not only that, given the connection between inflation and unemployment, it is also going to have a long-term effect on employment prospects in the economy.

Second, given Keynesian techniques of economic management and the cyclical nature of the economic cycle, the state sector emerges well in 'go' phases of the economy compared with the private sector, whereas during the 'stop' phase of recession, a disproportionate share of the costs fell on to the private sector. During an inflationary period government increases its own spending and a good deal of this goes directly on the types of state spending identified above, whereas during the 'stop' phase governments seek to do two things: one is to use monetary and fiscal squeezes which act directly upon the private sector, the other is to cut public spending.

On the face of it, this should hit the public sector, but in the view of conservatives a good many of these cuts are illusory. The justification of this argument is twofold. First, cuts usually mean not spending as much as the government had planned to do. So instead of *real* cuts Britain has experienced failure to *increase* expenditure at planned levels. Secondly, given the stop–go cycles of the post-war world, how can it be that real cuts have been made when public expenditure as a proportion of GDP has grown from two-fifths to two-thirds during the same period? Hence, with a large level of public expenditure, Keynesian remedies have favoured the public sector against private business.

The state sector and those industries supported by state subsidy are not required to earn a return in the market to match their expenditures and in this sense they are rather insensitive to the general economic environment. Given the size of the state sector and its disproportionate role in the economy, this means in the view of conservatives like Sir Keith Joseph that it acts as an inertial agent in the economy. The need to be competitive and profitable is reduced by the very existence of a huge sector relatively immune to market conditions.

Again, it follows from the size of the state sector that, to use Joseph's phrase, 'the state remakes the market in its own image'.[22] For example, for private firms to deal with the state sector leads to a growth in bureaucracy for those firms working with the bureaucratized rather than a market sector. This can be seen in the growth of licences, permits, planning permission, and general form-filling. All of this has had a deleterious effect upon private businesses which can get entangled in this web of regulation. It might not matter so much if the state sector were relatively small but, as it stands, it does bear down very heavily upon private businesses.

In addition, the state sector of the economy has almost inevitably become a field in which make work in highly subsidized jobs is to be found. Governments, in a democracy, have a strong incentive not to curtail employment by redundancy and staff reductions. Within the nationalized industries, it is argued, large numbers of people were kept at work, for example, in the late 1970s in British Rail, in the steel industry, and in coal mining, which could not be related to any criterion of economic return. Given the need to finance these jobs and given the monetarist view about inflation and unemployment, makework schemes are destructive of real employment in the longer term. The same is true of preserving jobs in private industry through subsidy: 'For every job preserved in British Leyland, Chrysler and other foci of highly paid outdoor relief, several jobs are destroyed up and down the country'.[23] Hence the conservative capitalist would not accept, at least in principle, the idea of state subsidy to 'lame duck' industries.

This has proved to be a very important and rather intractable issue. In 1972 the need to nationalize Rolls-Royce Aero Engines, which had become financially overstretched by the development of the RB 211 engine, led to the policy U-turn by Prime Minister Heath, who had up to that time accepted much of the above diagnosis.[24] During the early years of the Thatcher administration, Sir Keith Joseph and David Howell, both advocates of the above analysis, found it impossible to resist making large sums available to British Leyland and the coal industry on more makework schemes, as they would see them, when they were Secretary of State for Industry and Energy respectively.

There are two further features of the critique of public expenditure that led to the victory of the Thatcher forces. The first is the argument that the state sector 'crowds out' private-sector investment in both economic and human terms. The fact is that lending to government to satisfy the needs of the state sector seems secure, because it is not clear now, if at all, state industries or, for that matter, government itself could go bankrupt. This assumption is bound to influence lending decisions by banks and financial houses in favour of the public sector compared with the uncertainties and the disciplines of the private sector. This security also has an effect, so it is argued, on human resources. Public-sector employment is attractive to people whose skills are in short supply because of regular promotion and national salary scales.

This has an adverse effect on the labour market in the private sector. Therefore the limitation of the state sector, coupled with some attempt to limit what is seen as the attractive job security in the state bureaucracies, for example, by abolishing tenure in universities, is important for the supply side of the economy. It would remove yet another distortion of the labour market provided by state institutions and bureaucracies.

The size of the state sector and the extent of its labour force also has the effect of politicizing industrial disputes. These disputes can be turned into political, or indeed constitutional crises, just because government is seen to be responsible for the provision of the appropriate services, and for the conditions of service of these within such services. On the free-market view, this is fair enough for those limited services where the state is providing genuine public good. The criterion is supplied by the economists' sense in which these services could not be provided effectively through the market, as in defence or law and order. But the role of the welfare state goes far beyond this, providing all sorts of services which the private market could easily provide, so it is argued, and in these circumstances the possibility for the politicization of disputes is enormous.

The most obvious example of the politicization of economic disputes, and one which naturally has preoccupied the Conservative Party, is the history of the two major disputes in the coal industry. The 1974 miners' strike effectively brought down the Heath government, which itself turned the issue into a quasi-constitutional confrontation by fighting the first election of that year on the basis of who governs Britain? The issue was repeated during the pit strike during Mrs Thatcher's period of office when the government was successful in facing down the coal miners – but again there were constitutional issues involved in this dispute. One of the effects of privatization of the state sector of the economy would be to divest government of responsibility for the provision of goods and services, and for the terms and conditions of service and employment in state industries and bureaucracies, and thus to depoliticize many industrial disputes.

So the attention has to turn to cutting public expenditure. The appropriate level of spending cannot and should not be financed by taxation, or by borrowing and deficit budgeting which are inflationary. In the context of a new philosophical framework which sought to rethink the nature and functions of government, as we saw in chapter 3, this became a compelling political programme for the victory of Margaret Thatcher.

The programme targeted the unions and the way they were able to regulate both recruitment into specific areas of the labour force and the ways and the times at which jobs are done by rigid demarcation procedures and job definitions. This had produced a wide range of deleterious effects: inflexibility of working practices, resistance to change and innovation in industry, a restriction of the 'right to manage', and a baleful influence on training. A central feature of conservative thinking became ways in which the power of unions could be decreased. This was a particularly sensitive issue for two reasons. The first was that the Heath government had been brought down by the miner's strike in 1974; the Wilson government had been brought to a crisis point by the split between the Labour government and the unions over the White Paper, *In Place of Strife*, in 1969; and the Callaghan government was fatally weakened by a series of public-sector strikes in the late 1970s, culminating in the 'Winter of Discontent' in 1979. Second, at a more institutional level, for a very long period unions had been brought more and more into economic policy-making. The Heath government had offered the unions and the Confederation of British Industry a central place in economic policy-making in the latter part of his administration, while the Wilson government had formed a social contract with the unions from 1974 in an attempt to work out an agreed economic policy. Challenging the rights of unions therefore was a major issue in the free-market critique of growing collectivism, but at the same time the political risks were self-evident.

However, union reform was not the only reform necessary to

increase the flexibility of the labour market; other things were important too. There was a strong argument that labour mobility was restricted by housing policy and, in particular, by the control over private rented accommodation by government through various rent acts. This was a particular restriction on mobility because of the decline in property in the North of the United Kingdom. The South was much more prosperous, but a consequence of this prosperity was a large disparity in house prices between the North and the South. In the view of some conservatives this could be changed only by a liberalization of private rented accommodation and there was therefore a need for government to get out of rent regulation.

Other strictures imposed by well-meaning governments also served to distort the labour market. Wages councils were in place to secure a basic wage in traditionally low-paid industries, but it was the view of the new government that this led to unemployment. Employers could not always afford to pay the minimum wages set by wages councils, and it was argued that these should be abolished. What would follow, it was argued, would be a greater supply of low-paid jobs at a price the market could bear. Similarly, too, criticism was directed at nationally negotiated rates of pay in industries and in the public sector across the country. Although living costs such as housing could differ quite markedly, particularly between the North and the South, unions and employers, whether private or public sector, negotiated national rates of pay. This again was a distortion of the labour market.

At least in the public sector, it was argued, government could take a lead and try to offer different wage deals based upon local or regional conditions, in the hope that local authorities and private industry would follow such a lead. Again a labour-market rigidity could be removed by government's challenging a union-vested interest. Welfare, too, it was argued, contributed to labour rigidity and to unemployment. There was no incentive to take a low-paid job if a bread-winner could be better off on welfare benefits. A good deal of thought was given to ways of removing this disincentive from people coming forward to participate in the labour market, particularly at the lowest end of the wage scale.

Finally, education too, it was felt, contributed to these rigidities. It was argued that the new form of comprehensive education, introducing during the Labour government and carried on by Mrs Thatcher as Education Secretary in the 1970–4 Conservative government, had led to a decline in children's acquiring the sorts of skills which industry and commerce could use. Either the school curriculum had to be reformed or additional training in work-related schemes had to be introduced as a training tier placed on the top of the traditional educational system. It was also argued that the whole outcome of the British educational system was inimical to wealth creation, entrepreneurship, and a positive valuation of industry and commerce.

The rise to power of conservative capitalism was made possible by the foregoing analysis of the lessons of British politics from the 1930s through the 1970s. With Mrs Thatcher installed at 10 Downing Street, the time had come to attempt the implementation of this analysis in the form of specific policies. As we shall demonstrate in the next chapter, the impact of these initiatives was not what had been forecast by their proponents. After surveying some essential elements of the impact of the Thatcher government's policies, we shall turn to the question of how the left on both sides of the Atlantic might learn from and respond to the rise of conservative capitalism.

Chapter Eight

THE IMPLEMENTATION OF CONSERVATIVE CAPITALISM IN BRITAIN

So far we have been concerned with the attempt to explain the theoretical basis of the effort by the Conservative Party to break with the post-1945 social democratic or 'statist' consensus. In this chapter we shall focus on some salient areas of policy in which these underlying ideas can be seen as operative. The chapter will be dominated by economic policy because it is here that the heart of the critique of the 'statist' consensus is to be found. We shall concentrate on the central issues of economic policy and public expenditure.

MONETARISM AND INFLATION

Control of the money supply will over a period of years reduce the rate of inflation. The speed with which inflation falls will depend crucially on expectations both within the United Kingdom and overseas. It is to provide a firm basis for these expectations that the Government has announced its firm commitment to a progressive reduction in money supply growth. Public expenditure plans and tax policies and interest rates will be adjusted as necessary in order to achieve the objective.[1]

With these words Sir Geoffrey Howe, the Chancellor of the Exchequer, launched the Conservative government's Medium Term Financial Strategy (MTFS) on 20 March 1980. This book is not the place for a detailed appraisal of the economic performance of the Conservative governments since 1979. Rather our task at the moment is to consider the extent to which the policies of the government were inspired by a market conservative approach and to consider in rather general terms how successful they were on their own terms. The MTFS was at the centre of the government's economic policy and it represents in its most uncompromising form the view of the government about monetarism. There is, first of all, in the above statement a clear endorsement of the monetarist idea that there is a direct relationship between money supply and inflation. Second, there is the idea that by publishing money-supply targets the government would bind itself to the policy and make both it, and its associated parts, difficult to abandon, whatever the interest-group pressures. Mr Healey, the previous Labour Chancellor, had to learn this lesson in the hard way when the City of London detected an incompatibility between his published money-supply projections and his fiscal policies which led to a gilt-edged strike in the City, to be relieved only by a July package of expenditure cuts in 1978. Publishing money-supply targets would keep the government on the path of virtue and would, in addition, create a firm and predictable climate for businessmen, union leaders, and other agents in the economy to pursue their business.

In addition public expenditure and tax policies are mentioned in Howe's statement. Earlier we argued that monetarism is a thesis about the inflationary consequences of deficit financing; it does not of itself say how budget defects are to be eliminated, whether by cutting expenditure or by raising taxes. Clearly the combination of monetarism with the government's supply-side convictions about the effect of tax on incentives and its philosophical beliefs about the overblown nature of public expenditure led it to propose cuts in public expenditure in the MTFS rather than bridging any gap by raising taxes. In Sir Geoffrey's 1979 budget public expenditure was cut by £1.5 billion and, together with the sale of £1 billion of shares in BP (which counts as negative public spending), illustrated the government's strategy in regard to public expenditure, which will be discussed later in the chapter. So far as taxation was concerned, the basic rate of tax was cut from 33 to 30 per cent and the highest rate from 83 to 60 per cent and VAT was raised from 8 to 15 per cent. The MTFS made projections for all the elements in the monetarist equation. The chosen monetary indicator, sterling would be posited within the target ranges, shown in table 8.1.

Table 8.1 Money-supply projections

1980–1	1981–2	1982–3	1983–4
%	%	%	%
7–11	6–10	5–9	4–8

Source: Treasury Committee Report on 1983 Budget

The Public Sector Borrowing Requirement would also be reduced at an increasing rate as a percentage of GDP on the scale in table 8.2.

Table 8.2 Public Sector Borrowing Requirement as percentage of GDP (projections)

1979–80	1980–1	1981–2	1982–3	1983–4
%	%	%	%	%
4.75	3.75	3.0	2.25	1.5

Source: Official statistics

This was to be achieved not by raising personal taxes but by reducing public expenditure. There were three threads to this:

1 Planned expenditure would be reduced by 4 per cent in value terms between 1979/80–1983/4.
2 Cash limits would be continued and, if they were exceeded, the value would be reduced.
3 The first real cut would occur in 1981/2. Up to this financial year the other cutbacks would be in planned increases rather than real cuts.

Finally economic growth of a modest 1 per cent per annum was assumed. Partly because the government was so explicit about the basis of its policy, it is more straightforward than usual in such matters to assess the core of the MTFS which was that, 'There would be no question of departing from the money-supply policy, which is essential to the success of any anti-inflationary strategy'. So it is important therefore to consider the relationship between monetary targets, the PSBR, and the rate of inflation. The out-turns for the money supply and for PSBR are shown in tables 8.3 and 8.4 respectively.

Table 8.3   Money-supply out-turns, 1979–84

	1979–80	1980–1	1981–2	1982–3	1983–4
	%	%	%	%	%
Target	7–11	7–11	6–10	5–9	4–8
Out-turn	11.2	17.9	13.6	11.7	8.2

Source: Official statistics

Table 8.4   Public Sector Borrowing Requirement out-turns as percentages of GDP

	1980–1	1981–2	1982–3	1983–4
	%	%	%	%
Target	3.75	3.0	2.25	1.5
Out-turn	5.4	3.3	3.1	3.2

Source: Official statistics

Over the appropriate period therefore sterling M3, the chosen monetary indicator, rose by 70 per cent compared with a projected rise of 46 per cent. Consequently it would be difficult to argue that money supply was under control and it is not surprising that during 1980–1 a lobby developed for a narrower measure and, as Samuel Brittan has pointed out, in the 1982 Budget three monetary targets, using different indicators, were adopted without any indication of their relative weight.[2] By November 1985 sterling M3 had been abandoned as the appropriate monetary indicator and, since that time, without a clear indicator endorsed by the Government and without an external standard such as membership of the European Monetary System, there has been no very definite constraint against which to measure the performance of government. However, the important thing for the moment is to compare the British inflation rate with those in Organization for Economic Co-operation and Development (OECD) countries which had not adopted the same monetary policies.

From table 8.5 it can be seen that the best performance of the Thatcher government was to achieve an inflation rate which in the second half of 1982 was 1.8 per cent lower than the average in OECD. However, OECD countries had not operated monetarist policies and had not suffered the degree of recession induced by the highly deflationary budget in 1981, at the depth of the world recession, which undoubtedly increased unemployment beyond that

Table 8.5 Inflation in OECD countries 1978–84

% change	Difference from UK
1978 I	−0.0
1978 II	−0.3
1979 I	2.9
1979 II	9.0
1980 I	5.0
1980 II	1.8
1981 I	1.2
1981 II	1.4
1982 I	1.9
1982 II	−1.8
1983 I	−0.6
1983 II	0.3
1984 I	−0.9
1984 II	0.0

Source: OECD Economic Outlook 1984

Notes: * Minus indicates periods when UK inflation rate is below that of OECD countries
I First half of year
II Second half of year

induced by the recession. As we shall see later in the chapter public expenditure did not fall during this period; indeed it stayed above the level the government inherited in 1979 as a percentage of GDP. Hence most features in the monetarist equation fail to relate in the way projected in monetary theory, and yet inflation came down to broadly speaking the sorts of levels enjoyed in OECD countries which were not self-proclaimed monetarists.

There is very little wonder therefore that as early as 1982 the House of Commons Treasury and Civil Service Select Committee was able to argue that 'The relationship between monetary aggregates and prices has in the event, turned out not to be as simple as the Government originally thought.'[3] The Committee concluded that there is no discernible relationship between changes in the money supply and the rate of inflation. Monetarism as a doctrine was implicitly abandoned after the 1985 sterling crisis when, contrary to the theory, interest rates were changed independently of monetary considerations. The abandonment of strict monetarism became explicit with the dethronement of sterling M3 as the central monetary indicator in the Chancellor's Mansion House Speech on 17 November 1985, although in the view of some commentators its importance had been downgraded since 1982. Of course, this did not mean that the fight against inflation was to be dropped as the major aim of macro-economic policy[4] – indeed, this point was reiterated by the Chancellor recently. However, other factors are now used to explain the behaviour of the price index as well as figures relating to the growth in the money supply – for example, the strength of sterling, the slow-down in the growth of wages, and the fall in the price of many commodities.

So the defeat of inflation is still at the heart of macro-economic strategy, but the means to achieve a lowering of the rate of inflation are much more obscure than monetarist theory implies. The rate of growth in sterling M3 has been higher than it was under the preceding Labour government, and this failure of monetary control is in part a rejection of the government's failure to achieve its public expenditure targets. Remember the monetarist is concerned about deficit financing of government spending – if it is not covered either by a reduction in expenditure or by taxation, then the money supply will rise and inflation will occur. Hence we need to consider the government's policies in respect of public expenditure. However, even at this stage it is clear that, given the rise in public expenditure, tax cuts could only be achieved by utilizing some of the proceeds of privatization which will also be discussed later. Without the privatization policy the government's approach would be an impossible bind: that is, the burden of taxation makes the British economy uncompetitive and unable to preserve the levels of public expenditure projected in the long-term agenda of government; on the other hand, the inability to cut public expenditure makes tax cuts impossible. It was the policy of privatization of state assets which has enabled the government to break out of the impasse – to maintain public expenditure (politically necessary but against its better judgement) and to cut personal taxes – the basic rate was reduced to 25 per cent in the 1988 budget (from 33 per cent in 1979) and money was put aside to reduce the Public Sector Borrowing Requirement to 0 per cent of GDP. Without privatization these various policy imperatives would have been difficult.

It is therefore necessary to turn to an account of public expenditure, to be followed by an account in the next chapter of the privatization programme which was an unintended contribution dissolving some of the contradictions at the heart of the government's economic policy.

PUBLIC EXPENDITURE

The upshot of all the discussion in chapter 2 on the underlying diagnosis of the ills of modern politics presented by the market-based conservatives is that public expenditure should be cut and the concomitant role of government reduced. As we saw, this was based on a whole variety of interlocking reasons which do not need to be reproduced here. However, despite eight years in office, the government faces a crucial dilemma because its record on public expenditure has, on its own principles, been dubious, because in 1988–9 the planning total of public expenditure, plus net debt interest, will be 41¼ per cent of GDP at market prices, which is broadly what it was in 1979 when the Labour government left office, and the actual out-turn is likely to be higher than that. The Chancellor frustratedly defined the problem in the following way: 'we face a kind of Catch 22. High government spending requires high growth, but high growth will be achieved only by lower government expenditure.'[5] In table 8.6 (p. 163) the history of public expenditure during the period 1979–86 is illustrated. What we need to do is to describe briefly the policies which lie behind these totals and the government's reaction to the grave difficulties in cutting public expenditure. The Medium Term Financial Strategy White Paper of March 1980 set out the government's first specific intentions in relation to public expenditure. There were three elements to the argument:

1 That planned public expenditure was to be reduced by 4 per cent in value terms over the four years 1979/80–1983/4.
2 Stricter cash limits were to be imposed and, if costs rose higher than the limit, there was to be a trade-off whereby the value of the expenditure would be cut.
3 The first real cut, as opposed to the reduction in planned increases, was to take place in 1981/2.

Whatever is the correct interpretation of what has happened, it is clear that these proposals have not been achieved. Indeed, the possibility of securing overall real cutbacks in programmes has not been achieved and since the publication of the MTFS the policy has changed to one of seeking to maintain public expenditure in real terms, that is to say allowing for inflation, with the hope that it will decline as a proportion of GDP as the result of economic growth. If everything goes well and growth rates projected by the

Treasury are achieved, then the proportion of GDP taken by public expenditure will fall steadily by 1990–1, having been above the 1978/9 level of 43.25 per cent in the first seven years of the life of the government and having risen to a peak of 46.75 per cent in 1982/3. This 'consolidation' strategy is quite risky because the rate of growth projected might not be attained and the limitations on public expenditure might be exceeded by interest group pressure which at the time of writing in early 1988 seems quite likely to happen in relation to the health service.

Most free-market critics of the government's performance refer to precisely the sorts of pressures discussed in chapter 3 as the reasons behind what in their view is a rather poor performance. In a sense the record of the government on public expenditure has antagonized both critics and supporters, as Samuel Brittan has argued:

> Like most governments the Thatcher government has not reduced the range of its responsibilities for social security, health or any of the large spending areas. The result is that it has had to be as tight-fisted as possible simply to stay where it is. Thus the defenders of the welfare state see meanness and cheeseparing all round, while the Radical Right feels that it has been betrayed by the continuing rise in public expenditure and the pressures for still more.[6]

Some areas of public expenditure have increased markedly, particularly in the spheres of defence and law and order and some, particularly housing, have been cut back. It is instructive to look at table 8.6 which covers percentage changes in public expenditure for the period 1979–86. Thus the table refers to a period when the government hoped for substantial reductions in expenditure by real cuts rather than the consolidation strategy of reducing the proportion of public expenditure to GDP by broadly funding programmes at the general inflation rate (which actually left many badly underfunded) and by going for growth.

During the period covered by this table the economy grew by about 14 per cent and the value of public expenditure is at about the same level of increase. Clearly some of the increases, on defence for example, reflect the priorities of the government when it came into office in 1979 and no doubt some of the areas in which decline is most marked – in the housing sphere, for example, where invest-

Table 8.6 Percentage change in expenditure programmes 1978/9 to 1985/6
(in real terms)

1985–6 prices	% change from 1979–86
Defence	+29.8
EEC	−43.3
Agriculture	+62.6
Trade and industry	−56.0
Employment	+67.2
Transport	− 8.0
Housing (DOE)	−59.0
Home Office	+40.7
Education	− 0.6
Health	+19.7
Social Security	+33.7

Source: Government Expenditure Plans 1986/7 and 1988/9 (Cmnd 9702)

ment in new public housing has dropped by a half in a situation in which homelessness has almost doubled since the government came to power (see chapter 12 for further details).

Despite popular mythology on both the left and the right there has been no overall attempt by the Thatcher government to produce deep cuts in public expenditure, and the table just cited bears this out. What has been adopted is a decrementalist approach rather than one which went for large-scale cuts. The political advantages of decrementalism are obvious; they cause the least damage to the interests of pressure groups and voters.[7] Indeed the political dangers of a more root-and-branch approach to public expenditure were revealed in 1982 when the Central Policy Review Staffs (CPRS) submitted a paper to the cabinet on *Public Expenditure in the Longer Term*.[8] This paper appeared to have the backing of the then Chancellor, Sir Geoffrey Howe, who attached notes to the paper. The paper which was extensively leaked did present what the Thatcher government had clearly lacked up to that point, namely a coherent strategy for the reduction of public expenditure, and hence the role and agenda of government.

Despite its rhetoric and arguments in Opposition about the oppressive role of the state, the government had not tackled the problem head on. The CRPS represented an opportunity for doing this, but the consequences caused a major political storm, the paper was withdrawn, and the CPRS was itself abolished after the election in the following year. Among the CPRS proposals were: the introduction of private health insurance with the possibility of a minimum private insurance for everyone, together with charges for visits to a general practitioner, and higher prescription charges. On a low growth rate the CPRS argued that resources would not be available to maintain present standards. It was calculated that such charges could produce savings around £3–4 billion out of a budget of £34.2 billion in 1982/3. Second, in the field of defence, it was suggested that the NATO commitment which Britain had made to increase defence expenditure by 3 per cent per annum should be dropped by the mid-1980s and that its share of public expenditure should be frozen. In the field of social security it was argued that savings could be produced if payments no longer rose in line with prices.

Finally, the most draconian proposals were made for the state sector in education where it was argued that state funding of higher education would cease. In place of state funds fees would be set for courses at market prices, presumably derived from historic average unit costs for various courses, and access would be by payment of these market-priced fees with access facilitated by student loans and some state scholarships. In the field of primary and secondary education a voucher scheme was contemplated, although this would have produced no savings but would have had an effect on producer interest groups. Underlying these proposals were several assumptions: that the government had a philosophical desire to reduce the level of public expenditure, that it needed to reduce the level of taxation, and that growth would be at around 1 per cent per annum. It was argued by Sir Geoffrey Howe that it would be sensible to make pessimistic assumptions about growth and not assume that 'growth will float us over the rock'. This is particularly true because of the Catch-22 dilemma which Mr Lawson, Sir Geoffrey's successor as Chancellor, identified, namely that on Treasury assumptions, and indeed on the assumptions of the market capitalist, high growth could be achieved only by a reduction in public expenditure and tax cuts.

The paper discussed at Cabinet in September 1982 argued that the economy would need to grow steadily and strongly to permit the sort of expenditure levels envisaged. It is central to the government's view that this growth cannot be achieved without tax cuts. However, these proposals, which would have set a clear agenda for the reduction of public expenditure and the role of government, caused a political outcry with the result that, within the period between September 1982 when the Report was submitted to Cabinet and the start of the General Election campaign in 1983, the government reaffirmed its commitment to, broadly speaking, the general pattern of expenditure and government responsibility. So, for example, proposals about the Health Service were dropped by Mrs Thatcher who argued during the 1983 campaign that the Health Service was safe in Conservative hands, and in the sphere of education proposals for student loans were dropped. For the radical right the CPRS paper presented a radical opportunity which was missed because the government caved into the political pressures from all the interests discussed in chapter 3,[9] and thus the opportunity for a drastic reshaping of the agenda of government had gone. What was left was what we called earlier 'decrementalism'.

However, the free-market Right takes the view that this strategy is woefully inadequate for several reasons. In the first place the scope for cuts will be small and arbitrary and do very little to cope with the economic and political problems of the growth of the state which were discussed in chapter 2. Second, it leaves cuts far too much in the hands of bureaucrats. Clearly if cuts are not made at the quantum level suggested by the CPRS and other free-market economists, then they have to be made at the level of programmes within spending departments, and this will mean by necessity that the lead for initiating cuts will be taken by civil servants rather than ministers. This allows, to use the words of John Burton, one of the major critics of the policy, 'bureaucracies subject to cash limits to time their programmes in ways most suitable to themselves.'[10] Specifically it is possible to maintain the volume of inputs (especially personnel), whilst cutting the output of services and capital expenditure. Cash limits then run into the problem that bureaucrats may trim the meat rather than the fat of their organization.

This is a variation of the 'bleeding stump' argument which we met in chapter 3, particularly when the trimming is done in areas which may well increase the backlash on government by the consumers of the state services.

Hence, in the sphere of public expenditure, the government must be held to have failed in its crucial economic and political objective to reduce the role and size of the state and to change the agenda of government. Presumably all the defects of a large state consuming the wealth of the nation of broadly the same size as when the government came into office in 1979 are still with us. It is really only within the sphere of privatization that the policy can be considered a success on the government's own terms.

Indeed the massive receipts from privatization have contributed to the government's ability to deal with public expenditure dilemmas discussed in this section. Without the proceeds from these sales the problems of public expenditure would now be very acute. The question of whether the economy can grow sufficiently during the breathing space provided by receipts from privatization to finance future public spending remains to be seen. However, before moving on to privatization, we need to consider the place of local government in public expenditure and the financial, constitution, administrative, and policy dimensions of this.

LOCAL AUTHORITIES AND PUBLIC EXPENDITURE

One of the areas which contributes to public expenditure in which the government has shown itself to be particularly tenacious is local-government finance. Between 1979 and the start of 1987 there had been fourteen parliamentary bills dealing with local government, and certainly the structure of the constitutional relationships between central and local government has changed fundamentally with a much more centralized arrangement emerging. In its anxiety to control local-government expenditure, the government has produced a much more centralized constitutional arrangement which is certainly not obviously compatible with the decentralist views of the free-market Right and is incompatible with traditional conservative assumptions about the importance of local ties and identities and suspicions of centralized power. In the new 1987 Parliament, the government intends to introduce a whole new basis for local-authority finance, the community charge or poll tax which will be paid by everyone over the age of 18. This will be discussed in more detail shortly, but it is worth pointing out that the Green Paper, *Paying for Local Government*, produced in 1986, and which forms the basis for the new legislative proposals, is in flat contradiction with previous efforts by the government to rethink the basis of local-authority finance, particularly the 1981 Green Paper, *Alternatives to Domestic Rates*, and the 1983 White Paper, *Rates*, which unequivocally rejected the flat-rate community charge or poll tax which forms the basis of the government's new proposals. The issues at stake in trying to think about central–local relations are increasingly complicated on the constitutional, administrative, and financial side and clearly cannot be adequately dealt with here, but we shall concentrate on two major features: the way in which the government has sought to bring local-authority finance into its overall policy for controlling public expenditure, and hence the role of government, and, second, some of the deeper implications of the community charge which will be introduced into the present Parliament.

On the face of it, a government worried about public expenditure has to take a close interest in local-government finance, given the major contribution which it makes to the overall volume of public expenditure and the extent to which it contributes to the Public Sector Borrowing Requirement with all its impact, for the monetarist, on macro-economic policy. There are really two aspects to this. The first is to ensure that local authorities are constrained by the overall public-expenditure policies of the government. The second is to ensure that local authorities do not have the capacity to drive rates up with impunity to make up for a shortfall from central government under the first consideration. The impact of rates upon the inflation rate, pay expectations, and on the local business environment make it imperative on this view to control the level of rates, if the proportion of local-authority expenditure by central government is being controlled. At the moment government contributes about three-fifths of local-authority expenditure through the Rate Support Grant and clearly government has direct capacity to control this. What is more difficult is to prevent local authorities making up the shortfall by 'excessive' rate increases.

If we consider control of the Rate Support Grant first, the government's policy has been clear, namely to reverse a policy adopted by previous governments whereby grants were allocated to local authorities on the basis of past spending. Hence a high-spending local authority was able to increase its share of government grant through automatic increases based upon its historic spending. This has now been replaced by a block grant system in which grants are based on much more standardized spending levels rather than historic principles. These spending levels provide a kind of benchmark to determine appropriate levels of expenditure. Councils can still decide the level of their own expenditure but, when it rises above the benchmark to a significant degree, then central government reduces its contribution to the expenditure under the Rate

Support Grant. The only options facing councils at this point are either to reduce expenditure or to increase rates in order to meet the intended expenditure level.

The main countervailing argument to this policy, deployed by both Left-wing and traditionalist Conservative critics of the policy, has been that standardized ways of calculating expenditure reflect different needs in different parts of the country. Many high-spending councils are in areas of high deprivation in inner cities suffering multi-faceted social problems – decay, unemployment, problems in education, racial tensions, growing numbers of elderly in non-supportive neighbourhoods, etc. There has been support for such a view too from Conservative councils in prosperous parts of the country who have found that they have increasing populations with growing affluence, and that their level of spending has not kept up with these changes, and are not reflected in standard measures. Pressures of these sorts have led to a phasing-out of volume-spending targets in favour of a computerized account of each local authority's need to spend.

In the view of critics, historic expenditure recognized local differences and the differing needs of different areas. Standard spending levels however fail to recognize these differences and in doing so are at the best a blunt instrument and, at their worst, represent a failure to take into account that dispersed local knowledge which is not available to central government. This paradoxically forms a central feature of the radical Right's rejection of centralized planning. The government's response to this has been twofold. First, it is argued that many of the local authorities in question are Labour controlled and have highly overextended policies which are not really needed or required by their neighbourhoods. In this context, the government has been given a good deal of ammunition by local Labour authorities who, while claiming that their policies are in the interests of their area, pursue policies on Lesbian and Gay rights to take the usual example, or nuclear-free zones, which are thought by government to have very little relevance to the needs of localities.

Second, the government argues that the current system of rates encourages irresponsible voting, that is to say, voting for policies at a price when a good deal of the cost can be transferred to others. So, for example, many who vote in local-authority elections do not pay rates, at least directly, and they have therefore an incentive to be altruistic at someone else's expense. So, in the view of the government, there is a just case for moving away from historic grants, which are inflated by exaggeration of need and by irresponsible voting, towards a more standardized system which seeks a benchmark of appropriate spending across the community.

The second element of the strategy has to be to attempt to close off the possibility that local authorities could just put up rates to compensate for a down-turn in contribution through the Rate Support Grant. Initially there were a series of rather *ad hoc* measures to limit the capacity of councils such as Liverpool and Lambeth to do this. For example, measures were taken to abolish supplementary rates and to allow the Department of the Environment to adjust the block grant to individual councils to discourage overspending, impose tighter regulations on the operation of Direct Works Departments, a particular *bête noire* among the free-market conservatives, and make more extensive use of external auditing to reveal waste and inefficiency.

However, this was eventually superseded by the rate-capping legislation which gave the Department of the Environment (DOE) the power to cap the rates of the most blatantly overspending local authorities. The DOE could fix their rate for that year. The local authority had the power to appeal but, if that happened, then the Department would examine their budgets in great detail. In 1984/5 eighteen councils were rate capped, all but one Labour, and the twelve selected the following year (including ten from 1985) were Labour.

However, the most radical change will undoubtedly be the poll tax or community charge which will in effect make local citizens pay much more directly and individually for the policies and programmes for which they vote. The aim at least in part is to make people more aware of the costs of programmes and make fixing the level of local finance which has to be found a much more responsible process than it has been.

Hence, in the fiscal sense, the approach of the government has been clearly centralist, neglecting (in its view with good reason) localized knowledge and circumstances in order to take a firmer grip of public expenditure through the Rate Support Grant and to make local people directly foot the bill for their own political decisions. This policy has produced great tensions and an almost total breakdown of trust between central and local government. In narrow public-expenditure terms, however, it has been a relative success for the government in that the amount spent through the block grant declined from 61 per cent of local-authority expenditure in 1979 to 48 per cent in 1985. Given the scale of local-authority financing, the increasing scale of government's contribution to it, and the consequential impact of that upon inflation, borrowing, and unemployment, it is likely that any future government is going to want to continue to make use of similar mechanisms to control the contribution of central government to local-authority finance which the present government has introduced. After all, it was Anthony Crosland, then Secretary of State for the Environment in the 1974–6 Labour government, who announced at a local-government conference in Manchester that the 'party was over'. The paradox is, however, that a government committed to a smaller role for the state, and therefore committed to much greater control of public expenditure which, after all, reflects the agenda of government, has found it necessary radically to increase its control over local authorities which have been seen by communitarians of both the left and the right as important centres of local identity and independence from local authority.

While these arguments have been clearest in the context of the financial control of local authorities, there is an additional, and in some ways more fundamental, change in central-local relations at the policy level, not just the financial level. Again in this context we see the same phenomenon at work, 'centralization in order to decentralize', as Ferdinand Mount, at one time head of the No. 10 Policy Unit, once put the point. Take two areas which will be discussed in more detail later, namely housing and education. Since the war governments have relied very heavily upon local authorities to increase the public housing stock and to provide schools at the appropriate standard to fulfil the requirements of the 1944 Education Act. This worked very well in the post-war consensus years in which there were shortages.

However, as housing shortages were eliminated and schooling became more of a political issue with the introduction of comprehensive schools after 1965, many conservatives came to believe that local government was no longer the appropriate sphere of accountability, but rather that responsibility and accountability should be decentralized further. In the case of housing, responsibility and accountability are devolved to individual tenants who were to be given the right to buy and, afer the 1987 election, to housing associations and other agencies which would be offered the opportunity of taking on non-privatized public-housing estates. In the case of education, local authorities were compelled to cede some powers to school governors; school budgets are to be decentralized to head teachers rather than local education authorities, and schools are to be given the capacity to contract out of the system altogether.

Part of the reasoning behind these proposals, which will be discussed in more detail later, is the idea that government's reach has outrun its grasp. In the fields of the implementation of housing and educational policy, the policy of government is in the hands of local authorities, both local politicians and bureaucrats, whose priorities may be very different from the national government. The aim is therefore either to get rid of this level of accountability altogether, as with the privatization of council housing, or to bring in other countervailing forms of accountability, for example, by extending the powers of parents in local-authority schools and giving them the option of opting out of local-authority control.

Housing

The housing sector is the area within which perhaps the most consistent attempt has been made to change the relationship between private and public provision. The way in which it has been done has shown a very astute political sense and has achieved a major shift in the balance between public and private provision which could not have been attained, for example, in relation to the National Health Service. Peter Riddell has described the position in the following way:

> The Government's aim has been to introduce and to extend market forces, both by requiring the local authority sector to be self financing and profit making and by reducing the size of the public sector. . . . This has been described as a minimalist view according to which the private sector is regarded as the main provider of housing and the public sector as a safety net.[11]

This aim fits in very well with the view of market capitalists such as Sir Keith Joseph who argued that, in so far as government was concerned with welfare issues (broadly speaking), it should be concerned in terms of minimal standards rather than with greater equality.[12] If people wanted higher standards, then they should look outside the state sector for them.

The attempt to change the balance between the public and private sectors in the sphere of housing was to be achieved as Riddell notes in two ways: first, by attempting to make the public sector self-financing, and, second, by maintaining encouragement to the private sector in two ways: one by retaining and, on occasion, extending the scheme for tax relief on mortgages, the second by allowing tenants in the public sector, i.e. tenants in council accommodation to buy their own homes, and requiring reluctant Labour authorities to allow this to happen.

The public sector has to be made self-financing by the implementation of two policies. The first was to cut subsidies to local authorities for council-house building by more than 50 per cent. The second was to increase council-house rents to double in cash terms between 1979 and 1982. This policy, of course, made it rather attractive for council tenants to purchase their homes on favourable terms when they were given the legal opportunity to do so. Between 1979 and 1983 half a million homes were sold and this, together with other incentives for first-time buyers, saw the percentage of private homes rise from 54 to 59 per cent during this four-year period.

This policy fits very well with a number of features of the market-capitalist approach. First of all, the attempt to put the public sector on to a self-financing basis meant that housing policy made a substantial contribution to reducing the overall level of public expenditure, the reduction of which was, as we have seen, a prime aim of the government. Second, it led to another and very palpable shift in the balance between government and society and gave a very large number of people a stake in the housing market which they had not had before. Purchasing council property was seen as a way of securing greater personal independence and self-reliance and a move away from bureaucratic control of people's lives by government, in this case local-government officials. Extending people's freedom to paint their front doors with a colour of their own choosing was thought to be symbolic of a much deeper freedom which home ownership brought. Finally, it was an astute political move, because it created a potential constituency of people who were now more likely to vote Conservative. Of the new owner-occupiers, 56 per cent voted Tory and 18 per cent Labour in 1987.

Of those who voted Labour in 1979 59 per cent turned to either the Conservatives or the Alliance after purchasing their own homes. Given that change of ownership between private and public is irreversible, the potential further electoral pay-off to the Conservatives is tremendous and thus detracts from what was often seen as a Labour heartland.

Two effects of the housing policy are worth noting in terms of the general issues raised in this book. The first is that the tax relief available on mortgages, the limit of which has been raised during the Government's period of office to its current rate of £30,000, fits rather uneasily with free-market economics in that it is an explicit subsidy which is bound to distort the market price of houses. Many economists would like to see the policy phased out.[13] However, Mrs Thatcher is clearly behind it and, according to newspaper reports, unsuccessfully lobbied the Chancellor to have it raised in the 1987 budget. Clearly there is a major vested interest here which the government, despite its scorn for interest-group politics, is not prepared to take on. Second, despite the fact that the subsidy does involve a distortion of the market, it has been an essential feature of the strategy to shift the balance from public to private, from politics and public processes to the market. It has been justified as instrumentally compatible with market economics in these terms.

Obviously not everyone wants to buy a house and many people cannot afford it, so the privatization of the public-housing stock may well have increased inequalities between, for example, those who can afford to buy their own homes and the very poor and single-parent families who cannot. However, as we saw in the earlier chapter, it is part of the philosophy of the new conservatism that public policy should not be concerned with equality but rather with the maintenance of a decent minimum standard.[14] To attempt to do more will harm the economy in the long run and, in the view of the Conservatives, among those who would be the best clearly harmed would be the poor.

Education

In the sphere of education the proposal which accords most with the free-market conservative approach is the education voucher, espoused particularly by Milton Friedman,[15] and in Britain by the Institute of Economic Affairs. State schools would be privatized and fees set at a market level, probably based upon some idea of historic unit costs within the state system for education at various stages. Parents would then be given cash in the form of vouchers which could be redeemed only in the educational sphere. This would allow parents to choose where to send their children to school. Good schools would be likely to grow and expand, bad schools to decline and close. The voucher is the closest to a free market in education which could be attained and it has all the benefits, so its supporters argue, of the free market in other spheres. It gives the consumer choice between different sorts of schools, even if government set minimum standards, because within this constraint there would still be a wide variety of schools with different educational styles and traditions available. It weakens the power of professional producer-interest groups, in this case the teachers who will have to be far more responsive to parents' demands if they are to retain the enrolment of children. Indeed the expansion of the professional power of teachers may necessarily have been at the expense of parents whose views have been displaced by those of professional 'experts'.[16] As we saw in chapter 3, it is characteristic of the free-market conservatives that they argue that producer-interest groups such as teachers, doctors, or bureaucrats are able to define the interests of their clients in terms of their own interests, when in fact this is not true. Producer groups have interests of their own which do not necessarily coincide with the interests of client groups.

When Sir Keith Joseph became Secretary of State for Education, he saw himself as intellectually attracted by the idea of vouchers, and certainly Kent County Council had a long-standing interest, having set up a feasibility study in 1976. However, by 1983, Sir Keith declared at the Conservative Party Conference that the educational voucher was dead. Its demise seemed to be credited to two reasons: first, that at least in some versions of the scheme, it would be possible for parents to top up the volume of their vouchers and thus buy a better education by attracting better teachers to the better conditions and salaries available in a topped-up voucher school, and second, that educational vouchers were not really compatible with a sense of national community and a common culture. This argument was put forward in several ways which were not wholly compatible. The first is that schools could be set up on ethnic, religious, or sectarian lines and offer very narrow forms of education. At the other end of the scale it was argued that, if topping up of vouchers were allowed, then rich parents would tend to send their children to the same school, and that this would lead to a decline in social integration. Hence the ideas and values of common culture (a rather leftish notion) or community or a sense of national identity were used to argue against the voucher scheme because it could produce great educational diversity, some aspects of which would not be compatible with more traditionalist views (both left and right) about the common values which the educational system should serve.

However, given the death of the voucher scheme, alternative attempts are being made to bring in market surrogates and to challenge the interest-group status of teachers, but in ways which do paradoxically increase the power of the central state in a way which the voucher scheme would never have done. First of all, several mechanisms have been introduced to strengthen the role of parents on governing bodies of schools, and to ensure that there is an annual meeting for each school at which teachers and parents would meet to discuss the work of the school. On the whole this idea runs rather counter to the general ways to which free-market capitalists believe accountability should go. As we saw in chapter 3, in relation to bureaucracy, they are very sceptical about the capacity of democratic procedures to make interest groups accountable to those whom they are supposed to serve. Only a market relationship will do this properly in their view. However, coupled with the attempt to increase parental power, there are proposals to decrease the powers of local authorities, while at the same time increasing those of central government. Schools are to be given the capacity to opt out of the control of local education authorities after a democratic decision by parents and staff and to be directly funded by the Department of Education and Science, the central education ministry. While this is presented as a way of enabling schools to escape from what is considered to be the malign influence of Labour-controlled local education authorities, it does, nevertheless, increase the power of central government, as does the proposal to introduce a national curriculum.

Hence schooling provides a fascinating example of the tensions with conservative capitalism between traditionalists and free marke-teers. Traditionalists saw the voucher scheme as too libertarian and not securing communitarian values which, in their view, a state system together with a national curriculum would.[17] Free marketeers on the other hand preferred the voucher as the only realistic way in which actual control could be exercised over producer groups – namely through the cash-market mechanism. It remains to be seen whether the attempt to increase parent power through political as opposed to market means will be as useless as free-market critics would tend to assume. For the free marketeer the only effective form of accountability is through economic exchange. Traditionally the left has considered democratic accountability as the replacement for the market forum. In the case of education, the failure to introduce a voucher scheme has required the endorsement of what many will regard as a much less effective means of accountability.

HEALTH POLICY

While housing policy has been radical and consistent with market-conservative principles, and education rather less so, the same could hardly be said about the approach to the nature and funding of the National Health Service (NHS). The obvious market capitalist approach to the Health Service would be to adopt a similar strategy to that adopted in the field of housing, to use public provision as a basic safety net coupled with a system of private insurance made compulsory for those who were insurable. On the face of it, such a policy should have been attractive in the light of the inexorable growth in the cost of the NHS. It was believed by the government's own interdepartmental committee that expenditure would have to rise by 2–3 per cent a year in real terms to keep up with need and to meet clear deficiencies in the service. The possibility of a radical solution was produced in 1982 by the Central Policy Review Staff, the Government's own 'Think Tank' which did propose a system of compulsory health insurance on the same basis as many continental countries. This paper appeared to have the blessing of Sir Geoffrey Howe, then the Chancellor of the Exchequer. However, the paper was extensively leaked and there was a massive outcry and, during the 1983 General Election campaign, Mrs Thatcher stated that the National Health Service was safe in Conservative hands.

Other less dramatic possibilities of changing have also been discussed including paying for the 'hotel' aspects of hospital treatment and payment for visits to general practitioners. Given the rejection of such wholesale policies to change the financial basis of

medical care, a number of less dramatic policies have been introduced. First of all, there has been an attempt to encourage private
medicine. Income-tax relief on employer-employee medical
insurance schemes has been restored up to a relatively modest level
of income (£8,500 in 1982–3 the year the scheme was introduced)
and attempts have been made to encourage joint use of high technology between the public and private sector and voluntary and
charitable contributions to medical care. The net result of this is
that, while the number of people insured privately has increased
markedly from 2.5 million in 1979 to 4.2 million in 1982, and the
number of beds has risen to 34,000 with a particularly marked
increase in beds in private 'rest homes' for geriatrics, the overall
effect of this compared with the National Health Service provision
is very marginal: the Health Service has nearly 400,000 beds in
over 2,000 hospitals.[18]

Hence, while private insurance has produced some relief for the
financing of the Health Service, it has not shifted the balance to the
private sector in a very substantial way. In addition, the private
sector is heavily dependent on the infrastructure of the National
Health Service and the Health Service has responsibility for treating
types of cases which are not attractive to the private sector. Hence
the government has had to remain committed to the maintenance
of a National Health Service which goes far beyond the minimum
standards (whatever they may be in the health context) which the
market diagnosis would prescribe. It has to try to maintain a very
high level of Health Service against a background of attempting to
reduce public expenditure.

Although it has spent much more on health, the nature of medical
need and demographic factors have made it very difficult to
convince the public on this issue that all that should be done is
being done. Attempts have been made at the margins to reduce
expenditure, largely through three strategies. The first has been an
attempt to change the management structure of the Service by
employing new types of managers who will be paid partly by results.
This was in the wake of the Griffiths Report on the management
of the Health Service, Griffiths being the managing director of
Sainsbury, one of the country's most efficient and effective retail
chains. Second, there has been an attempt to introduce some
element of privatization through contracting out hospital catering,
cleaning, and laundry services. The benefits of contracting out are

supposed to be those which the conservative capitalist would usually associate with the market.

1 That in-house, publicly-financed services are more concerned with satisfying the needs of producer interests than with the consumer.

2 Competition allows for regular recontracting to enable the management to review costs.

3 Competition leads to innovation and breaking old and inefficient working practices.

4 Because the requirements of hospitals are so open-ended, in-house provision of services also tends to be open-ended and there is no clear limit to cost. Private contracting, however, requires that the job to be done is clearly specified and related to a particular cost.

So far this policy has not impinged upon central medical services but, during 1987, there have been press reports of some examples where operations have been contracted out to the private sector on a limited basis in order to reduce waiting lists for routine surgery. At the moment this is not explicit government policy, but the contracting-out principle may well become policy now that the government has been returned to power.

The final way in which government has sought to reduce costs is through a requirement to prescribe generic drugs rather than graded drugs in the NHS. This was bitterly resisted by the medical profession which regarded it as an infringement of clinical freedom. The government, however, regarded this as a typical reaction of a producer-interest group and went ahead anyway. However, it must be stressed that, given the rejection of the 1982 proposals for an insurance-based scheme, the effect of these changes on the NHS are going to be rather marginal. Currently the government is committed to the maintenance of a national system which seeks to provide the best service available and not merely a minimum standard. Clearly the public-expenditure consequences of this are very clear and would have been much more acute, had it not been for North Sea Oil revenues and for the benefits to the Exchequer of the privatization programme.

SOCIAL SECURITY

In broad context, social security policy looks set to be changed in a way influenced by the dependency theories developed in the US by Murray, Mead, Nathan, and others (discussed in chapter 3). In March 1987 these figures attended a seminar at the Centre for Policy Studies (which Plant also attended), the aim of which was to expose leading conservatives to this kind of thinking. By the autumn of the same year Mr John Moore, by then Secretary of State for Social Services, made a speech which reflected most of the thinking of the dependency theorists. Indeed, Social Security ministers and officials have met Murray and discussed his ideas with him. In his autumn speech Moore contrasted what he saw as the 'sheer delight of personal achievement' with the sullen 'apathy of dependence', and there is an attempt to break down what is seen as the entitlement and benefit culture. This is becoming apparent in a number of areas.

The first is that the Youth Training Scheme is now being seen essentially in workfare terms, although this designation is being avoided. From September 1988 16 and 17 year olds who refuse the YTS scheme will lose all entitlement to benefit. In the field of long-term adult unemployment the autumn of 1988 will also see the introduction of the Manpower Services Commission Unified Adult Training scheme to deal with the 600,000 a year long-term adult unemployed. The scheme, which will include a cut in benefit coupled with a £10 premium for those who take part in it, is not compulsory in the strict legal sense, but given the economic circumstances of the unemployed, a premium of £10 per week to take part in the scheme coupled with a cut in benefit could come close to what political philosophers sometimes call a coercive offer.

Second, people who leave employment for reasons other than redundancy are liable to be disqualified from unemployment benefit for three months. In addition, their supplementary benefit is cut by 40 per cent during this period. In 1988 it is being proposed to extend this period to six months. This is a reassertion of Victorian values with a vengence. In 1834 the Poor Law Amendment Act sought to make the position of those on charitable relief less eligible than that of the least well-paid in work. The proposal mentioned above is a clear modern example of this principle being applied to someone who leaves employment on a voluntary basis. This of course empowers management against workers and would enable new conditions of work and wages to be imposed which employees could resist by leaving that employment only if they were prepared to put up with the consequences of a cut in benefit as the result of voluntary unemployment. However, the government does not regard this as coercive because as Hayek argues in *The Constitution of Liberty*, except in monopoly circumstances, contracts of employment, whatever their character, cannot be coercive. Indeed, Patrick Minford, a New-Right economist has argued that the real aim of the proposals is precisely to drive wages down (*The Listener*) 18 February 1988, p. 4).

The final way in which entitlement has been attacked in favour of breaking down the benefit culture is through the introduction of the Social Fund. Hitherto, people living on supplementary benefit have been entitled to apply for a grant for basic necessities such as furniture and cooking implements. This is now being replaced by a social fund, the total amount of which is much less than was available under the previous system and which will now be available only as a loan and not a grant, the loan being repayable out of supplementary benefit income. The idea is that people will learn the skills of budgeting if a loan is granted and this in turn will make people more independent. If someone is refused a grant they will be directed to local charities. There could be no clearer way of exhibiting the desire to end entitlement and to attack the benefit culture.

TRADE UNIONS

The final area in which we wish to explore the impact of conservative capitalism in Britain is in the relationship between the government, trade unions, and the labour market. As we saw earlier, the unions played a central role in the market-conservative diagnosis of the ills of British society: they were seen as having too much political power and having been encouraged by corporatist governments to cross the threshold to political influence; they were seen as a deleterious influence on the labour market, using their coercive powers to drive up wages for members and to price potential entrants out of jobs; they were seen as antagonistic to civil liberty with closed-shop agreements which required workers in particular industries to join a union or lose the job; they were seen as offering support, particularly financial support, to the Labour Party which was not really subject to the democratic control of members. Finally, and more generally, it was argued that the leadership had no real democratic mandate, frequently being elected for life and being able to manipulate decisions over strikes, for example, at mass meetings and the like, rather than through private ballots. On all of these points the government has taken a lead. In addition though, the unions have suffered on other fronts. First of all, the recession and growth of unemployment have led to a slump in union membership (see table 8.7); second, the government's rejection of Keynesian techniques of economic management has effectively frozen unions out of any role in macro-economic policy-making and has in recent months devalued NEDO, one of the institutional survivors of the 1960s economic consensus; finally, the upturn in the economy has been in areas, particularly of part-time female work, which are not and are unlikely to be heavily unionized.

Before we go on to discuss the policy of the government in relation to unions, it is worth, first of all, getting some idea of the decline in union membership.

Table 8.7

Year	Total number of unions	Total number of union members
1893	1,279	1,559,000
1914	1,260	4,145,000
1920	1,384	8,348,000
1933	1,081	4,392,000
1939	1,019	6,298,000
1948	735	9,319,000
1968	584	10,193,000
1979	454	13,498,000
1985	373	10,716,000

Source: George Sayers Bain and Robert Price in Bain (1983) (ed.) *Industrial Relations in Britain*, Oxford: Blackwell. The figures have been updated by Plant's colleague, Dr Jon Clark of the Department of Sociology and Social Policy, University of Southampton, on the basis of figures provided by Robert Price

In the late 1970s union power appeared to be immense and a power with which government had to deal carefully. After all, the Heath government had been brought down by the miners' strike, and the winter of discontent caused by public-sector union strikes contributed to the decline in legitimacy of the Callaghan government. By 1987 the unions had lost membership, power, and influence on government and it would be difficult to deny that the union movement was on the defensive. Although the membership figures show some dramatic losses, nevertheless this is not the result of union members quitting unions, but rather the result of union members' losing their jobs and their membership's lapsing. In addition, we have to be careful to consider the figures over a longer period before drawing too apocalyptic conclusions from the figures. While in the mid-1980s union membership had fallen to about 50 per cent of the workforce, compared with 55 per cent in 1979, nevertheless at the end of the 1960s the density of union membership was 44 per cent of the workforce. Similar considerations apply to the decline in the closed shop. This decline too is not the result of people's opting out of closed-shop agreements, but rather the reduction of numbers of people employed under such terms.

We need to turn now to a brief discussion of the legislative actions taken by government to curb the power of the unions, partly for political reasons – the government had become convinced since the 1970s that the unions were too powerful – and partly for economic reasons on the market-conservative view that the unions were pricing workers out of jobs, and that, only if this power was curbed, would the labour market work efficiently. However, as we shall see, the government's legislative actions are not the only important features of the market-conservative offensive against union power; power has also been reduced as a consequence of other policies in the fields of employment, manpower services, and other spheres. First, however, we turn to legislative action. There have been three major pieces of legislation on the unions: the Employment Acts of 1980, 1982, and 1984. These pieces of legislation embodied the following changes: the provision of public finance for secret ballots on proposed strikes and elections for union office; protection to individual employees against dismissal for refusing to join a union operating a closed shop; the possibility for employers of ending closed shops unless the closed-shop agreement was supported by 80 per cent of the workforce in a secret ballot; picketing, at places other than where the industrial dispute is taking place, to be made liable to civil damages; secondary picketing of companies supplying firms at the centre of dispute to become subject to civil damages; requirement of unions to hold secret ballots on membership of national executive committees of unions, on strikes if immunity to civil action for breach of contract was to be retained, and on the setting up of union political funds. One of the central assumptions of the policy was in relation to secret ballots to ensure that what were assumed to be moderate majorities would emerge through secret ballots in a way that was not possible at factory-gate mass meetings. Of course, this may cut both ways: while on occasion strike appeals may be rejected in a secret ballot, equally, if a strike is supported in this way, it may well gain legitimacy. Certainly the laws against secondary picketing have had a major impact on the conduct of industrial disputes since the late 1970s when secondary picketing was endemic.

Unions have also been placed on the defensive by the consequences of other policies. First and foremost, of course, the dramatic rise in unemployment up to 3.1 million in 1985 has, as we have already said, weakened unions in terms of membership and has also led to a less militant attitude on the part of union members over potential industrial disputes. This has been very clear, for example, in the case of the National Union of Railwaymen whose members on several occasions have failed to support the leadership when the latter was keen to pursue industrial action. Privatization, as we shall see, has also weakened unions which were formerly in the public sector by making them more responsive to consumer demands and market pressures. Finally, the government has also acted against tripartite and corporatist arrangements by lowering the profile of the National Economic Development Office, by the abolition of the Industrial Training Boards on which unions were represented, and by dealing with youth training through the Manpower Services Commission to which unions have had a very ambivalent attitude. In addition, the abolition of wages councils to protect the low paid and the attack by government on nationally negotiated rates of pay are also likely to fragment unions and to reduce their power. Rather like privatization, it is very difficult to see this policy's being revised in the short term at least, particularly in the sphere of the internal democratization of unions. Again we see the same feature which we have noted before, namely government centrally taking an initiative in relation to autonomous groups in society in order to decentralize them and make them more accountable to their members. The general thrust of this policy across a wide range was well summed up by Brian Walden, once a Labour MP, and now a firm Thatcher supporter, in the *Sunday Times* on 26

183

July 1987 when he argued: 'Her Government can be used as a suction pump to draw responsibility from a range of agencies and send it back whence it came and where it belongs.' This quotation captures a good deal about the strategy of taking centralist initiatives with the aim of decentralizing power and responsibility, usually to the market and the consumer, which the conservative capitalist regards as the most effective vehicles for accountability. However, there is a deep paradox here. The anti-state strategy of the conservative capitalist has led to an increase in centralization over both local authorities and the educational system, which seems to neglect precisely the strictures about the capacity of government and bureaucracies which lie at the heart of the conservative capitalist critique of the statist consensus of the post-war world.

To complete our account of the development and implementation of conservative capitalism in Britain, it is important to devote special attention to the issue of privatization which forms the theme of the next chapter. In this sphere Britain has set the pace in the international context and many countries, both capitalist and socialist, are following suit. It is a sphere of policy in which many of the ideological issues discussed in chapters 2 and 3 emerge with a good deal of clarity.

Chapter Nine

PRIVATIZATION IN BRITAIN

We shall now consider the privatization programme in relation to nationalized industries and state assets, undoubtedly one of the central successes of the market-capitalist programme.

The privatization policy of the British government since 1979 fits closely with the policy imperatives that follow from the conservative-capitalist, anti-statist and anti-interventionist assumptions discussed in chapter 2. When the government came to power in 1979, the nationalized industries accounted for about one-tenth of the retail price index. Taken together, the nationalized industries employed about one and a half million people. If all the industries scheduled for denationalization were to be returned to the private sector of the economy, the proportion of GDP created by the public-sector industry would have dropped to 6½ per cent. Over 600,000 jobs would be transferred to the private sector.

This policy of privatization, more than any other, perhaps demonstrates most vividly the break with the 'statist' consensus, as Sir Keith Joseph has recently called it. It will be recalled from previous chapters that post-war Conservative governments did very little to upset the nationalization position achieved by the 1945–51 Labour government, privatizing only steel and road haulage. When steel was renationalized by the Wilson government in the 1960s, the Heath government did not seek to denationalize it, presumably because the market position of steel was so adverse, and indeed came to nationalize Rolls-Royce Aero Engines. However, the Thatcher government has, since it assumed office, pursued a vigorous policy of privatization and, as we shall see, as a policy it meets not just one, but very many of the ideological assumptions of conservative capitalism.

In addition to privatization in the strict sense of the word, it has also sought, where possible, deregulation, particularly in the field of bus transport. As we shall see, this policy has not only been consistent with the assumptions of the market-capitalist case, but has also brought likely political benefits. With the disposal of ownership to small as well as large investors, it becomes politically very difficult for the Labour Party to try to renationalize these undertakings. A large constituency of small shareholders now value their stake in these companies and, it is argued, the Labour Party would be unwise to antagonize them by threats of renationalization. In fact, the Labour Party has now abandoned its approach to this, only promising to renationalize British Telecom. However, it has forced the Party to think about different forms of public ownership. In particular, the Labour Party has been concentrating on ideas of 'social ownership' that move away from the old centralized Morrisonian state corporations which now seem to be regarded as obsolete on all sides of the political spectrum.

IDEOLOGICAL RATIONALE

The conservative policy on privatization has gone a long way toward changing the agenda of politics on these issues, even among those who believe that the undertakings currently privatized should come under some form of state control. So what are the ways in which the privatization strategy follows the institutional critique mounted by market conservatives as we saw it in the earlier chapter?

It will aid discussion to itemize the points of congruence:

1 The privatization programme will diminish the size and scope of government, thus serving a major aim of the market wing of the Conservative party and allowing government to concentrate on narrower areas of proper concern, so that it can act more effectively and more authoritatively within its proper and more limited sphere.

2 It will increase economic freedom in the sense of expanding consumer choice because, it is argued, the nationalized industries are not responsive to consumer choice and are dominated by producer interests.

3 It will lessen the government's role in pay negotiations and the inherent politicization of industrial disputes in the public sector where government is perceived as being the final paymaster.

4 It will decrease the Public Sector Borrowing Requirement when state industries no longer have to look to government for investment but, as privatized undertakings, will raise the capital needed for investment from the public sector. The diminution of the Borrowing Requirement is a central part of the monetarist strategy discussed in a previous chapter.

5 It will increase the efficiency of the industries by making them more responsive to pressures from shareholders and customers who in the case of some privatized undertakings are one and the same.

6 It will allow investment decisions to be taken more rationally in terms of the needs of the industry rather than as the result of political decisions arising from interest-group pressures.

7 It will help to generate an enterprise culture by bringing more people into the ranks of shareholders who will then feel more of a stake in economic success.

8 It will diminish the power of public-sector unions, while at the same time offering to those who work in the newly privatized industries a boost in morale by being members of more efficient and consumer-oriented industries.

9 Given the inherited size of the public sector, it is bound to influence the whole of the British economy. Given the problems of the nationalized industries, particularly their economic inefficiency and their bureaucratic structure, to privatize the industries is likely to have a beneficial effect on the rest of the economy.

IMPLEMENTATION

However, before we go on to discuss these arguments in more detail, it is important to grasp the scale of the privatization programme. In the first table we give details of the programme, and in the second the sums raised by the programme which as we shall see are important in relation to the argument about the Public Sector Borrowing Requirement (PSBR).

Clearly the scale of the operation shows it to be a very radical programme. It has swayed the balance in the economy between the public and private sectors in ways suggested by the diagnosis of the defects in British society as understood by the market conventions discussed in the previous chapters. We now need to turn to discuss the arguments in detail.

Table 9.1 Privatization receipts

Date of issue	Company	Value of issues (£m)	Government proceeds (£m)	% of equity
November 1979	British Petroleum	290	290	5.0
February 1981	British Aerospace	150	50	50.0
June 1981	British Petroleum	293.5	15.2	5.6
October 1981	Cable & Wireless	224	189	49.0
February 1982	Amersham International	71	65	100.0
November 1982	Britoil	549	549	51.0
February 1983	Associated British Ports	22	−34*	51.5
September 1983	British Petroleum	566	566	7.0
December 1983	Cable & Wireless	275	275	22.0
April 1984	Associated British Ports	52	52	48.5
June 1984	Enterprise Oil	392	392	100.0
July 1984	Jaguar	294	294	100.0
November 1984	British Telecom	3,916	2,626	50.2
May 1985	British Aerospace	551	363	59.0
August 1985	Britoil	449	449	48.0
December 1985	Cable & Wireless	933	602	31.0
December 1986	British Gas	5,434	7,720	100.0
February 1987	British Airways	900	900	100.0
May 1987	Rolls Royce	1,363	1,080	100.0
July 1987	British Airports Authority	1,225	1,275	100.0
October 1987	British Petroleum**	7,240 minimum	5,727 minimum	31.5

Total: 23,055.2m.

Source: *Sunday Times Business News*
Notes: * After writing off debts
** Projected only

In a recent book the economist Cento Veljanowski has called the privatization programme 'Selling the State', and it is the impact of privatization on the role of government which goes to the ideological heart of the issue. Certainly a good deal of the argument between the parties, and indeed within the Conservative Party, has been about the issue of selling national assets or selling 'the family silver', as Lord Stockton (previously the Conservative prime minister, Harold Macmillan) put it in a famous speech in the House of Lords.

The argument here turns on two central themes. The first is that an extended state that has within its grasp such a large sector of the economy is bound to suffer from overload. In Professor King's telling phrase, cited earlier, its reach will exceed its grasp so that it cannot govern effectively. The second is the market-conservative response to the claim that government, rather than the private sector, has a kind of moral responsibility for 'natural' monopolies such as gas and water.

Industries were originally nationalized by the Labour government in the post-1945 period as part of the fulfilment of the basic ideology of the Labour Party as set out in Clause IV of its Constitution which refers to the public ownership of the commanding heights of the economy. To have basic utilities covering such a large section of the economy in public ownership would facilitate economic planning because only in these industries would government have a direct say about the level of investment, the type of investment, the scale of service to be provided, and the location of the plant – important, for example, in regional policy. In addition, natural monopolies should be under government control so that they could be used for the overall public good rather than for the benefit of shareholders. Without this kind of ownership, pricing might become unresponsive to public need. Uneconomic activities by natural monopolies might be discontinued despite the high social costs involved. So, for example, if the telephone system were to be privatized, there would be no guarantee that vital services such as call boxes would not be discontinued because they were uneconomic, even though there could be devastating social effects. Public ownership, so it was argued, would enable some degree of cross-subsidization to occur between profit-making and loss-making parts of the enterprise in response to social need. This could not be expected or imposed on a normal commercial company responding both to market conditions and the desire of shareholders to seek a return on their investment.

Given the more modest assumptions about the role of government in relation to economic management which the Conservative government holds, as we have seen, the need for government to own basic industries is removed. The authority of Keynes himself could not be invoked to justify a large state sector. However, in the view of market conservatives, the argument in favour of nationalized industry as a necessary means to planning is part of what they regard as the discredited collectivist, Keynesian, interventionist consensus which had dominated British politics with dire results since 1945. Given the view of the government that the state should play an economic role only in the narrow sense of producing a stable framework of monetary and fiscal policy within which business could make its own decisions, there could be no intrinsic case for a publicly owned sector of industry. This would follow additionally from the capitalist critique of planning, deeply indebted to Hayek and the Austrian school which we discussed earlier in the book.

PRIVATIZATION AND PUBLIC UTILITIES

If economic planning, in whatever mode, is off the political agenda, then the argument for the public ownership of basic utilities as a necessary instrument of planning policy also falls. Government should have a limited and sustainable role in economic policy and that is defined in terms of providing a stable monetary and fiscal framework. State ownership of industry is positively inimical to this. In order to raise the cash necessary to meet the investment demands of the nationalized industries, government will either have to borrow, which will crowd out investment for private industry, or it will have to raise money by taxation with baleful effects on incentives. So it is, on this view, a necessary condition of stable monetary and fiscal policy that the state should be, as far as possible, disengaged from direct responsibility for funding the forward investment of nationalized industry.

The second argument in favour of nationalization was that many of the utilities involved with it always were natural monopolies, as in the case of water, or are in effect natural monopolies, as in the case of gas supply because of the colossal cost of laying down alternative infrastructures of supply. Given these infrastructures (which apply also in the case of telephones, electricity, and the railways), such utilities are effectively in a monopoly position. If this is so, then the nationalization argument would claim that they should be a publicly owned resource. If they are not, the monopolistic position may be exploited by private owners and the distribution of the utility will not be sensitive to social cost. Public ownership, rather than operation in the private market, is the only way of ensuring that such utilities are directed by considerations of the public interest, of which government is the custodian, rather than the shareholder or market pressure. Given that the infrastructure of such monopolies cannot be broken up, even if the services provided can be regionalized, there can be no case for private ownership in terms of increasing competitiveness, and hence nationalization for the public good is the only legitimate response. Mr John Moore, formerly the Financial Secretary to the Treasury, and the person most responsible for the privatization programme characterizes the argument for nationalization from natural monopoly as follows:

> Conventional wisdom was that monopolies were so powerful, so prone to take advantage of their customers, so liable to become fat and inefficient, that the only safe place for them was in the public sector. Only politicians and civil servants could be entrusted with monopoly power because only they would exercise it with restraint, justice and good sense.[1]

Ministerial responsibility to Parliament for the overall oversight of a nationalized industry was, in the conventional view, the way of ensuring that a monopoly was exercised for the public good. However, the *laissez-faire* capitalist rejects this argument for a number of reasons.

In the first place, when politicians are custodians of resources, they are not merely responsive to vague ideas like the 'public good' but are also concerned with interest-group pressure.[2] So, for example, in the 1974–9 period when the Central Electricity Generating Board saw no need to build a new coal-fired power station the pressure of the National Union of Mineworkers on the Labour government ensured that it was built, despite the professional and managerial views of the electricity-supply industry. Politicians cannot resist such pressures when they are custodians of such immense resources, and arguments about the overall public good are likely to be overcome. Second, with the privatization of monopolies, it is inevitable the case that shareholders are also customers. So Moore argues:

> The existence of large numbers of shareholders who have both paid for their shares expecting a reasonable return and are customers interested in a good service at a fair price is an irresistible combination and a powerful lobby in favour of both efficiency and price restraint.[3]

In the third place privatized utilities will have to raise capital for investment in private markets and thus be subject to investigation by bankers and financial analysts. This will impose its own discipline on the performance of these monopolies which, in the view of defenders of privatization, is much more effective than political trusteeship. Finally, in the view of defenders of privatization of effective monopolies, it is perfectly possible to impose on privatized utilities a regulatory regime to ensure a fair use of the monopoly. In the case of the privatization of British Telecom, a regulatory Office of Telecommunications was established which, in the view of conservative capitalists, will provide a model of how the public interest can be secured, even in the context of the privatization of a national monopoly.

It is also, of course, possible to hold open the possibility of competition to break the monopoly. So, for example, the Mercury system has been allowed access to British Telecom lines and an Act of Parliament allowed alternative access to gas mains hitherto installed and monopolized by British Gas, although at the moment no business has sought to take advantage of this.

The final argument is about social cost. To what extent will private monopolies be responsive to uneconomic operations which may well yield important but unquantifiable benefits in particular areas?

PRIVATIZATION AND THE PUBLIC INTEREST

The counter-argument here is threefold. The first is that nationalized industries are not always responsive to social factors either. The classic case here was the Beeching Plan for British Rail which drastically reduced British Railways track and with it the policy of keeping open uneconomic lines as a social amenity. Hence the defender of privatization will argue that responsiveness to social factors is not intrinsic to nationalization. One cannot draw a categorical distinction between the public and private sector on this basis. It is more of a continuum rather than a difference of kind.

The second counter-argument is that some regard for social considerations could be part of the brief for the regulatory agencies which will accompany privatized monopolies to ensure that monopolies at least take such claims seriously into account. However, the strongest argument is that the entrenched need to make nationalized industries responsive to social factors – which followed necessarily from political oversight – led to difficulties in four ways. First of all, political interference to ensure responsiveness meant that managers always had incommensurable purposes to pursue: to run a profitable business and to be responsive to social factors. Once monopolies are privatized, the social costs will clearly

become a political responsibility rather than a managerial one, and there will be a clear division of labour between politics and business. The second argument is that the requirement to be responsive to social factors in fact meant that nationalized industries had to run cross-subsidies between profitable and uneconomic activities. However, supporters of privatization argue that this is inefficient and, if there are uneconomic social obligations to meet, this should be a transparent political responsibility rather than an accounting exercise within a nationalized industry. So Beesley and Littlechild, who have both advised the government on privatization, argue as follows:

> Procedures for establishing non-commercial obligations need to be clearly specified. Each privatization act should define which services are potentially of social concern. Any company claiming that such a service is uneconomic should be required to provide relevant financial data to support its case accompanied by a request to withdraw unless a subsidy is provided. A specified public body (e.g. a local authority) will then consider whether the case is plausible, whether another operator is willing to provide the service,* and whether a subsidy should be provided.
>
> Where should the subsidy come from? One of the prime aims of nationalization has to facilitate cross subsidies from more profitable services. However, cross subsidization largely hides the extent of the subsidy and opens the door to political pressures. Also, it entails restricting on competition so as to protect the source of funds. . . .** For these reasons economists have long recommended that explicit public subsidies should be provided in preference to cross subsidies.[4]
>
> * Obviously not applicable in the case of a monopoly
> ** Again not applicable in the case of monopoly

Again, in the view of those who favour privatization, the state can discharge its obligation to all members of the community by subsidizing in an explicit and transparent way such social costs, rather than through nationalization with all the baleful effects which, in the view of *laissez-faire* capitalists, will inevitably follow from a large public sector.

Hence, to summarize the argument: the state has no basic duty or competence to plan the economy, hence public ownership of basic utilities is not a 'core' function of government, once planning is eschewed. Second, while government, of course, has a duty to all members of society and has to treat their interests in an equal manner, this does not necessarily imply public ownership of industry, since needs can be met when they are uneconomic by explicit subsidy rather than by the direct ownership of the industry.

PRIVATIZATION AND DEMOCRACY

The second main argument in defence of privatization and of reducing the state sector in industry, is that it increases economic freedom which is a necessary counterpart to political and civil liberties. There are perhaps two aspects to this case which are important in relation to nationalized industries specifically: the first is that nationalized industries may well limit the economic choices open to consumers; second, that nationalization requires coercion in relation to property rights. When taking an industry into public ownership, the state coerces individuals to relinquish property rights – then shareholdings – on a basis dictated by the state. In using public resources to buy and to sustain industry, government requires citizens, or at least taxpayers, to have implied property rights in state enterprises, even though the normal rights in relation to property cannot be discharged, and an individual taxpayer may, if he or she had the choice, decline to become a property owner in a particular enterprise. In these two specific ways, so it is argued, nationalization restricts economic freedom leading to a more generalized threat posed by the general growth of government and its impact on the rest of the economy.

Market-based conservatives argue that nationalized industries limit choice in two main ways. The nationalized industry may use its monopoly power to charge an unfair price for a commodity for which there is no other competition allowable under the monopoly. For example, before the privatization of British Telecom, prices for installing phones were rigidly fixed and there was no alternative to paying the price under the monopoly guaranteed by statute. Second, either by using market strength or monopoly power, nationalized industries are able to prevent new products coming on to the market. So again in the case of the telephone system, a wider range of telephone instruments is now available to customers than was the case before British Telecom's denationalization. Some of these may be inferior instruments, but they respond to consumer demand.

The break-up of monopoly in this view increases economic freedom in the sense of consumer sovereignty and this is an important fact of political freedom. Other examples can also be cited. Perhaps one of the most dramatic has been the expansion of the range of choice in express-bus services as the result of deregulation of route licences. This has clearly led to an expansion of routes available. The general lowering of prices has, in its turn, had some effect upon the pricing policy of British Rail which is currently still fully nationalized.

The third argument in favour of privatization relates to public-sector pay. In this case there are several different considerations at work. This has been a particularly sensitive issue within the Conservative Party since the collapse of the Heath government over the miners' strike in 1974 and the 'Winter of Discontent' which affected the Labour government in 1978/9. The Conservative Party leadership commissioned Mr Nicholas Ridley, a leading market Conservative, to produce a report on the attitude which should be taken by an incoming Conservative government to the problem of public-sector pay. This report was secret but was leaked to *The Economist* and published on 27 May 1978. In it Mr Ridley argued that, when the nationalized industries 'have the nation by the jugular vein the only feasible option is to pay up'.[5]

There are two aspects to Ridley's argument which are worth exploring. The first is to do with the lack of a budgetary constraint at the end of the day in the nationalized industries. In the private sector a company can go bankrupt and pay negotiations have to be conducted against the background of that fact. Hence union negotiators will be likely to moderate their demands if it is thought that bankruptcy will result from their action. In the public sector no such final constraint exists. If excessive pay settlements are made, then these can be passed on directly to the consumer by putting up the price of the goods and services. Alternatively, nationalized industries will be able to gain access to money from the Treasury either because government fears a strike in basic utilities or, for reasons of inflation, does not wish to see increased costs passed straight on to consumers.

This links up the economic argument in relation to public-sector pay with what might be called the legitimacy argument. Because of the lack of an internal financial constraint within a nationalized industry, the government is perceived in reality to be the final paymaster. This is so, even if nationalized industries are cash limited as happened under Mr Healey as Chancellor of the Exchequer from 1970 to 1979. The presumption is that cash limits are not the ultimate bottom line, on a par with bankruptcy, because they can always be altered by political pressure. Government is the ultimate guarantor of the finances of nationalized industries. Hence the industrial disputes which arise in nationalized industries over pay almost inevitably become political disputes in which the authority of government is put at risk, as was the case in 1974 and 1978/9. It is another case of government's responsibility outrunning its power actually to control events.

Privatization again is thought to be a solution to this problem because, once an industry is privatized, it is cut off from Exchequer funds. Bankruptcy, rather than potentially movable cash limits, becomes the basic financial discipline. Union negotiators have to operate against this background as well as the fact that, with an actual or potential liberalization of the market, it becomes much more difficult to pass costs on to customers directly. So, for example, in the case of a recent strike in British Telecom, the small but significant access to the system of a market rival, Mercury, had to be borne in mind by union negotitators, and the strike was relatively short lived. In principle, privatization cuts the link between government and a particular industry so that, in the conduct of an industrial dispute, the standing and legitimacy of government are not directly involved.

Of course, there is still a long way to go to fulfil this as a strategy. The gas industry is still nationalized, and in the miners' strike government was directly involved and its legitimacy was seen to be on the line from the point of view of both the government and the miners' union. The same would be true in the case of a prolonged national strike in the electricity-supply industry or the railways, though competition with deregulated buses would be a factor.

PRIVATIZATION AND ECONOMIC STRATEGY

Privatization also plays a central role in the government's ability to pursue its 'monetarist' strategy. Given the intellectual case for monetarism described earlier, government borrowing is seen as inflationary and as having a bad effect on the capacity of private industry to borrow at reasonable rates of interest. The revenue which accrues to government as the result of privatizing industries will allow the government to reduce the Public Sector Borrowing Requirement as part of what it needs to raise to fund its more appropriate functions. Second, because government is no longer directly financing the investment of nationalized industries, it no longer has to find that money as part of its overall spending. Thus, it is argued, privatization will reduce the size of government spending and increase its revenue. This strategy was most clearly revealed in the 1987 Budget when the Chancellor, Mr Lawson, was able to reduce the size of the PSBR to about 0 per cent of GDP, while at the same time reducing the standard rate of tax by 2p. It was partly revenue from the sale of nationalized industries that allowed this to be done.

This is where the issue of selling the nation's assets, or disposing of the family silver, becomes most controversial. On the one hand, there is no doubt that the privatization programme has led to an immediate short-term easing of the government's revenue and expenditure position. However, critics have argued that this is very short term and reflects the extent to which at least some of the privatized industries could in the longer term have led to returns to the government. The capacity of the government to restrict monetary growth has certainly been improved in the short term by privatization, but in the longer term privatization could lead to a reduction of income to the Exchequer. This is clear from the consequence of compelling British Gas to sell its offshore oil interests and would clearly follow from the privatization of British Gas which has made substantial payments to the Exchequer. It was also true of the denationalization of BNOC – the British National Oil Corporation. Because denationalization can really only be secured for industries such as these and British Airways which are profitable and attractive to investors, it follows that the gains from privatization in Exchequer-revenue terms are likely to be only short term, and the gains in terms of the long-run reduction of PSBR will commonly be secured by other reductions in public expenditure. This might therefore indicate the need to privatize the coal industry and the railways in some way, because these are a constant drain on government borrowing. However, precisely because they are loss making as currently constituted, the possibility of privatizing these industries on the same basis as others seems rather remote. It would be wrong to regard this as a direct issue of ideology between Conservative and Labour since the Labour Party in office, 1974–9, sold off shares in British Petroleum in order to reduce the Public Sector Borrowing Requirement as part of the agreement with the International Monetary Fund.

In addition, critics of the PSBR argument point out that in the case of some privatized industries a great deal of public money has been put into 'fattening' them up to make them attractive to private investors, many of the issues have been underpriced as revealed by the degree of oversubscription, and very large sums of money have been spent on advertising the privatization issues. Although by the middle of 1987 the programme will have raised £12 billion pounds for the Treasury, in one case alone, the privatization of British Gas, the Institute of Fiscal Studies has estimated that the cost of advertising plus the cost of underpricing has been in the order of £3 billion.

Several of the arguments cited in the initial list of discussion points can be brought together under the heading of efficiency. We have seen already that the argument about economic freedom and about financial disciplines connected with the market have efficiency connotations. The argument about economic freedom implied that privatization would restrict consumer sovereignty in relation to these undertakings. The necessity to be more responsive to consumer demands, for example, will make enterprises more competitive and efficient. This is particularly so, it is argued, in the case of monopolies because in those cases the consumer and the shareholder are necessarily identical and this is bound to lead to increased efficiency. Second, operating against market conditions with the removal of an Exchequer safety net will require firms to adopt more financial discipline, negotiate with unions more realistically, and manage more effectively. In addition, privatized firms will be able to make their own investment decisions without political interference. Such political interference may itself be the result of interest-group pressure as, for example, in building new power stations in areas of unemployment or keeping open uneconomic plants for social reasons, as, for example, the British Steel plant at Ravenscraig in Scotland. Issues like this can still, so it is argued, be a legitimate area of government concern, but separating out the business and social function of a nationalized industry will bring a clarity to managerial objectives which cannot be achieved by a regime of cross subsidy. The point has been made clearly by Mr John Moore, then Financial Secretary at the Treasury:

Not only are the industries constantly at risk from political and bureaucratic interference, the managers must at times wonder what it is they are supposed to be managing. Are the industries businesses or social services? Social and commercial objectives interact to the detriment of both. Tell any able manager to create and build up a prosperous company and he will know what to do. Tell him at the same time to carry out a host of non-commercial functions and he will be hopelessly muddled. The commercial and social objectives then both suffer.[6]

Privatization therefore, in the view of its defenders, leads to greater efficiency by reducing political interference and interest-group pressures, restoring the discipline of the market, and producing more discipline for managers and workers. This makes the industry more responsive to consumer choice and leads to a greater clarity of objectives.

In addition, it is argued it brings benefits to its workforce. Most privatization schemes have given a preferential position in buying shares to the workforce and, so it is argued, this will lead to greater involvement on the part of workers with the running of the company and its success in the market. The most obvious success here is the case of the National Freight Corporation which was subject to an employees' buy-out and has become hugely successful. Second, given the greater efficiency which is likely to occur as the result of privatization, workers in such industries will experience an increase in morale because they will become members of profitable industries rather than ones which depend, partly to meet social functions, on state underwriting and interference.

Critics of privatization often argue that employees are at risk from the greater prospect of unemployment once industries are privatized. Defenders of the programme disagree with this. They draw attention to the history of the nationalized industries over the past fifteen years where there have been constant job losses, particularly in coal (losses here accelerated since the pit strikes) and the railways, but also in more successful nationalized industries. Between 1978 and 1983 employment in the gas industry fell by 19 per cent and in electricity by 22 per cent. On this view, nationalized industries cannot remain overmanned indefinitely, partly because of the consequences for the rest of the economy and the government's responsibility for that. Recall what Sir Keith Joseph argued in

Stranded on the Middle Ground: 'For every job preserved in British Leyland, Chrysler and other jobs of highly paid outdoor relief, several jobs are destroyed up and down the country.'[7]

The cost of financing overmanned nationalized industries cannot be sustained in the long term by any government because of the impact that this would have on either borrowing or taxation. Freed from the strait-jacket of statutory control and placed in the context of market disciplines, privatized firms will, like all other firms, have to look to new products and new methods if there is a decline in demand for their historic products. However, because of statutory controls, nationalized industries have to pursue the same products and aims. Innovations which are the only things that can lead to new jobs are stifled:

> The statutory strait-jacket limits their means of adjustment. They struggle on and turn their backs on the real world. In the end circumstances force abrupt and traumatic change. But too late. Jobs are lost forever. Nationalization may create a spurious sense of security but it is not a means of insuring continuing employment. . . . Competition, on the other hand, breeds jobs. It forces modernization and technological change.[8]

This fits very well with the classical liberal idea of the market as a learning mechanism. Individuals using limited knowledge are much more able to adapt to changes in the environment than bureaucratic or political processes which are not responsive in a direct way to the price mechanism which signals where innovation and investment should go. In the absence of a competitive market price for the products of nationalized industries this capacity for change and innovation is lost and as a result there are considerable risks to employment.

POLITICAL DIMENSIONS

The final element of the case for privatization arose as perhaps an unforeseen consequence of the programme, and this is the widening of share ownership among the population. This was not originally part of the intention behind the privatization programme but it has been subsequently a major element of it. First of all, it is important to get some of the factual issues clear. Many of the large privatization programmes did succeed in attracting a large number of people into share ownership for the first time. Up to mid-1983, shares were owned by about 5–6 per cent of the adult population. By 1983, and largely as the result of the privatization programme, this proportion had risen to 16 per cent. British Telecom, which was privatized in 1984, attracted 2.2 million shareholders of whom slightly more than half had not owned shares before. Although many were sold in initial profit-taking, there are still 1.7 million shareholders on BT's books. The Trustee Savings Bank sale attracted 3 million shareholders of whom 2.5 million remain on the register. The British Gas privatization in December 1986 attracted about 4.5 million of whom 4 million remain registered. In the first two cases the extent of ownership was clearly encouraged by quite marked underpricing of the assets but this cannot account for the large numbers for British Gas shares which were more fairly priced. More recently the British Airways and Rolls-Royce issues were also oversubscribed. In the case of Rolls-Royce (privatized in May 1983) the offer was oversubscribed 9.4 times with private investors putting up £2.65 billion, applying for the 3.15 billion shares. In the case of British Airways 1.1 million people applied for shares. The numbers of these remaining on the registers after initial profit-taking illustrate the extent to which the vast majority were not enticed by the desire to make a quick profit. Certainly the privatization programme has extended the range of shareholding, if not the overall proportion of shares in British companies held by private individuals which has fallen from 59 per cent in 1963 to 25 per cent in 1986.

This increase in the range of shareholding as a percentage of the population was perhaps not initially expected by government but since that time it has been encouraged. Again John Moore argued in December 1984 that 'Our aim is to build upon our property owning democracy and to establish a people's capital market.'[9]

This aim is clearly consonant with the conservative-capitalist approach. It has been one theme of conservative writers that Britain has never really assimilated capitalist values, valuing professional and public service employment over trade and industry. Wider share ownership is one way of attempting to diffuse capitalist values more widely and make people more aware of the workings of markets and companies within markets. It has to be said, however, that the industries which have attracted most small investors have been those with very little risk attached to them. It has been argued that interest would fall off with more risky ventures, but so far this has not deterred applications for Rolls-Royce and British Airways shares.

The extending of share ownership is thought also to extend the stake which people have in the private enterprise, non-socialist system and it is felt that this could be politically important in two ways. First of all, the wider share ownership of privatized companies makes it less electorally attractive for the Labour Party to seek to renationalize such companies, although it has made such a promise in the case of British Telecom. Second, it is argued that share ownership has increased in social class C2 which consists of skilled manual workers who deserted the Labour Party in 1979. Of this group 16 per cent now own shares, mainly in privatized companies, and all together 40 per cent of the shares in privatized companies are held by classes C2, D, and E who collectively own only 26 per cent of the shares in non-privatized companies. So it does seem that the privatization programme has extended share ownership substantially among groups which held shares in only limited numbers before. This includes the stake in the private-enterprise system, limits the choice of the Labour Party over renationalization, and provides a powerful group of floating voters who may well favour the Conservatives, or at least are likely not to favour Labour if it continues with policies of further public ownership.[10]

The success of the privatization programme has led the government to seek other ways of facilitating wider share ownership. For example, granting tax relief for approved employee share-option schemes and personal equity plans. There has also been an amendment to the Companies Act and the Stock Exchange rules to allow private-sector companies to promote and sell their shares to individuals. In all of these ways, it is hoped, interest in and attitudes to the market economy will be altered favourably and the political agenda in relation to nationalized industries will be changed in an irreversible manner.

However, existing privatizations have taken place against the background of a buoyant stock market. The crash of October 1987 seems likely to have shaken the faith of many small investors and certainly since that time Building Society receipts might well indicate that many small investors have become more nervous about direct investment in stocks and shares. It remains to be seen how far the 1987 experience affects the capacity of future privatizations to attract small investors.

Part Three

RESPONSES FROM THE LEFT

Chapter Ten

THE MARKET AND THE STATE

The central theme of this book has been the extent to which modern, market-based conservatism has sought to roll back the frontiers of the state and, where possible, to increase the role of the market. Earlier chapters explained this theoretical basis and estimated its recent impact on politics in Britain and the United States. It is clear that the conservative record is very patchy.

The pursuit of this policy has caused severe tensions within conservatism itself – between conservative traditionalists and those who emphasize the free market. However, it is now time to discuss in some detail the ideological framework against which market-based capitalism has developed, and to consider the possible response of the left to this attempt to shift the political agenda away from public collective provision towards private market provision.

In a sense this attempt to change the political agenda goes to the heart of the most fundamental issues of political theory. After all, the central political institution is the state and its nature and functions. This is the pivotal point of political theory and, as we have seen in the past few years, it has been the core issue of political practice. In what follows, we shall concentrate upon three main issues: the moral basis of the market; the role of political institutions compared to market-based institutions; and the nature of the left's response to the changed agenda.

For some time, the left in Britain and the United States has been somewhat conservative – a defender of the government's role in public finance as bequeathed by the New Deal in the United States and the post-war political settlement of the Attlee governments in Britain. Until the left confronts the intellectual self-confidence of the free-market right, it will remain on the defensive. There has been a great deal of moral indignation generated by the left in reaction to the 'New Right', but the intellectual response has been a long time in coming. However, there are now signs that a more cogent critique of the free-market right is developing, especially in Britain.

While the case for less government and an increased role for markets has been couched in terms of modernization, growth, and efficiency, there is lying behind this a moral and political thesis about markets and their superiority over public provision in many spheres. This must be confronted directly here. The moral case by the left has rested on counter-arguments that markets restrict freedom, vitiate social justice, cause poverty, do not promote equality, and infringe rights. In each of these cases conservative capitalists have developed a position which requires an answer from the left. We shall now consider these issues.

In the conservative capitalist view, the suffering which may be caused by the operation of the market is not to be rectified by claims to rights, justice, and equality. The provision of a welfare safety net – whether by voluntary or political action – is a gift to be bestowed, not a right to be claimed. There might be good pragmatic goals for the limited provision of welfare, but for redistributive purposes it has no moral legitimacy.

We saw the reasoning here in chapter 3. Because the outcomes of the market are not intended or foreseen by anyone, market outcomes cannot be coercive and limit freedom, nor can they cause injustice or infringe rights. Infringements of this sort can result only from intentional outcomes which markets do not produce.

These arguments about liberty and justice are a radical strike at the normative basis on which the left justifies the welfare state as a promoter of liberty and rectifier of injustice. Any defender of the welfare state who seeks to portray it as a more than pragmatic phenomenon – to buy off social discontent or to create a reasonably healthy workforce – must come to terms with this critique because he will not be able to trump pragmatic claims in favour of diminishing the welfare state with claims about freedom and justice. Obviously, in the context of freedom and justice, Hayek's argument depends crucially upon his claim that economic outcomes are unintentional and unforeseeable and therefore cannot produce coercion or injustice which depend upon coercers and distributors being identified as specific human agents. However, these claims need to be disentangled a little.[1]

In the case of foreseeability, we need to go back to Hayek's pivotal assertion: 'These shares are the outcome of a process the effect of which on particular people was neither intended nor foreseen.' However, it is not clear that the left's critique of the market in relation to the lack of freedom of the worst off has ever been made on the basis of individual cases. Usually the argument has been in terms of groups – that, as a general rule, those who enter a market with least will end up with least. Hayek has to accept existing inequalities in property, income, and power as given because to seek to change these would be an illegitimate exercise in distributive justice. Given this initial inequality, then it does seem plausible to suggest that those who by and large enter the market with least in the way of income and property will have less capacity to act effectively in the market. If this can be foreseen as a rule of thumb, and we believe that it can, then Hayek's argument about foreseeability loses much of its power.[2]

Even if the outcomes of markets could be foreseen for the poor as a general category, this would still not, in the capitalist view, limit their freedom because freedom does not consist in having the positive power or the resources to satisfy desires; it consists in freedom from intentional coercion. However, the sharp distinction which Hayek, for example, draws here is dubious even in the context of his own work. In his discussion of coercion in chapter IX of *The Constitution of Liberty*,[3] Hayek makes the wholly sensible point that a monopolist could be regarded as exercising coercion if he controls what Hayek calls an 'essential commodity' or an 'indispensable supply'. But it is not at all clear why this should be regarded as coercive unless there is some conceptual link between such basic goods and the exercise of liberty. Unless there was this analytical connection between certain basic goods and liberty, we might regard the actions of the monopolist as being economically inefficient and morally abhorrent in various ways, but not coercive. The point can be made in a more general way about coercion.

If a coercive restraint is removed on my conduct, then I am enabled to do something which I was not realistically able to choose before. Of course, in my new-found freedom I may choose not to do it, but nevertheless the limitation on coercion is an enabling factor. Alternatively, the imposition of coercion may make me realistically unable to do what I was able to do before. Before the gun was held to my head, I was able to walk through the door. Now, realistically, I am unable to do so. On these grounds therefore, there is a basis for saying that there is some connection between freedom and the capacity to exercise agency.

The second reason there could be thought to be a connection between freedom and ability is to take up another theme in Hayek's work, namely the value of liberty. Hayek rests his case for the value of negative freedom on the basis of our ignorance:

> If there were omniscient men, if we could know not only all that effects the attainment of our present wishes but also our future wants and desires there would be little use for liberty. . . .
> Liberty is essential in order to leave room for the unforeseeable and unpredictable; we want it because we have learned to expect from it the opportunity of realising many of our aims.[4]

Now, of course, this is very important and has to be preserved in a full account of the value of liberty but, as Hayek himself makes clear in this passage, liberty is an opportunity-related concept. He clearly wants to restrict the idea of opportunity here to mean the opportunity to capitalize upon the accidental and the unforeseeable which is important for human progress and this is fair enough; but surely this is too restricted a view of opportunity. I value negative liberty because of the private space it offers me to do what I want. I value liberty because freedom enables me to advance my ends and purposes and it is surely the case that to do this means that I need resources, powers, and opportunities of a more substantial kind than merely the openings which my ignorance reveals. This is central to Rawls, for example, when he speaks about the value of liberty: 'the worth of liberty is not the same for everyone. Some have . . . greater means to achieve their aims.'[5]

This is not to say that their liberty is unequal, only that the value of freedom varies in relation to their powers and opportunities. This is, we believe, the fundamental idea behind the proposal by MacCallum in which freedom is defined as the freedom of x from y to do or become z.[6] The opportunity to do or become z is what makes the absence of constraint (y) valuable to us; it is that in which the worth of liberty resides and as such requires powers and abilities as well as Hayek's opportunities to exploit ignorance.

On these views, therefore, there are strong reasons for rejecting the right's account of liberty as having nothing to do with abilities. However, even if we have given reasons for seeking to link ability with freedom, at least in explaining in an intelligible way why liberty is precious, we still have to respond to Hayek's point that, if we make this connection, then we get into the absurd position of not being able to distinguish between freedom and omnipotence. There are two issues here. The first is an account of the abilities/ powers/capabilities which are indispensable to the value of liberty. We have to put some restriction on this list, otherwise we fall foul of Hayek's strictures. The second is to say something about the relationship between the list of basic powers/capabilities/abilities on one side, and freedom on the other, because not all the restrictions on my abilities can be said to lower the value of liberty.

Hayek's argument is that, if we link freedom and ability in the way we have done, then the value of my liberty declines in proportion to my abilities. This is absurd because there are many things which I am unable to do which have no bearing upon the value of freedom – I cannot be in two places at once, I cannot prove Golbach's conjecture, I am unable to run a four-minute mile, I cannot afford to go on a round-the-world cruise, and all these differently based inabilities would lower the value of liberty. If this argument is to be rebutted, because as it stands it is quite powerful, we need some idea of which abilities/powers/capacities relate most directly to the value of liberty and thus of the conditions and resources which will allow free and independent citizens to flourish. The most plausible answer to this problem is to say that these are the powers and capacities which bear most directly on the possibility of agency.[7] Our capacity for agency clearly must have a bearing upon the value of any liberty. If someone is unable to act at all, not for this or that particular purpose, but at all, then negative liberty will be of no value.

So, are there any basic needs which an agent has to satisfy in order to act at all? If there are, then this will answer Hayek's criticism, because we could then distinguish those basic goods/ powers/opportunities which an agent would need to make liberty valuable from those other powers and abilities (such as the ability to run a four-minute mile), the lack of which it would be absurd to regard as restrictions on the value of freedom. In his discussion of monopoly Hayek has already conceded that there are certain necessary goods or indispensable conditions for human beings to be free, and it can be argued that the most obvious way of character-izing these goods is in terms of the necessary conditions of agency.

What are these goods? At the most basic level it seems clear that physical survival is a necessary condition of agency and that, as such, survival is a basic human good – this good, of course, has to be cashed in terms of specific goods such as health care and the minimum economic conditions of survival. In addition, autonomy is a basic good because it too is a necessary condition of agency. Autonomy is to be understood negatively and positively too in terms of the possession of those resources which secure the necessary condition of autonomous action. This type of argument has been developed by a number of writers in a range of places.[8] The termin-ology of these arguments differs and does reveal different concep-tions of the issues involved as well as different philosophical assump-tions. Nevertheless, for the purposes of this chapter, the thrust of the arguments is very similar and could be couched in the more familiar language of basic needs – those necessary for the exercise of liberty in an effective manner.

A theory of needs is central to a left critique of markets because it provides the beginning of a justification for arguing that there are certain goods which are so necessary for individual agency and action that they should be provided for collectively and intentionally rather than through the market which is the forum within which wants and preferences are satisfied. However, the basic goods of physical survival and autonomy and the specific ways in which these are cashed in terms of health care and income maintenance are fairly minimal as they stand. They would not take the defence of the welfare state in terms of the value of freedom much beyond the idea of the welfare state as a residual institution (although this is useful in defending the welfare state against libertarians such as Nozick who really see no role for a welfare state at all, even at a residual level, and against neo-liberals such as Hayek and Acton who see a residual welfare state as justifiable only on pragmatic and not on moral grounds).

Nevertheless, one can go beyond this minimalist idea towards a more comprehensive view by arguing that sheer physical survival and autonomy are not the only generic goods relating to agency and thus to the value of liberty. One has to think also in terms of well-being. Sheer survival is a necessary condition of agency, but it is clearly not a sufficient one, because someone can literally survive on a respirator; clearly the possibility of purpose fulfilment requires more than this. What it in fact requires cannot be specified except in a culture-dependent way, but in our society the ability to act as an agent is going to require, first of all, negative liberty but, more than this, the ability also to act effectively. For liberty to be valuable, a person is going to require possession of resources both material and psychological, and these will specify various sorts of welfare goods such as education, etc. In order to make negative liberty meaningful and valuable, these resources, however they are defined in a particular society, which comprise the power to act at all in an effective manner are going to be basic goods of agency and will define the conditions of citizenship.

However, while this argument defines a class of basic goods and basic needs in relation to such goods, it does not of itself say anything about distribution. The link with the idea of the value of liberty, however, gives us the clue for a distributive principle. If we accept liberal assumptions about equality of respect due to each citizen, together with the kind of view to be found in Hayek, that we lack criteria for saying that one person is more deserving than another, then there are no moral grounds for saying that some people deserve to have more effective basic liberty. In these circumstances, therefore, those welfare goods which define the conditions of effective agency and the value of liberty should be distributed equally just because there are not any *a priori* moral reasons for any other sort of distribution.

THE DEGREES AND KINDS OF COERCION

So far the argument has been couched in terms of the value of liberty but there is a second strand to the argument which has to be deployed in order fully to meet the market-capitalist argument that can be mounted in terms of liberty, namely in relation to coercion. It will be remembered that part of the argument is that the outcomes of markets are non-coercive because they are neither intended nor foreseen in relation to individuals. We have already argued that the point about foreseeability is irrelevant in relation to individuals and that it is possible to argue that the poor are coerced. Certainly this principle works at the level of personal morality: if I intend to do y and I know that x is a foreseeable consequence of doing y, even though the occurrence of x is not part of my intention, it would be difficult to evade the responsibility for *x*. So in a market, if it is a foreseeable consequence of the operation of a free market, with the existing highly unequal distribution of resources, that some will be made poor as the result of its operation, and if something can be done to change this – for example, through a redistribution of resources, then it would be difficult to evade responsibility for this outcome, even if it was not part of any individual's intention. In this sense, if we can link foreseeability and responsibility together, the market socialist can argue in favour of the redistribution of resources in order to give to individuals the capacity to act as effective and free agents in market transactions.

None of this in any way lessens socialists' commitment to markets. Like most social institutions markets can be characterized in more than one way. The market capitalists' characterization is tendentious and seeks to avoid collective responsibility for the means which people have at their disposal when they enter markets.

EQUALITY, LIBERTY, AND SOCIAL JUSTICE

In our society equal political liberty is taken for granted. While political philosophers may argue about the exact way in which equal political rights are to be grounded, for the citizen at large the issue is uncontroversial. It is only when we come to the sphere of social equality that controversy arises, and this is because social equality articulates a claim to a share of goods which are the objects of competition and are in short supply. However, it is a naïve and mistaken view, although one characteristic of free-market theorists, that formal political equality can exist independently of a high degree of material inequality.[9] The objection to this point has been made very forcefully by John Rawls:

> Historically one of the main defects of constitutional government has been the failure to insure the fair value of political liberty. The necessary corrective steps have not been taken, indeed, they never seem to have been seriously entertained. Disparities in the distribution of property and wealth that far exceed what is compatible with political equality have generally been tolerated by the legal system. . . . Moreover, the effects of injustices in the political system are much more grave and longer lasting than market imperfections. . . . Thus inequities in

212

the economic and social system may soon undermine whatever political equality might have existed under fortunate historical conditions.[10]

This can prove to be a powerful defence of social equality, if it is linked in a defensible way with uncontroversial equality of political rights.

Equal liberty understood in negative terms will have unequal political results. While equal political liberty may be defined in terms of procedural rules, the fact is that, without a greater equality of material resources, political liberty is likely to be of unequal worth. Studies in political science have demonstrated the differential levels of political participation and political influence generally between groups with different command of resources. Universal suffrage grants all citizens the same voting rights, but it is very clear indeed that the wealthy will have more ability than the poor to influence the selection of candidates, the media, public opinion, and political authorities.

Politically equal liberty can turn very easily into an unequal worth of liberty, and the same arguments hold true within the legal system: the rich and the poor have the same rights, but differences of wealth at least allow better counsel to be employed, not to mention the questions of whether the better-off members of society can in fact secure laws which favour their interests, or whether they can exercise influence upon what kinds of crimes are prosecuted (for example in the field of tax evasion).[11] The same is also true in terms of the equal right to free expression. Those in better circumstances are able to utilize this liberty more effectively and it is of greater value to them. If we see greater equality as increasing the worth of liberty, and thus link our defence of a greater degree of equality with support for a fairer worth or value of liberty, we shall be on stronger ground in resisting the free-market conservative assault on equality. The free-market defence of liberty is disingenuous because it neglects the resources which would make the formality of equal liberty more of a reality for the worst-off members of society. The egalitarian is concerned with the maximization of the worth of liberty between individuals, although, as we shall see later, this may in certain circumstances mean that some inequalities are to be seen as legitimate by egalitarians.

MARKETS AND SOCIAL JUSTICE

Having made and defended some of these distinctions, we are now in a position to deal with the market-conservative strictures on social or distributive justice. It is central to the argument here that the outcomes of markets which adversely affect the position of an individual do not result in injustice. Of course, the person may be poorer, he may suffer, but he does not suffer injustice. The difference is crucial for, only if he suffered an injustice, would this generate a moral claim on the resources of the state to rectify that injustice. The key to this argument is that considerations of justice are irrelevant because the outcomes of the market were not willed or intended by anyone and maldistribution can occur only where there is a distributor intentionally making a maldistribution. However, this degree of intentionality is lacking in the case of markets and thus injustice cannot arise.

However, first of all, it is not clear that injustice is only a matter of how a particular outcome came about, but rather is as much a matter of our response to the outcome. Certainly someone who was born with a severe handicap does not suffer an injustice because of the genetic lottery, but where justice and injustice come in is in our response to his position. If we fail to compensate him when we could have done so, at no damaging cost to ourselves, then this is where injustice lies.

In addition though, the argument deployed in the context of freedom becomes relevant here. In a sense, Hayek's own argument about justice parallels the case of freedom as turning upon intentionality. Because there is no intentionality, there is no injustice. However, as we have seen, the situation in respect of intentionality is much more complex than Hayek allows. Although my intention in the market is to buy and sell for my own particular reasons, nevertheless, if it is a foreseeable outcome that individuals will do badly in the acquisition of basic or general goods which bear upon the value of freedom and citizenship, then that outcome is unjust, given that there is an alternative available – the redistributive welfare state.

The foregoing arguments which were deployed in Plant's Fabian pamphlet, *Equality, Markets and the State*,[12] have been considered and rejected in a recent book on *The New Right*[13] by David Green, a research fellow with the Institute for Economic Affairs which, as we saw earlier, was an important base in Britain for securing the revival of free-market approaches to public policy. The grounds on which Green rejects the argument are very instructive. On the argument concerning the fact that those with greatest initial property and income will derive greatest benefits from markets and those with least will derive least he says the following:

> clearly if at any given moment some people have more resources at their disposal than other people, then those already well endowed will have an advantage. But this does not only apply to markets. It also applies to every type of society so far known. Whether you live in a pluralist democracy or under democratic socialism, or in the Communist bloc, there will be an advantage in possessing power and wealth. This advantage explains why the middle classes benefit disproportionately from the welfare state, as many collectivists frequently observe. There is no escape from human differences, and consequently no escape from differences of material wealth and power, but what we can do is to ensure that those who hold power at any time can be easily dislodged for poor performance. With political power this is the role of free elections, and with economic power it is the role of competition. Bad performers in the market can find themselves driven out of business by alternative suppliers more attuned to the wishes of fellow citizens.[14]

This objection misses the point. The argument is that, without a redistribution of income and property rights, the market will not be a fair and neutral mechanism. To say there is no escape from human differences begs the question over whether it is possible to narrow the range of differences and to minimize the costs of failure and the rewards of success without changing economic performance. We shall look at this argument in more detail later on in the chapter when we consider incentives and their role in economic performance.

The second argument which Green considers is the case where it is argued that injustice is not merely a matter of how something arose, for example, by the impersonal forces such as the weather on the market, but how we respond to misfortune. It is possible to describe our reactions to misfortune as just or unjust. Green argues against this as follows:

This claim is valid, but care should be taken not to assume that the existence of hardship or misfortune provides a rationale for government intervention. It provides a moral basis for action to help any person suffering misfortune. But it still leaves unresolved what sort of action should be taken. If it could be shown that private action to assist the poor or victims of misfortune was always less adequate than government action, then a case could be made for state intervention, but no such general claim can be made. Indeed, in some cases private action may be superior. Thus, the existence of misfortune morally requires that help be offered, but what form this should take is a pragmatic question, depending on which available types of help are most effective.[15]

However, this avoids the point about injustice. If those who suffer misfortune can be regarded as suffering an injustice, then it can be argued that this does provide a rationale for state provision in that the rectifications of injustice are not a matter of private charity any more than it is a matter of private action when property rights are unjustly infringed.

POLITICS AND WELFARE

So far then we have argued that there is a defensible view of the obligation to provide welfare both in terms of freedom and justice. The worst-off members of society do suffer a constraint on the value of liberty and they do suffer injustice given that there are alternatives. However, this last phrase brings us back to some of the more practical considerations discussed in the earlier part of the book because, of course, the argument at that point was that the alternative actually produced major problems of its own, particularly its cost and the welfare state's relation to the rest of the economy. While it may be that there are strong moral arguments in favour of the welfare state, if there are great practical and economic difficulties they may, so it is argued, override the moral considerations. One of these practical objections relates to the ambiguity and indeterminacy of welfare. It will be remembered that part of the free-market critique is that, because the claims of welfare are indeterminate, the welfare state has an in-built tendency to grow. There is no plateau to be found, new needs are constantly being discovered (invented?), and being put on the political agenda, requiring an expansion of the welfare state. Because needs are politicized in this way, the welfare state becomes like a financial bottomless pit with no clear limit to the resources it can claim.

This idea received official backing in a recent Treasury document:

> Since there is no clear 'right' level for any particular social security benefit, there are constant demands for both real increases in benefits and for extension of benefit coverage to those who do not at present qualify.[16]

In the view of the market theorists the coupling of this open-ended welfare commitment with electoral politics drives up public spending on welfare inexorably.

In our own argument about the generic goods of welfare as basic needs, we conceded the case that such goods are socially relative and that there will therefore be disputes expressed in political ways about what would satisfy such needs, and it does seem that there can indeed be no alternative to this. There can be no context-independent, purely conceptual answer to the question of how extensive basic goods would be, and to this extent the basis of the free-market case is conceded. However, the search for a non-politicized answer to this question is fruitless, but it does seem to us that there are some limits and constraints which make sense, even within a welfarist perspective. The first and most basic one is that there is no obligation to provide for the basic needs of some individuals if this puts at risk the satisfaction of similar needs of others. This principle certainly works at the level of personal morality. Similarly, there can be no obligation on society to meet basic needs, if to do so would imply a comparable cost or risk. In this case the onus would be on the critic of welfare to show that providing for well-being would be likely to put at severe risk the economic resources necessary to continue to provide for the well-being of all citizens.

The second constraint would be the Rawlsian one.[17] There is no duty to continue to try to equalize well-being if in fact the economic consequences of so doing would actually mean that there would be fewer resources for well-being. That is to say, there might be a level of provision of welfare which falls short of equal provision, because an attempt to go beyond that towards equality would be likely to make everyone, including the professed beneficiaries of more equal treatment worse off. On this view, it would be irrational, if our concern is with well-being, to prefer a system of strict equality of well-being, if this actually lowered the level of welfare to everyone, including those whom the egalitarian was most trying to help.[18]

Additionally, most free-market conservatives, unlike libertarians such as Nozick, do in fact concede a minimal safety-net welfare state and it is clear that such a view has to depend upon a clearly defined concept of absolute poverty, but it is, of course, notoriously difficult to define poverty in such non-relative terms. To concede a residual welfare state without a clearly limited notion of poverty which is publicly acceptable is to open up the free-market conservatives' own conception of the welfare state to the same kind of expansion for which they criticize 'welfarists'. Their own conception of poverty may well become open-ended with all the consequential pressures for further welfare additions to relieve it.

Sir Keith Joseph, cited in an earlier chapter, argued that the welfare state should be concerned with a minimum rather than with equality. But this minimum is *not* defined, although he implies that it is more than subsistence. If this is so, then it is equally capable of being expanded by political pressure. Hence the only safe answer for those who fear for the politicization of welfare is to argue against the existence of a welfare state as a whole, as do libertarians such as Nozick. However, it is very important for the left to recognize the constraints of the economy and to seek to lower expectations about the resources which can be devoted to welfare, both in terms of the moral reasons, but also in terms of its effect on the economy. It is important that the left emphasizes the centrality of production to distribution and does not assume as, for example, Crosland did in the 1950s that the problem of production was solved with only distributional problems remaining.

EQUALITY AND CITIZENSHIP

We saw earlier that it is central to the development of the conservative capitalist case that it should provide cogent reasons for rejecting the left's ideas about equality. Greater social equality was seen as a vice in all sorts of ways: it yielded tax systems which reduced incentives, it led to uniformity, impeded economic development and growth, and bedevilled the welfare state in that it led to a confusion about its purposes as between equality and minimum standards.

However, these arguments need to be disentangled. Although they are abstract, they are of the very first practical importance in the sense that even market conservatives believe that the state has a duty to maintain some form of equality – civil and political and even some forms of equality of opportunity; one's view about the national role of the state and the appropriate sphere of the market will be clearly influenced by one's view of equality.

Equality of opportunity seems on the face of it to be a very persuasive conception of equality, and perhaps the most consensual form which it could take in modern society. It is concerned with fair recruitment procedures to jobs and can be portrayed as an important factor in increasing efficiency because it matches recruitment to ability, not to birth, race, or sex. However, the principle has to be subjected to a good deal of interpretation and, when this is done, it becomes clearer that it is at bottom very vague and ambiguous and its widespread acceptance in society may well depend upon its remaining ambiguous.

In a minimalist interpretation of the principle we might say that it is concerned with the progressive removal of legal impediments to job recruitment and with giving all children a fair start in schools. It is a procedural notion concerned with making sure that the race for positions is a fair one.[19] It is this procedural aspect of equality of opportunity which makes it attractive to free-market theorists such as Hayek. They argue that more substantive forms of equality, such as equality of outcome, will involve intolerable interferences with personal freedom, whereas a procedural form of opportunity will involve few if any interferences with freedom.[20]

However, this easy compromise is illusory. A fair equality of opportunity cannot be attained on a purely procedural basis. Otherwise, we shall be in the position of maintaining that there is equal opportunity for all to dine at the Ritz. There are doubtless no legal impediments against dining at the Ritz so long as one has the resources to do so. If we are concerned with an equal or fair opportunity for the development of talent and ability, then more substantial policies than the removal of legal and procedural limitations on recruitment will have to be involved. Granted that background inequalities between individuals and families are going to affect the development of talent, if we are to equalize opportunities, we shall have to act on these background inequalities.

However, if we seek to do this then two problems arise in the view of the critic. In the first place, if we try to compensate for background inequalities which bear upon the developments of talents in children, then it might seem that this is going to threaten the personal freedom of families to live their own lives in their own way; and thus the claim arises that equality of opportunity and personal freedom may not be so compatible as is usually supposed.

Second, if a policy of seeking to compensate for background inequalities, which make a difference to the development of talent, is adopted seriously, the redistributive consequences of such compensation would make the principle of equality of opportunity merge into that of greater equality of outcome which liberals reject. In this sense, equality of opportunity is not a stable position but, as we have argued, unless we are to stick to a disingenuous procedural conception of equality of opportunity, the ideas of equalizing starting places in the competition will take on a very substantial role of compensating for unmerited inherited disadvantages and in restricting rights of bequest for the better off. Only strategies of this sort are likely to be able to equalize opportunities, but such strategies pose severe problems for liberty.

The basic objection of the left to equality of opportunity is concerned with the fact that there is no critical approach to the differential positions to which equal access is being proposed. It takes the existing structure of inequality for granted and is concerned about recruitment to it. However, this is not satisfactory to the left: it will want to probe the legitimacy of the differential reward structure, otherwise greater equality of access may give a greater legitimacy to a structure of rewards which those on the left may regard as unjust. Of course, if the left has a defence of differential reward structures, as we have suggested earlier, then, of course, fair equality of opportunity for recruitment to such positions would only be consistent with the general values of the left. However, this equality of access to legitimate inequalities must include substantive compensatory techniques for background inequalities which bear upon a fair development of talents.[21]

The obvious alternative to equality of opportunity, given the difficulties which it involves, would be to endorse greater equalities of outcome in terms of income, wealth, and welfare. The reasons for this can be developed out of an internal critique of equality of opportunity. We have already suggested that the redistribution which would be necessary to secure a fair development of talent would itself make inroads upon the reward structure and thus narrow differential outcomes. However, there is an important subsidiary aspect to this argument.

If we seek to compensate those who do not have a fair chance to develop their talents because of circumstances beyond their control – their genetic endowment, their family background, their sex, their colour – there will, in fact, be very definite limits to which this can be done consistently with the maintenance of the family and individual freedom. There is a point beyond which the attempt to secure a fair background for the development of talent cannot go without being intolerably intrusive.

So what do we do at this point? There are two alternatives. One is to endorse the existing differential reward structure, admit that there are limits to which equality of opportunity can go, and argue that it is an unfortunate fact that some individuals will be penalized in realizing their life chances because of factors which are outside their control but which cannot be altered by government in a way compatible with individual freedom. This approach, when coupled with the view that markets do not cause injustice, defines the approach of market-based conservatism.

The other alternative is to argue for a greater compression of the reward structure and in favour of greater equality of outcome. If the family is to be maintained and personal liberty secured so that measures to secure greater equality of opportunity must be limited, then it is wrong to reward as prodigiously as we do a narrow range of talent for which the individual does not bear full responsibility,[22] and to make the costs of failure so heavy for those whose opportunities have been more modest, and who similarly do not bear full responsibility for their condition.

This is the general ground for equality of outcome, and it follows fairly naturally from a recognition of the defects of equality of opportunity. The obvious difficulty with it is that, in endorsing a wholesale critique of an income-and-status hierarchy, it may well embody very weak demands in terms of efficiency, while at the same time failing to recognize the positionality of certain goods which cannot be distributed in a substantively equal manner. The obvious solution to this difficulty is to seek to develop a theory of legitimate inequality.[23]

DEMOCRATIC EQUALITY AND CITIZENSHIP

Earlier we argued that the defence of equality should be linked to that of liberty in order to secure a fair or equal worth of liberty. This argument was developed in the light of the idea that political and social freedoms and rights could be credited on an equal basis to citizens, but differences in social and economic circumstances would mean that these liberties had differential value for individuals. As purposive creatures, liberty to pursue our own good in our own way is central to us; but this means that we cannot be indifferent to the worth of liberty to individuals, and to the resources they have to pursue their conception of the good.

Consequently a theory of equality satisfactory to the left will be concerned with the distribution of those resources which are necessary basic goods for experiencing a life of purpose and agency and making full use of the rights of citizenship. In our society these will include health services (unless people have the greatest degree of physical integrity of which they are capable, they will not be able to act effectively), education, and welfare goods generally. These resources are also going to include income because, as Le Grand has shown, differences in income lead to marked differences in the use of other sorts of basic welfare goods.[24] A fair distribution of the worth of liberty is therefore going to involve far greater equality of income and wealth as well as the provision of services. It also follows from what we argued earlier that these basic resources, which are necessary to live a life of active citizenship, should so far as possible be distributed in cash rather than in kind, in order to enhance the ability to live life in one's own way and avoid bureaucracy and paternalism. This linking of equality and a more equal worth of liberty should demonstrate to critics that the left is serious about freedom.

INEQUALITY AND INCENTIVES

The most obvious free-market response to these arguments is to claim that equality is incompatible with efficiency since incentives are necessary for the dynamism of the economy. This, it is argued, is as true of the interests of the poor as well as the rich. The poor will be better off through the trickle-down effects of the free-market economy, even though there may be an increase in inequality. This

222

strategy clearly lies behind the tax policies of the Conservative government in Britain and the Reagan government in the United States. In Britain the standard rate of tax has been reduced to 25 per cent and, during the election campaign in 1987, Mrs Thatcher explicitly endorsed the trickle-down theory. There are two issues here: the first is to do with the necessity of incentives, the second with whether the trickle-down mechanism helps the poor more than redistributive policies. We turn now to arguments about incentives. It should be borne in mind, though, that we are defending a view of equality which allows for considerable inequalities if they are justified on broadly Rawlsian grounds, and hence there is scope for the recognition of incentive arguments.

It would be ridiculous for an egalitarian to dismiss arguments about production, precisely because high productivity is necessary to achieve his distributional aims. What, therefore, can be said about the view that there is a big trade-off between equality and efficiency? How far is it true and how far are incentives necessarily incompatible with equality?

The first thing we should say is that, if there are trade-offs between equality and efficiency, they are going to be extremely complex. Certain sorts of egalitarian strategies can be seen as enhancing efficiency. We could perhaps take two examples here. Greater equality of opportunity in the sense of fair and open competition for jobs must be more efficient in matching talents to jobs than restrictive job recruitment. Fair equality of opportunity must be more economically efficient if it involves more than just the removal of legal and conventional restrictions on recruitment and extends to some positive attempts to encourage groups of people to enter a particular area of the job market which they have not typically done before. A wider pool of talent together with fair equality of opportunity ought to be the best way of matching abilities and jobs.[25] Similarly, positive training programmes which would improve the skills and earning capacities of manual workers could be defended both as a gain in efficiency and a gain in equality. Forms of education provision which involve spending more money on the children of unskilled manual workers could again be defended as much on grounds of efficiency as equality. We should beware of slogans in this field and over-simplified views of the nature of the trade-off. However, this is not to deny that there are trade-offs to be made. The important point is to be aware of where they occur and to see what consequences there are for egalitarian policies.

The fundamental argument here is about incentives and the extent to which incentives are needed to make people work more productively and efficiently. It should perhaps be said in passing that the empirical nature of this claim is shrouded in mystery. Many confident assertions are made about the need for incentives without its being at all clear what evidence there is for this view beyond anecdote. Indeed, as even some conservative commentators have realized, arguments about incentives can be stood on their head, so that, if incomes above a certain level are taxed at a differentially high level, individuals will work harder to maintain their standard of living. However, it is no doubt also true that they will resent doing so and we should take seriously this resentment, just as we ask the better endowed to take seriously the justice of the resentment of those less well circumstanced.

Let us therefore accept as fact, although it may not be, that incentives are necessary for higher productivity and efficiency. Perhaps the first point then to notice is that, if this is the ground on which the inequality of income is being claimed, it has nothing whatsoever to do with moral qualities like merit and desert. What society is being asked to pay is a rent of ability[26] to mobilize skills which otherwise would no longer be mobilized and without which we should be worse off. Incentives are not ends in themselves; they are means to ends, and they are linked to justice only in the sense of the degree of economic rent which is required to be paid to generate prosperity for the welfare of citizens.

What the incentive argument asks is that we pay a differential rent to mobilize abilities for which the individual may claim only some modest responsibility. Abilities and talents are not engendered by individuals in a vacuum; they are rather in some large part due to genetic inheritance, fortunate family background, and education, for which the individual concerned bears little or no responsibility.[27] If I deserve something, it must be in terms of a feature of my life for which I am responsible. Individuals are not the sole bearers of the responsibility for their abilities, and in some respect they already represent a considerable investment of social capital which in turn is being rewarded by more expenditure on the individual.[28] So we should not be confused by the moralistic fog[29] which in a free-market discussion envelops the issue of incentives. We are talking about a pure economic criterion: that sum of money which will get a job done and without which society would be the poorer.

We do believe we have to recognize and accept this notion of incentives. It is true that some socialist societies and some socialist theories try to do away with the notion of incentives altogether, but they presuppose some fundamental change in consciousness and human attitudes which seems utopian and unrealistic. Certainly societies – such as China during the Great Leap Forward – which tried to do away with the rent of ability were not particularly successful. So on empirical grounds there do seem to be good reasons for accepting that there is an ineliminable role for incentives in economic relations, and this fact must place a constraint on the operation of the principle of equality. The point could be put in a more theoretical way which would link together incentives, efficiency, and personal liberty: if we believed in absolute material equality, so that we fixed 100-per-cent taxes on incomes above the fixed level and 100-per-cent subsidies below it, then there would be no reason at all to move economic resources such as labour, capital, equipment, land, or whatever to areas and occupations in which the marginal value of the occupation was higher. This must limit efficiency and innovation and, if there was no incentive to respond to these technological and other changes, without which society would be worse off, there would have to be direction of labour and therefore a considerable loss in personal freedom. Given this powerful argument, what place can a recognition of the need for incentives have in egalitarian political theory?

Apart from those incentives which could be seen as compensation for doing dirty, risky, or health-threatening jobs, where the incentive is compensation for the diswelfare experienced, it is in the nature of the case that incentives are going to create inequalities. Thus it follows that socialists are going to be concerned with the range of *legitimate inequalities*, that is with those considerations which will give the structure of differentials some legitimate role in society. No one is suggesting that there is a way in which a pay board could produce a hard and fast scientific answer to the question of the proper rent of the ability to be paid; rather that there is an onus to justify incentives and the level at which they are set.

MARKETS, PROCEDURES, AND DECISIONS

So far we have considered the relationship between the market and equality, social justice and welfare. We need now to move to another set of considerations, namely markets and consumer sovereignty, a moral case which lies behind a good deal of the political defence of market mechanisms. For Hayek, Friedman and others, part of the justification of the market is that it allows individuals with limited knowledge and imperfect information to record their preferences. That is to say, the individual is able to make small decisions, each of which is within his competence to make. What could be more free or more liberal than that? The trouble with small decisions, however, as Hayek implicitly acknowledges, is that, when taken together, they may well have unintended consequences which the individuals making the decisions did not foresee and would not have chosen had they known.

This may seem a very abstract and rarefied point but it is part and parcel of everyday experience. For example, one may live in an area in which there is a corner shop, within walking distance, which one uses for convenience and a supermarket, two or three miles away, which one uses, together with the car, for the week's shopping. Prices are lower at the supermarkets as their bulk purchases mean discounts from the suppliers. Obviously, for any particular individual this arrangement is best for all concerned, but the overall effect of rational individual choice, using the supermarket for most purchases and the shop only on occasion, is to drive out the corner shop which we all find convenient and do not wish to see disappear. The driving out of business of the shopkeeper was an unforeseen, unintended, and unchosen consequence of rational behaviour in the market. It is an outcome which none of us wanted and none of us would have chosen, but it emerges as a consequence of our choices.

It is very difficult on a very decentralized market basis to take rational strategic decisions which may be of great importance to the overall quality of our lives, and to make choices more important than the small decisions which are characteristic of the much vaunted freedom of choice of the market. The example which we have used may seem rather trivial, but it is in essence the one which bedevils, for example, the provision of public transport on a rational basis, and other forms of public provision.

THE MARKET AND THE STATE

These are not arguments against markets as such but they do go some way to weaken the hold of the idea that markets are the bastion of choice. Sometimes strategic decisions taken by democratic governments, overriding market considerations, may well reflect the strategic choices of individuals rather than the tyranny of small decisions in the market.

These strategic decisions are going to be far more crucial to the maintenance of an equal value to liberty than are the small decisions made in a market. So long as these more strategic decisions are taken by democratic governments, there is no reason to fear for freedom, particularly when as we have argued, the planning or strategic decisions of governments may well reflect people's more general choices taken in the polling booth rather than the unintended outcomes of small-scale decisions in the market.

In a sense, the decentralized decision-making characteristic of markets and the more strategic decisions characteristic of politics lead to a deep issue at stake between politics and markets. On the individualist conservative view, if a market procedure is fair so that individuals buy and sell according to fair contractual and quasi-contractual procedures, then the outcomes of the aggregate decisions are just.[30] Justice is not, as Nozick argues, a patterned or end-state principle to be applied to the pattern of outcomes in a market, but is rather a procedural principle about whether individual actions are just, whether people have a right to what they exchange, and so forth. Consequently justice is a process, not a pattern or an end state to be secured by political action. However, this can be doubted. It could be a consequence of individual actions of legitimate buying and selling, small decisions as Hirsch calls them, that leads to a concentration of incomes and wealth in a few hands. Such a concentration of economic power, if it is the result of individual choices, would be just.[31] There can be no principle of social justice in terms of which this outcome could be criticized. Justice is a matter of procedure and not of outcomes. Outcome or end-state theories are a mirage for reasons which we have discussed earlier. However, if the outcome of individual fair decisions does lead to concentrations of wealth and income, this can also lead to concentrations of power and political influence for reasons which were mentioned earlier.[32] Society cannot be deprived of the right to criticize and to seek to change outcomes just because they are the outcomes of individual fair actions, understood in a procedural

227

sense of fairness. Because of the political and power implications of concentrations of income, this must be a matter of concern for a liberal democratic society. In any case, it can be argued that procedural fairness can itself be doubted, if the procedures are superimposed on a society in which there are sharp differences in life chances, and in the opportunities to enter markets on fair terms. A socialist society must be concerned with the dispersal of political power but this cannot be separated from concentrations of economic power, however much these may emerge as the result of individual 'fair' procedures. In this sense, issues of the distribution of economic power must lie at the heart of democratic socialist politics, and end-state principles of justice and greater equality must have political salience, and cannot be dismissed from the political agenda.

This bears directly upon the issue of the ownership of capital in a free market. If capital ownership is concentrated, this will enable those who own capital to exercise power over others and will lead to coercive exchanges between those who do and those who do not own capital. This will typically occur in a firm. The workers in a firm who do not own capital will have to work on terms to a degree dictated by the owner of that firm, particularly if capital becomes concentrated and there are, in a particular community, no realistic work alternatives. This gives the capitalist a considerable degree of power over workers who will not be in the position of independent subcontractors, but rather will be subject to discretionary power, either exercised by the capitalist or those appointed to oversee his business for him. The free-market conservative will see nothing wrong in such inequality of power and again will not see it as a potential restriction of liberty. This is for two reasons. In the first place, as we have seen, inequalities, however large, in the distribution of material resources are not a restriction of freedom because freedom and the possession of resources are different things. Only if the capitalist is a strict monopolist will his behaviour be potentially coercive. Otherwise a worker has freedom to work or not to work for a particular firm, and, while this option is open, whatever the position of the worker in terms of resources, he is not coerced by the behaviour of the capitalist. Second, in a free market capital is accumulated through a process of free exchange. So long as the capitalist does not acquire capital as a result of coercion, then the ownership of capital, however concentrated, is not unjust. It could only be regarded as unjust on the basis of some socialist end-state principle which he rejects. Hence, however concentrated capital may become as the result of free exchange, its ownership is not unjust and the power which it confers is not illegitimate.

However, socialists will be minded to reject both of these arguments. We have already seen the grounds for rejecting the first in the earlier argument about the nature of freedom. The second argument is more complex and contains both empirical and normative elements. The empirical element would be that we lack sufficient historical information to determine whether present concentrated holdings of capital were justly (i.e. non coercively) acquired and, given the threat to equal freedom which such concentrations of capital and power pose to society, a reasonable principle would be to undertake the dispersal of that capital and property rights in the means of production more widely in society. This is the view adopted even by Nozick, one of the arch defenders of free-market capitalism.

There are various ways in which the ownership of capital could be dispersed: individual and group dispersion. Individual dispersion would give to individuals some entitlement to the ownership of shares as a function of working in a firm over a period of years. Another proposal would be for the state to lease capital to producer-owned co-operatives. An additional method of capital dispersal would be to direct public policy so that producer-owned co-operatives would receive favoured status regarding investment and taxation.

None of what we have argued should be taken as a root and branch rejection of markets, only that markets have to be operated in a democratic socialist society against a background of legitimacy which concerns freedom, justice, and equality in a much richer sense than that accepted by free-market theorists. Free-market theorists are fearful about the politicization of social problems, but they are naïve about economic power and its impact upon politics.

We have therefore seen good reasons to disagree with the individualist conservative case described in its essence by Fred Hirsch in relation to issues of distributive justice:

One broad solution which is propounded by the economic libertarian school of Hayek and Friedman is to deal with the distributional issue by taking it off the agenda . . . the economic outcome is legitimized not as just but unjustifiable. Those who have drawn trumps in the existing allocation of resources are merely fortunate, those who have drawn blanks unfortunate; all will be damaged by attempts to get a legitimated distribution by deliberate adjustment.[33]

This view, combined with a negative view of liberty, rights, and citizenship, together with an individualized account of the nature of coercion, forms the basis of the market-conservative case and, as we have seen, it is to be found wanting.

All of this may sound rather abstract and theoretical, but we do not believe it is, because at some point the failure of the trickle-down effect will become clear, as will its consequences for the effective exercise of liberty and citizenship, as, at the opposite end of the scale, will greater concentration of economic power and its consequential effects on political power. Unless some consensus can be agreed about distributive justice, and the broad pattern of market rewards, and the range of collective responsibility and provision, we shall face an uncertain future. As John Goldthorpe, one of the finest sociologists of industrial society, has argued:

> Such a consensus cannot be achieved without the entire structure of power and advantage becoming principled – becoming, that is, capable of being given consistent rational and moral justification . . . in other words the advancement of social justice has to be seen not as some lofty and impracticable ideal . . . but rather as an important precondition of mitigating current economic difficulties.[34]

Indeed, much the same point is to be found in the writings of Samuel Brittan who sympathizes a good deal with a libertarian approach to political economy, although not in its current conservative mode when he argues that:

> If the rational arguments for accepting a system that does not aim at complete distributive justice are too abstract and sophisticated to command assent; and if there is an emotional void which cannot be met by rising incomes and humanitarian redistribution unrelated to merit then the outlook for liberal democracy is a poor one.[35]

THE LEGITIMACY OF MARKETS

As we have seen, it is central to the view of influential market-based theorists, such as Hayek and Friedman, that egalitarian social justice is a mirage which threatens individual liberty. Instead of seeking social justice we should cast off substantive constraints on markets, and, so long as the market procedures are fair, we should accept the outcomes of market transactions as morally legitimate, whatever they may turn out to be. On this view, the market is neutral between political and moral principles; these are for each individual to determine for himself. Most market theorists regard this as one of the greatest strengths of markets, but there are weaknesses, and attention has been drawn to these as much by non-Thatcherite Tories as by socialists.

The basic difficulty is this. If, as the free marketeers hope, the market is to come to dominate more and more of our lives, and as much as possible is to be turned over to private markets, then the market must have some legitimacy in the eyes of ordinary citizens who will perhaps be unable to appreciate the complex economic arguments which favour markets. Some kind of citizen commitment has to be mobilized behind the market, and this has to at least equal the weight of the loyalty spread throughout society to non-market institutions such as the National Health Service.

We do not want to deny that markets are important and should be fostered; rather the arguments we deploy are aimed to weaken the idea that markets should be the wholly dominant mode of allocation and that therefore egalitarian socialism is a threat to the values which markets represent. What then are these values and are they sufficient to secure citizen loyalty? The usual answer, as we have seen, is that markets secure freedom, and we have already seen grounds for doubting this in the sense in which it is usually put forward. Does it therefore have a more substantive moral basis? The answer to this is clearly no, as Hayek has the courage to admit. It does not secure social justice, whether understood in terms of need, desert, performance, or anything else; it does not secure a fair worth of liberty; it does not secure equality. The market is neutral and amoral. Success depends upon luck as much as anything else, the luck of birth, of upbringing, of education, of being in the right place at the right time, and certainly not solely upon merit or desert. In the light of this, meritocratic conservatives and liberals ought to

231

be rather wary of linking their ideas with those of the market. This point is made very effectively by Irving Kristol in his influential essay 'When virtue loses all her lovelieness' in which he argues:

> The distribution of power, privilege and property must be seen as in some profound sense expressive of the values that govern the lives of individuals. An idea of self government, if it is to be viable, must encompass both the public and private sectors, if it does not you will have alienation and anomie.[36]

In fact, Hayek sees this. In *The Mirage of Social Justice* he argues that, while the market does not reward merit or desert, or any other principle for that matter, most political defenders of the market believe that it does, and this is the basis on which the claims of the market are legitimated with the electorate. Citizens' allegiance to the market may thus depend upon the existence of false beliefs which may at the same time be functionally necessary, because citizens would not feel loyalty to an institution which was totally indifferent to their moral claims and capacities. This does not seem to be a very secure moral basis for the market and, if it cannot meet its promise of increasing prosperity, which hitherto may have disguised its indifference to moral claims, its legitimacy may be very unsure.[37]

The dominance of markets can also be combated by reflecting upon the basic elements of a more traditional socialist critique which could be developed. There may well be a place for markets in a humane society but they must be kept in their place, because they encourage some forms of behaviour rather than others, viz. egoism over altruism, and rational calculations of advantage over trust. The wider market values extend, the more they will displace these other attitudes, the maintenance of which may well be central for the operation of the market itself as much as for other social institutions. The second aspect of the argument is that the operation of markets is likely illegitimately to extend the range of goods which we want to turn into commodities because, in some admittedly vague sense, there is a feeling that to treat certain things as commodities is to undermine human respect and integrity.

The point of these arguments, when taken together, is that there are substantive moral limits beyond which we would not want a market mentality to go and that the very legitimacy of markets depends upon their remaining within these limits. The first form of the arguments is that the attitude of rational self-interest, which market operations have to presuppose if they are to operate effectively, has very definite limits, otherwise the defence of the free market itself becomes incoherent. For example, it is very difficult to give the rational egoist an answer to the question of why he should not seek subsidy, monopoly, and other special privileges which, if generalized, would make the market work inefficiently. Of course, one could argue with him that these actions will not benefit society or the maintenance of the market in the long run but, without some restriction on egoism and orientation towards some notion of the public good, it is difficult to see how these arguments could be persuasive. Rational egoism, devoid of a sense of the public good, makes for free riders, which in turn may make the market as a whole less efficient, although it will benefit the individual. Thus markets themselves run up against moral limits. Some shared moral values and some conception of the public good are needed to provide an environment within which the market can flourish. Not everything can be made a matter of competition and the recognition of these limits is a necessary condition for the market to operate legitimately.

However, the second part of the argument, which has been deployed most recently in Richard Titmuss's Book *The Gift Relationship*,[38] looks at ways in which the sphere of markets can be seen to overstep the boundaries of moral legitimacy and despoil the objects which it seeks to turn into commodities. Titmuss's own example is blood for donation and how this altruistically given gift would be despoiled (and made less efficient). If it became a commodity, he argues, then anything can. Most people would argue that in the case of buying and selling human tissue – whether it be blood or body parts – the commercial mentality had overstepped its limits. Again, however vague and intuitive they may be, there do seem to be very definite moral limits to markets in terms of the commercialization of goods and services which are central to the life opportunities of individuals. Any sensitive defence of markets will make some reference to the general environment within which markets operate because, for the reasons which we have discussed in this section, it is very doubtful that markets can secure their own legitimacy.

Indeed, in one sense this is a clear tension between free-market and traditional forms of conservatism. Many conservative traditionalists hold the view that the market cannot secure its own legitimacy and that other values which are crucial to society can be threatened by free markets. This point was made forcibly by Sir Ian Gilmour, a dissenting member of Mrs Thatcher's first administration, when he argued in *Inside Right*:

> The preservation of freedom is a complex business. But if people are not to be seduced by other attractions, they must at least feel loyalty to the state. Their loyalty will not be deep unless they gain from the state protection and other benefits. . . . Complete economic freedom is not therefore an insurance of political freedom; indeed, it can undermine political freedom. Economic liberalism, because of its starkness is liable to repel people from the rest of liberalism.[39]

One way in which this is made clear in the contemporary debate is the relationship between the market and family life. The present government has been keen to pursue policies which strengthen family ties and indeed set up a Family Study Group on it but, while it has been concerned about the effect of things like violence, pornography, and social security on families, it has not really addressed the question of the relationship between the free market and the maintenance of families and family networks. We shall see later in the book facts about growing impoverishment of people, and regional changes too have acted as a magnet to people to move away from local communities and networks. The 'on your bike' view of labour mobility, characterized by Mr Norman Tebbit, the Cabinet minister, at a Tory Party Conference, threw this tension into relief. The issues here are wide and deep and cannot be gone into fully here. However, there is the argument developed by the German philosopher and social theorist, Habermas, in his book, *Legitimation Crisis*, that capitalism, because of its individualism and the demands of mobility, reduces traditional values, on which it actually rests for its own legitimacy in a broader sense. The issue has been well focused by the American theorist, Christopher Lasch when he argues:

> It is the logic of consumerism that undermines the values of loyalty and perseverance and promotes a different set of values that is destructive of family life. The need for novelty and fresh

stimulation becomes ever more intense, intervening interludes of boredom are increasingly intolerable.[40]

Again, the values of the market, from the point of view of the traditionalist right as much as of the 'communitarian' left, are placed in jeopardy by the unconstrained market. Both stress those forms of values and integration which must be sustained and not undermined by the operation of markets and for the left this requires attention to distributive justice.

There is quite a deep issue here for the coherence of the market-capitalist outlook. Part of the strategy is, as we have seen, to argue that in modern society there is not sufficient moral agreement to seek to constrain market outcomes through public policy. Such policies would have to embody end-state or patterned principles of distributive justice, and the market theorist denies that these can be agreed in a free, morally pluralist society and yet, so far as personal morality is concerned, the conservative capitalist wants to argue in favour of the maintenance of certain sorts of traditional values, and indeed, there is on the right an interest in resurrecting Victorian values. What is not at all clear is whether this is a coherent project, given the strictures on the impossibility of moral agreement to guide public policy in the distributive arena. The project depends upon an unargued and very implausible view that agreement is possible, so far as personal values are concerned, and that these could be encouraged by government, while at the same time the degree of moral pluralism in modern society could be stressed as a way of undermining distributive politics. Here we see a clear case of the way in which traditional conservative preoccupations sit very uneasily with free-market assumptions.[41]

Chapter Eleven

A VIEW FROM THE LEFT: THE UNITED STATES

The focus of any new initiative on the part of the left has to be on providing the real choices that make freedom meaningful. As Gar Alperovitz and Jeff Faux suggest,

> The pre-requisites of independent decision-making for most people boil down to some practical considerations: enough income to pay the rent, to put food on the table, to be free of worry over medical bills, to afford a child . . . these are the nitty-gritty economic freedoms of everyday life. On any moral scale, an economic strategy that aims to establish secure footings to enable everyone to exercise such freedom holds more weight than the provision of still more income and wealth to those who already enjoy an immense amount of freedom of economic choice.[1]

It is toward this goal that the left must direct its energy. An approach to accomplishing the goal requires first an assessment of what conservative capitalism has meant, how the public perceives the problems, what the limits of liberal capitalist approaches are, why the public is willing to trust the market rather than the government, and, finally, how a specific response to this analysis can be generated.

WHAT HAS CONSERVATIVE CAPITALISM ACCOMPLISHED?

Recent studies of Great Britain and of the United States have concluded that the economic policies of both governments have delivered hard times to the poor, while their political approaches haven't been strong enough to cut means-tested benefits significantly, so leaving more people dependent on government transfers. Summarizing the British study, Sheldon Danziger and Eugene Smolensky report that, 'The growth of transfers, in other words, while limiting the growth in inequality, has been accompanied by rapid growth in the numbers of people dependent on means-tested benefits and living on or around the poverty line.' Similar conclusions are reached regarding the United States.[2]

While we cannot claim that Reagan and Thatcher were always ideologically consistent in their policies, that is not the same as claiming that ideology played no role in their governments. It wasn't concrete evidence that persuaded these governments to embrace the proposition that big deficits and slow growth were caused by redistributive programmes – because the evidence isn't there.[3] In the event, neither of the correlations predicted by supply-side theory, between increasing the job-participation rate and cuts in social spending, or between higher job participation and decreasing taxes, worked out in fact.[4]

What both governments did, in a context of declining competitiveness, was to gain power by blaming the victims, while offering political and economic policies that worsened their situation. The prospects of rescue by the trickle-down method were always bleak.[5] To the extent that the US economy 'recovered', it was a combination of a reduction in inflation and interest rates brought about by a huge recession in the domestic economy, coupled with an enormous rise in military spending. The effect of the latter was a kind of military Keynesianism that resulted in a stimulus to employment that was felt disproportionately in the parts of the economy that service the military.[6]

Clearly the manipulation of ideology at the expense of demonstrated performance was essential to the rise to power of conservative capitalism. Ideology was deeply involved in the shaping of policy and in the cultivation of public support. While some of the ideological inconsistencies can be attributed to the necessities of political manoeuvring and to the requirements of adding together disparate elements to form coalitions, there is also a division, as we have shown, that is inherent in conservative-capitalist ideology itself.[7] Consequently the problem of the left is to break through the ideological smokescreen of the right and demonstrate that it has empirically valid answers to the desire of the public for sound economic growth with equity in the form of a fairer distribution of opportunity.

The irony may be that, if the Reagan and Thatcher initiatives come to be perceived as mistakes, the blame may be placed on government, not on the market-place. Reagan's personal popularity, rather than a consensus on his programmes, made these initiatives possible. Since these movements are the work of highly visible political leaders, the negative consequences may attach to government, rather than to the market, the *deus ex machina* of conservative-capitalist policy. For the present, however, the larger irony is that the Reagan administration has apparently succeeded in restoring some of the public's trust in government which had been badly eroded by the events of the 1970s.[8]

To the extent that political processes in both countries have become a cipher for the distribution of advantage in the market-place because of the role of campaign financing, manipulation of the media, the hidden nature of many subsidies, and various kinds of corruption, the public will be in the position of blaming the wrong institution. To fully understand the interaction of conservative-capitalist policies with public opinion, however, it is necessary to consider some lessons learned from several decades of research in the dynamics of opinion formation and change.

THE STRUGGLE FOR PUBLIC CONFIDENCE

The achievement of the conservative-capitalist movement in changing the terms of public debate is, in one sense, superficial and, in another sense, fundamental. The development of a rejoinder from the left will require an assessment at both levels. The simple advocacy of a return to the New Deal in the United States, or to policies of nationalization in Britain, would, we think, complicate the task of the left in reorienting those public expectations and perceptions that are most essential in changing the direction of political behaviour.

The superficiality of the supposed swing to conservatism is illustrated by any of a number of polls. In the United States, the number of people who identify themselves as conservative rose only slightly from 1972 to 1982, and then only among the most attentive sector of the public, and then declined by 1985 to pre-Reagan levels. On specific issues such as the environment and government programmes for the poor, the public in many respects became more liberal between 1980 and 1986. Support for increased military spending has essentially collapsed: 61 per cent favoured more funding in 1981; only 16 per cent were favourable by early 1985. Two-thirds of the population think that there should be no more substantial cuts in social programmes.[9]

The argument for conservative capitalism in the United States enjoyed its ascendancy because it had an effective exponent in Ronald Reagan, not because it has markedly increased its hold on the basic orientation of opinion on issues. In this sense conservative capitalism is a superficial movement. It is a media event more than it is a sea change in public opinion.

However, it is a mistake to assume that doubt about conservative policies may easily be converted into the arousal of support for liberal or socialist policies. The fundamental part of the conservative achievement has been to frame the argument so that the *means* of changing direction, the re-empowerment of government, has been undercut – even while support for specific policies of the left remains fairly high. The evidence of this shift is that party-identification data in the United States indicates that the long run of Democratic Party superiority based on New-Deal-era political socialization may be coming to an end. Everett Carl Ladd has reported that, among those who reached political maturity after depression memories had faded, party identification is about even (as it is for those of the pre-depression generation).[10] These generational changes mean that the political impetus behind the New Deal is fading. Government has fallen out of favour, especially with the young, even if the market remains rather suspect. Thus the political response to conservative capitalism is blurred by generational shifts.

In order to address this new situation, those who see government action as the key to changing the fortunes of the disadvantaged need to understand some dynamics of public opinion that were noted in the 1970s by political scientists such as Murray Edelman and various social psychologists.[11] What we have currently is political *quiescence* in Edelman's terms. The public is not particularly persuaded of the wisdom of Reagan's or Thatcher's course of action, but this doubt does not translate into positive arousal for the cause of the opposition party.

According to cognitive-dissonance theory, on which these observations are based, quiescence is the response that occurs when *expectations* are consistent with *perceptions*. This happens whether the expectations are positive or negative. By this theory, the reason there has been so little social unrest as a result of the damage done to the poor by Reagan's policies is that he led everyone to expect less government assistance. The perceptions were consistent with expectations and the result was a kind of negative quiescence that shows up as alienation from the system. The evidence is in declining performance rates for minorities in schools, rising numbers of crimes of violence, and an increasing incidence of self-destructive behaviour.

Reagan and Thatcher have harped repeatedly on the ineffectuality of government solutions. They have sought to shape the specific expectations that are consonant with the experience of unchanging inequities in society. All that is needed to validate expectations in inequity are the daily observations of the personal vagaries and fortuities of life in a capitalist society. Conservatives try to close the door on altered expectations by concentrating on negating the alternative, namely government action. The conservative strategy is to implicate government in all of the inequities that do obtain by virtue of 'free-loading', bureaucratic mistreatment or inefficiency of response to public demands. This alteration of political expectations is the fundamental achievement of the movement currently.

At the same time, the conservative-capitalist movement has a way of shaping perceptions of experience. Continual predictions of economic improvement, or of deficit reduction, or of a 'new spirit', are blatant attempts to manipulate perceptions. We would venture to say that this is the superficial part of the achievement, as these claims can be, and are, challenged by data on the economy, the distribution of income, the amount of the deficit. It is characteristic of politics, however, that public perceptions are distant from the realities, heavily mediated by interpretation, keyed to symbolic arguments, and therefore subject to distortion based on expectations.[12] In the absence of solid information, it is easier to view the world as we expect to find it than as it really is.

By the same theory, the source of political arousal is a divergence of expectations and perceptions. It was in good part the disappointed expectations of the disadvantaged in the 1960s that led to an explosive period of social unrest. Conversely, it was Reagan's ability to communicate optimism and a positive attitude against a backdrop of public negativism and cynicism that gave his personal leadership such a powerful boost.

Consequently mounting an effective response to conservative capitalism requires attention to the shaping of perceptions of experience – and that is what Walter Mondale did as the Democratic candidate for president in 1984 and what Labour Party Leader, Neil Kinnock, attempted in the 1987 British election. Yet the failure to convert uneasiness with the policies of the Reagan and Thatcher governments into political arousal is not because the reality of conservative priorities is pleasing to the public. As David Stockman points out in the US context, Reagan will leave office having tripled the accumulation of debt by all of his thirty-nine predecessors put together! He will, in addition, leave the United States in debt to the rest of the world by upwards of one-half trillion dollars.[13] These results have diminished support for the Reagan administration but have not yet delivered a decisive shift toward the ideological perspective of the left.[14]

The failure to mobilize a large-scale turn to the left comes about, quite simply, because negativism about government is the controlling expectation generated by conservatives – and critics on the left perforce validate that expectation when they cite the evidence of policy failure, whatever the parentage of the policy.

The keys to change at the fundamental level are in the expectations part of the equation. The credibility of political action must be restored. The instinct of the left for maintaining the legitimacy of public processes will need to be revived if we are to reach the first step toward the return of governmental activism. Myths about the equity of the market-place must be examined critically. Realistic policies must be developed that will reassure the public about the capacity of government to moderate the market and offer assurances to individuals of fairer treatment than they otherwise would receive in a world of unequal wealth and economic power.

However, the error of the 1960s must be avoided in the next revival of the left. Presidents Kennedy and Johnson and popular advocates for the poor such as Martin Luther King were able to generate new expectations of change. The substantive programmes that would have made genuine long-term change possible were undermined by the Vietnam War as well as by the tentative and limited nature of the programmes themselves. A new day for the left depends upon more than the rhetorical inflation of expectations – it depends on developing credible programmes that will answer the basic needs of the public. New expectations have to be based on substantive reforms that appeal to public opinion.

In approaching the task of cultivating public support, we will consider first the likely course of perceptions of conservative capitalism, contrast those perceptions with liberal-capitalist alternatives, and then propose some aspects of a response that would generate new political arousal based on expectations that can be sustained by substantive changes.

CONSERVATIVE CAPITALISM v. LIBERAL CAPITALISM

In comparing conservative capitalism and liberal capitalism, Bowles and Gintis argue that the latter is a spectrum of pro-capitalist responses to the natural tendency of capitalism to erode.[15] Rather than being tied to liberal capitalism as an ideal type, they see it in Marxist terms as a bundle of relations interacting dialectically and changing over time. From their perspective, the extended fight over the level and form of subsistence rights illustrates the process. Yet reducing these tensions to the language of 'dynamics' and 'contradictions' runs the danger of obscuring the distinctions that are clearly evident in the policy initiatives that have been taken by these two governments.

In the eyes of many critical theorists, the rebirth of conservative capitalism signals the failure of the class compromise that relied on economic growth along with moderate reforms to deal with inequality by lifting up those on the bottom.[16] To the extent that it is truly libertarian in policy, conservative capitalism also means the disestablishment of traditional élites, the randomizing of cultural values, and the subordination of all aspects of society to materialism and short-term self-interest.[17] As for the power of the market to put the economy right, the presence of competition does not mean that the will and the resources are in place to meet the challenge. The fault may be in myriad other factors, not least the rigidities of the capitalist class itself.[18]

The real splits are felt when industries are sold off for speculative gain, resulting in dislocation to workers, the disruption of communities, and even the expatriation of jobs and capital. Control is placed in the hands not of traditional élites, but rather of international capitalists holding little or no loyalty to nation, class, or the other ties of custom, mutual interest, and association that organize conventional politics.[19] Foreign investment in assets of US businesses are at record levels.

For the present, the hybrid of conservative capitalism allows conservatives to present themselves as both defenders of the past and as modernizers, while casting off the left as failed deviationists.[20] That and the palpable gains for the incomes of the traditional élite keep the movement in motion, even while the traditionalist element of its ideological base appears to be eroding.

At the same time politicians have been known to straddle contradictory elements of a coalition. There will doubtless be many variations on that art as the politicians hold together what philosophy would divide as between individualists and traditionalists. David Broder, for example, in discussing the presidential prospects of Senator Paul Laxalt of Nevada, a Reagan confidante, reports: 'Asked if he thought he could straddle the gap between libertarian and moralist conservatives in the GOP, Laxalt replied with a smile, "That's where I am." And that is exactly where the Republican Party may choose to be.'[21] The remark turned out to be prophetic with respect to the Presidential campaign of George Bush. What suggests itself as a formula for getting elected is less and less, as Reagan has demonstrated, a formula for governing.

Guaranteed-income programmes are a political dead-end for both right and left. While the rationalization of welfare at the national level is a necessary progressive step from the chaos of state-operated programmes in the United States, this cannot realistically be done without addressing the jobs issue first. What happened when the guaranteed-income approach was tried in the Nixon years was indicative of the problem. Traditional conservatives could not get the support of individualist conservatives within the Republican Party. Liberal Democrats could not deliver the moderates and conservatives in their party. The clientele for these programmes are never likely to find the benefit levels to be sufficient.

Tying the political future of the left to an income strategy, and to all of the contradictions of the welfare state, is the road to political ruin. That is the longer term significance for the left of the current conservative resurgence. It is a resurgence based not on a new-found credibility for conservative capitalism as much as on an unhappy experience with the alternative. Nevertheless conservatives can seize upon the public's dissatisfaction with abuses of the welfare system to undermine efforts to rationalize the programmes.

Aid to Families with Dependent Children (AFDC) is the successor to a line of policy that began as an alternative to the institutionalization of poor children. The intent was to aid the mothers as surrogates for the community in looking after impoverished children. Successive versions of the programme since the 1930s have tried to put the focus on aiding the children rather than the mother in order to counter criticism of 'welfare mothers'.[22] A new initiative would look upon child-raising in the absence of a conventional family as work and deal with it in an institutional framework appropriate to the organization of work.

Leaving under-age welfare mothers to fend for themselves with a cash grant is not a particularly defensible way of getting the job done. Quite aside from questions of competence, there are the incentives to play the game for all the benefits that can be obtained. This is no more than self-interested economic behaviour, though it is often criticized by libertarians, who otherwise celebrate self-interested economic behaviour, as moral turpitude. Even if the economic incentives are removed, the bleak existence of marginalized women makes having children a source of meaning and status.

It is not only the poor who find the market society difficult to live with. The capacity of ideologies to provide an anchor for class identity through myths concerning 'ensembles' or 'exploitation', based on class differences, confronts, in modern capitalism, a force fundamentally indifferent to the continuity of personal identity.[23] While socialists and progressives provided liberal capitalism with a scenario for the preferred identity of the reformers and the disadvantaged, traditionalists have given to conservative capitalism a sense of class identification with the establishment. Capitalism, by promoting the entrepreneur as the only truly legitimated role, celebrates a transitory figure ever at risk of displacement – thus undermining its class alliances whenever it becomes too closely realized in policy. As Sheldon Wolin noted,

A traditionless society that conserves nothing; ruling groups that are committed to continuous innovation; social norms that stigmatize those who fail to improve their status; incentives that require those who move up must move away: such a society presents a formidable challenge to the conservative imagination.[24]

These considerations of identity and its relationship to politics

244

mean that conservative capitalism is not necessarily in a strong position for the long term.

This discussion is intended to make clear the nature of the challenge to the left posed by conservative capitalism. There is one more challenge, and it goes to the core of the kind of programmatic challenge that the left needs to face. The public is not only suspicious of government, it is inclined to believe that the market is superior as a means of making distributive decisions. Understanding and accommodating this fact are the tasks of the final two sections of this chapter.

THE MARKET v. THE GOVERNMENT

The hallmark of the 1980s is a powerful shift in the basic ideology of the system toward an allegiance to free enterprise and away from government.[25] It is vital to the assessment of conservative capitalism that this shift from government to market be understood. Why is it that the public has moved away from faith in government toward placing greater trust in the market?

Robert Lane, after reviewing a variety of American survey data – though with some reference to British findings – concludes that, in a culture where self-interest is assumed to be the universal motivator the intrinsic public appeal of the market-place is that, 'in the market . . . self-interest is thought to be both fruitful for the common good and policed by competition, while in the polity self-interest is seen as neither fruitful nor properly constrained.[26] Rewards in the market-place are perceived to be earned, while politically determined rewards are the result of 'political muscle', in Lane's phrase.[27] The terms of that perception are, of course, arguable. There is nothing particularly just about the fact that, in the market, some can pursue their self-interest with considerable means, whether earned or not, while others have none. In politics the voting system, if not the other processes that impact on the choice of candidates, relies on an egalitarian distribution of one person – one vote. To the extent that control of the media, campaign financing, and corruption mitigate voting processes, the inequities of the market are reproduced as inequities in government. Government is blamed for a distribution of influence that originates in the market-place.

Seymour Martin Lipset identifies a similar value split in the history of American politics as a rivalry between equality and achievement.[28] As Lane demonstrates, the market lays claim to achievement as an ordering principle and to equality as well. The latter is the case not so much because of an equality of result, but for the twin reasons that an approximate equality of opportunity is thought to operate in the market; and an *in*-equality of influence is thought to operate in politics. Yet, as Lane points out, there is no reason why government can't stimulate achievement as government has through myriad projects and initiatives across the decades.[29] And it is surely clear from experience that without anti-trust and other forms of regulation, and the governmental enforcement of civil rights in the market-place, equality of opportunity would hardly characterize the life chances of minorities, women, the handicapped, most of the ethnic groups in the country, and, indeed, anyone not born with either wealth, a strong constitution, a scarce talent, or good fortune.

It is widely assumed that rewards in the market-place are deserved, though in fact wealth often reflects the advantage of position, whether by inheritance, the vagaries of scarcity, luck, or the power to control other people's access to the means of production.[30] The two sides of this argument are sufficiently complex, and public opinion is sufficiently ambivalent, that the advantage goes to those who have the means of shaping public perceptions.[31] In the 1980s, the advocacy of the market rests largely with the movement we have identified as conservative capitalism. It is up to the left to restore perspective to this crucial institutional argument, though it must avoid its own propensity for overburdening the capacities of government.

BEYOND LIBERAL CAPITALISM: ELEMENTS OF A PROGRAMME

There are costs to living by the market alone that sometimes are neglected in the rhetoric on the pleasures of individual freedom. The costs of constant competition, endless personal striving, and individual alienation from society are seldom accounted for. Therein lies opportunity for the left; however, seizing that opportunity will require a rethinking of traditional policy nostrums and even of basic attitudes concerning the uses of competition and the role of co-operation. There are four aspects to this rethinking: the question of guaranteed employment, the problem of dependency, the relationship of government and the market to the process of human development, and the issue of personal economic mobility.

Guaranteed employment

The premier value that binds together modern societies is the work ethic. Around the legitimacy that attaches to work, great political formations can be built. The conservative-capitalist movement has made its advances by placing the market in the foreground of institutions legitimated by the work ethic. They have striven mightily to make of government a symbol of that which hinders honest and useful work and obstructs the system of rewards that flow from it.

However unfulfilling much modern work may be, it does offer a specific and intuitively acceptable measure of one's usefulness to society as well as one's individual entitlement to reward. The left has sometimes carried its analysis of the alienation of labour to the point where work itself is discredited. The working public has occasion to be sceptical of this approach. If the left is to carry on the struggle for more meaningful ways of structuring and directing work, it will have to happen as a result of earning the confidence of the majority that reforms can be made that will deliver demonstrable results in terms of productivity as well as the fulfilment of personal goals.

The humanization of work remains a vital part of the programme of the left; however it needs to be put forward in an appropriate context. The late prime minister of Sweden, Olaf Palme, once suggested that a principal reason for the decline of working-class support for the left in his country was the disparity between the kind of schools and other public facilities the government financed with the taxes of working people, and the unchanging character of work in the private sector. A monotonous and unrewarding job cannot entirely be compensated for by first-rate public services and facilities for other aspects of life. So the restructuring of work must be part of the agenda, but the creation of viable jobs must be at the top of the list.

The substantive policy response that addresses the most fundamental priority would be a public jobs programme, nationally funded and locally administered, oriented to jobs productive of economic value, if not profit, and structured by standards of employment that allow for motivation, advancement, and continuity. There is a huge backlog of neglected work to be done in the areas of urban reconstruction, transportation, public housing services, social services, utilities, and research and development. There are, as well, areas of opportunity where public investments could be used to explore new technologies and enhanced services in nutrition, preventive medicine, child care, elder care, and environmental rehabilitation. Rather than paying the costs of neglect through police services, prisons, drug rehabilitation programmes, and hospitals, public investment could be directed toward positive programmes that would reduce these social costs through preventive action to establish a more humane environment. The latent productivity of the unemployed and underemployed could be tapped through a public-investment strategy for achieving useful social goals.

The purpose of publicly controlled economic activity must be to do public tasks well, and to do them in a manner most conducive to civilized norms of human development. Rather than a single large programme, these goals can better be accomplished by a variety of institutions co-ordinated by public policy-making processes. The means of administering these programmes would include publicly operated institutions, model programmes intended for private emulation, and incentives for privately operated businesses and co-operatives. By these means, the purpose of economic activity can be reoriented from simple wealth accumulation toward making a productive life possible for all citizens of the society.[32]

By elaborating on the model of child-care facilities operated co-operatively or administered with the assistance of public agencies, welfare children could be better looked after. Channelling subsidies partly through these agencies would increase the chances that the children would be assisted in a useful fashion. By specifying a contribution of time or effort on the part of welfare parents, and by encouraging their employment in the facility's programme, work skills could be combined with parental responsibility.

For the left to advocate such a programme would join the historic commitment by government to assure equal opportunity to a programme that is both urgently needed for economic reasons and consistent with public approval. Sidney Verba reports that 81 per cent of the US public favours guaranteed *jobs*, while only 32 per cent favours guaranteed *incomes* – and this is consistent with polling done over the last fifteen years.[33] The left could lay claim legitimately to the fruits of the work ethic, an attachment the right advertises as the advantage of the market-place. However, the worsening inequalities, the increasing dependency of minorities, the feminization of poverty are all unsolved by the market-place.

A programme of public employment, funded by a shift from military spending to domestic spending, would have productive consequences for the economy and would reach beyond the indirect assistance of the Great Society programmes to address the core of the problem: the productive engagement of the impoverished in economic activity. The support for cutting defence spending has risen to the point where a poll by the US Advisory Commission on Intergovernmental Relations (ACIR) revealed that by 1984 a majority of the public supported cuts in defence spending as opposed to less than a third who supported non-defence cuts as a way of keeping the budget more in line with revenues.[34]

It is not enough to solve the problem of poverty of income; the problem of dependency must also be addressed. Rather than funding dependency, the left should argue for the funding of productive public enterprises that address real economic needs, provide income to the poor, and attack the problem of dependency by supplying meaningful jobs.[35] The best means of doing so is expanded by public-works programmes. The Reagan administration has cut federal infrastructure expenditures by 13 per cent in the period from 1980 to 1985 – as contrasted with increases of 24 per cent in the decade of the 1960s, and 46 per cent in the decade of the 1970s.[36]

Franklin Delano Roosevelt envisioned a public-employment strategy as the next step for the New Deal, one which was never fully taken.[37] The Reagan administration's response to the problem of dependency is simply to reduce or cut off benefits. They have proposed, for example, that AFDC benefits should be denied to the children of teenage mothers who do not live at home.[38] This approach focuses attention on a growing segment of the poor, but not the fastest growing segment. Poverty rose by 32 per cent in married-couple households from 1979 to 1985, compared with 23 per cent in female-headed households. Yet an initiative of this kind distracts attention from the real structural problem at the expense of children living on welfare.[39]

Lest a public jobs-investment programme become another version of socialist nationalization, the left needs to return to its historic commitment to genuine democracy by considering locally based means of administering such a programme. Contracts with producer co-operatives would, for example, foster local initiative and democratic internal control outside the bureaucratic apparatus of government.[40] A significant sector of the French and Italian economies consist of producer co-operatives and there are interesting and successful examples of industrial co-operatives to be found in Spain and in England as well as in the United States. These appear to operate most successfully when a maximum of initiative is retained by the producers themselves. However there are key elements of support that can be provided through publicly guaranteed incentives for investment in co-operatives, the provision of expertise for those interested in this approach, and other forms of accommodation.[41]

Private enterprise that operates according to publicly determined guidelines for employment practices and accountability can also play a role. There are companies that have achieved favourable growth rates over the long term while maintaining a guaranteed employment policy for their workers.[42] Encouraging employee participation in decision-making and goal-setting has become a widely approved management technique following surveys of successful companies, as reported by the authors of *In Search of Excellence*.[43]

Establishing public standards for private companies has a long tradition. The elimination of child labour, the regulation of job safety risks, and the implementation of affirmative action policies are examples of its fruitful application. The tradition could be extended to encompass the requisites for a more sophisticated understanding of human development while, at the same time, addressing the goal of providing guaranteed employment.

Competition, dependency, and the family

The left has to overcome its aversion to competition if it is to participate fully in what the public understands by the work ethic. In the first place, there is a difference between competition by choice and competition by necessity. Competition that is chosen is often healthy, psychologically rewarding, productive to self-discipline, and socially useful. To the extent that it is freely chosen, personal competition is an expression of a basic democratic right.

Competition arising from necessity in a context of scarcity has a different character. While it can be productive of short-term gains, even the modern literature of management science recognizes that fear has only short-term uses, and that its destructive side-effects can well be counter-productive for the firm as well as the individual. The purpose of any civilized society is to reduce the impact of scarcity, not to encourage the threat that arises from it as a way of advantaging one class as against another.

The hero of conservative capitalism is the entrepreneur – and, given the allowances that conservatives would make for entrepreneurship, that is an invitation to a class-based society riven with inequality. The hero of the left has always been the worker, though the programmes it has advocated have often benefited rather more the bureaucrat, the politician, or the party member. The entrepreneur is but one link in the chain of productivity. The role is significant, but there is nothing about it that entitles its players to untrammelled dominion over the well-being of all others who labour in the economy.

In fact, much of the entrepreneurial activity of major corporations is the product of research and development teams in concert with a marketing organization. Research organizations directed toward public priorities and equipped to evaluate the utility of projects by standards of safety, economic efficiency, environmental impact, health and welfare consequences, and other socially useful considerations could take on a part of the role of entrepreneurship and place it in a responsible context. Genius should have its reward as it does in such organizations as universities where endowed chairs, research funds, and prestige appear to be adequate incentives for fiercely competitive research programmes.

At the other end of the spectrum from enforced competition, dependency is also a social evil. It undermines the sense of integrity and competence that is fundamental to human identity. As Daniel Patrick Moynihan points out:

> Being poor is often associated with considerable personal qualities; being dependent rarely so. This is not to say that dependent people are not brave, resourceful, admirable, but simply that their situation is never enviable, and rarely

admired. It is an incomplete state in life: normal in the child, abnormal in the adult. In a world where completed men and women stand on their own feet, persons who are dependent – as the buried imagery of the word denotes – hang.[44]

Dependency leads to the particular brand of corruption that goes with powerlessness. Welfare programmes have thus acquired a reputation, effectively exploited by the right, as the nemesis of the work ethic. Neither competition out of necessity nor dependency are adequate approaches to the development of humane living standards.

Dependency combined with poverty is a sure road to the destructiion of the family. All of the delicate dynamics of identity formation that rely upon role-modelling within the family are disrupted by the twin forces of social and economic pressure. A programme of productive public employment allows those structures to be rebuilt.

The family, as an institution, has been failed by all modern points of view. Liberal individualism is too casual about the social structures that families require. Daniel Patrick Moynihan points out that the neglect of the family by liberals is nicely illustrated by the obscurity of Alva Myrdahl's book, *The Nation and the Family*, written at the same time and under the same Carnegie Corporation commission as Gunnar Myrdahl's *An American Dilemma*, a classic on the problem of racism in America.[45]

Joel Krieger suggests that Reagan and the New Right play upon a strategy that capitalizes on the divisions that the decline of the family produces. The social programme of the New Right appeals to the sense of displacement shared by traditionalist men and women. Yet the 'jobs' rhetoric appeals to those who need two incomes to support a family, or finance a divorce. The disintegration of the family and the demands this places on social programmes makes those on welfare the targets of morally justified political opprobrium.[46]

The left needs to restore the economic basis for the family through establishing secure means of employment, especially for those who are marginalized by the operation of the market-place. The family is the best hope of humane social reconstruction; no set of state interventionist policies can make up entirely for the damage to human development that decomposed families can inflict. Families require at least a minimal level of economic security.

As an example, providing a structure of laws that enhances the position of part-time workers with families would remove some of the stress associated with two-earner households. A stronger public role in protecting pension and medical-insurance rights would make it harder for firms to fire employees whose benefit costs are rising with seniority. Rewarding firms for longevity of employment would counteract market pressures to keep turn-over high as a means of keeping wages low. There never has been a completely free market in labour, nor should there be if we are to avoid slavery, unsafe working conditions, and a host of other abuses. The only question is in whose interest the regulation is to take place. The suggestion here is that the development requirements of encouraging strong families should be given the first priority.

Government and the process of human development

Each ideological persuasion has its vices. The left has sometimes been captured by equality for the sake of equality, just as the libertarian right is attached to freedom for the sake of freedom, or the traditional right to order taken to an extreme. None of these simply stated values encompasses the subtlety of a process of human development that requires equality, liberty, and order in various mixes at various stages of life.[47]

Engagement in a socially responsible process of human development is a better statement of the classic objective of the left. Yet the main burden of human development as a process cannot fall on conscious policy made by governments. It is a process seated principally in private psychology, common sense, and communal sensitivities that can be nurtured but not, in the end, directed.

The role of government, if not at the structural centre, is vital to the framework of human development. Where there can be no other guarantee of physical safety, the government must provide it. Where there is no assurance of continuity and reward for effort, governmental means must be enlisted. Where there is segregation and discrimination by class, gender, or race, governmental power can combat such restrictions. Where the physical, social, or psychological environment becomes destructive of human development, government has to take a hand. Government, imperfect as it is, provides the only method by which all the people can hope to

253

make decisions that are equitable, regardless of the distribution of advantages between individuals.

Failing equitable policy, government does not disappear. It simply becomes the captive of interests, as Reagan and Thatcher illustrate, that have something other than equity on their agenda. Yet the means must be appropriate to the end. Governmental action that supplants socially useful individual initiative is counter-productive. That is why private charitable activity must be seen as the partner rather than the rival of government activity. The replacement of capitalist power by bureaucratic power does not, in the end, lessen class-based inequality; it merely changes the basis of class. The classical liberal principle that power flows from the office rather than the person and the limitation and counter-balancing of power are essential. On these bases, the left can argue that public power is socially superior to private power.

What disappoints the public about governmental activism on behalf of the poor is not the intent or even the design of the programmes. Anti-poverty programmes generally command majority support. The problem lies in the perception that the government is the handmaiden of powerful and entrenched inter-ests. Paradoxically the institution that operates on the basis of one vote per person is perceived to be corrupted by the concentration of power, while the institution that operates on the basis of gross inequalities in wherewithal, the market, is perceived to be 'fair and wise'.[48] Consequently, the *means* of activism has to be rehabilitated from the obloquy that has been deliberately created by conservative capitalism. A majority exists for the *ends* of the left, now a majority must be won for the *means*.

The distance that has to be travelled for public opinion to shift toward validating government action is not very great. At the height of Reagan's popularity in 1984, about a third of the public thought that the federal government had too much power, one quarter that it had the right amount, one third that it should act more vigorously (with the remainder having no opinion). The change in these percentages since 1978 was significant but not overwhelming (-3,+7,-2).[49] A majority would oppose more vigorous action however, so the type of action has to be carefully justified.

The very strategy of coalition of interest that is fundamental to organizing on the left presents a validation of negative stereotypes of special interests controlling politicians and government policy.

254

Whether it be the unions in Britain, or labour, feminists, and minorities in the 1984 campaign of Walter Mondale, the public suspicion is that fairness to all will not be the guiding principle of such governments. In the public's eyes, the means belie the ends. Theodore Lowi, in his *The End of Liberalism: The Second Republic of the United States*, observes that it is the self-serving character of interest-group liberalism that has cost liberal capitalism its impetus as the ideology of the world's reformers. The stalemate that has resulted as rival clients for public benefits have competed for favour at each other's expense has undermined and bankrupted public authority.[50]

Therefore it is this crucial question of whether the government will give people what they deserve that must be responded to. If the government provides people with benefits in return for work, that will meet the test of fairness; benefits in return for a status arrived at by failure in the market-place are far more dubious. Those whose identity is validated by the market may be excused for suspecting that people who fail in the market, or refuse the encounter altogether, are somehow less deserving. As Lane points out, the market is identified with a *process* that, for a majority, seems to result in just desert. Politics, on the other hand, is identified with *outcomes* that are perceived by most as unfair.[51]

The key to the problem, then, is to validate the process of politics by making it apparent that politics can have substantively fair outcomes, such as jobs for the unemployed. By that standard of comparison, the outcomes side of the market will be seen for what it is: grossly unequal and the result of an unfair process as well. It was government's ability to help those distressed by the malfunctioning of the market-place that made Progressivism and the New Deal possible in the United States, and legitimized the Labour Party in Great Britain.

To complete the restoration of political means in the public favour, it will be necessary to devise methods of delivering public jobs that can be insulated from the pressures applied by powerful interests that can distort fair assessments of efficiency and need. The fundamental principles that must guide this effort are the allocation of resources by publicly verifiable standards of need, and the enforcement of fair supervisory and contracting procedures by agents who are accountable for their actions. There is no accountability in private enterprise short of the 'bottom line'. The means of ensuring accountability are the essence of democracy.

Examples of the successful use of publicly accountable means for the enforcement of large-scale social and economic change include the civil-rights revolution in the United States, the wartime mobilizations of the economies of Britain and the United States, and the creation of the National Health Service in Great Britain. The repertory of techniques is very great; what is lacking is a will to discover the best mixes of public and private, centralized and decentralized, democratic and administrative devices. Our suggestion is that the will to do so flows from a clear conception of the ends that government action is to serve: the common characteristic of the civil rights, wartime mobilization, and National Health Service examples. A public-employment strategy could well provide the same directing energy for a renewed initiative by the left.

Private enterprise, by contrast, operates outside public scrutiny. One reason for the myth of the efficiency of the market-place in the allocation of resources is that so little is known about the mistakes, failures, and false starts that are part of the normal course of private enterprise. The failure rate of new businesses is very high. Major corporations frequently make mistakes that cost huge amounts of money. Increasing the level of public accountability in the operation of businesses so that workers can be informed of the financial condition of their employers, for example, will generate pressure for more responsible behaviour in the market-place.

Changing expectations: the left and economic mobility

The fundamental expectation upon which conservative capitalism bases its appeal is that of personal economic mobility. The left currently has no real strategy for claiming that the enactment of a leftist programme will match what is thought to be the potential of the market for elevating the lowly – and subjecting the mighty to the rigours of competition. The changing of these assessments of the comparative merits of right and left must be partly the result of a serious effort to develop an economically sensible full-employment strategy, as described above. The other part must consist of bringing realism to people's perceptions about what the current system in fact accomplishes by way of mobility.

The residue of genuine mobility is the accumulation of wealth in such forms as savings, stocks, assets in businesses, property, and other financial instruments. Wealth is what allows individuals to insure temselves against the vagaries of employment in the labour market.

The facts are that wealth is distributed most unequally in the United States, and the inequality is getting worse under conservative capitalism, not better. The share of wealth held by the top 10 per cent of the US population has increased over the last two decades. In 1963, the top 10 per cent controlled 65.1 per cent of all the wealth. By 1983, that share increased to 71.8 per cent. The converse of these statistics is that the bottom 90 per cent lost nearly 20 per cent of its relative share of the nation's wealth during that period.[52]

For the purposes of understanding the relative impact of liberal-capitalist and conservative-capitalist policies, it is important to know whether these changes in shares of wealth took place during the period of the Great Society programmes, or later as conservatism became the order of the day. While there is no data on the year-by-year share of the top decile, the evidence is that the share of the top 1 per cent was declining until 1976, the point at which the last data based on estate taxes was collected. This tiny segment typically holds more than a majority of the share of the top decile. This finding is, therefore, inconsistent with the major increase in the share of the top decile over the twenty-year period. Consequently there is reason to believe that sometime after 1976, when the Great Society programmes began to be undercut, the increases in the wealth share of those at the top moved up sharply. There is additional evidence that the share of the top 1 per cent increased even faster than the rate for the top decile as a whole.[53]

The sense in which wealth translates into power over people's livelihoods is apparent when it is realized that almost 90 per cent of all of the corporate stock is owned by the top 10 per cent of the population. The top 1 per cent owns a majority of all the stock. The same picture is true of assets of businesses, only more so. The bottom 90 per cent controls only 6.3 per cent of all business assets.[54] Furthermore, the share of the wealth that the richest citizens own is the more productive share – their assets have increased in value faster than those of the population generally. Apart from sheer monetary power, the amount of control vested in this tiny class at the top is enormous.[55]

Whatever has happened, it is clear that the rise of conservative capitalism has not led to an increase in the chances average people have of joining the economic élite. The data, reported earlier, on the distribution of income and the losses suffered by the poorest segments of the population in the last few years make it highly likely that this imbalance continues to grow. The only way in which these inequities can be addressed is through government action.

CONCLUSION

These data on the distribution of wealth, combined with analysis of the loss of real family income that has occurred over the last few years, make it apparent that liberal capitalism may even out the chances of individual advancement, but it can't necessarily deliver increasing living standards or even a reduction in the poverty rate independent of subsidies and transfers.[56] Conservative capitalism, on the other hand, can't deliver either increasing living standards or enhanced opportunity for anyone but the rich.

The two versions of capitalism remain in stalemate. Liberal capitalism cannot accommodate the propensity of workers and other interests to organize to demand a larger share of the pie. Ultimately the politics of the 'broker state' overwhelm the economic logic of capitalism. Conservative capitalism, on the other hand, gives social control to the market-place and loses the capacity to bring the society together around a productive process that supplies security as well as engagement for all levels of the society. As Andrew Gamble points out:

> The basic practical weakness of the social market strategy is that because it grasps capitalist societies not as systems of production but as market orders, it logically requires that the independent organizations of the working class be first destroyed or made impotent for the strategy to succeed.[57]

Yet it is through unions and collective action that workers achieve such security as they are able to find. As Joel Krieger comments, the political success of the Reagan and Thatcher governments 'involves the manipulation of fears to divide populations'.[58]

This conundrum of capitalist politics remains unsolved and awaits new conceptualizations of policy that may well lead away from an exclusive reliance on either the market or the government as the dominant agent of change. The way may now be open for a realistic consideration of how the two, together with a reordering of national-local relations, can be brought into a working arrangement that is productive for all levels of society.

Traditional conservatives suffered their political decline earlier in this century largely because they came to be perceived as an anti-democratic force in a century riven by struggles for increasing democracy. While libertarian conservatives seem to endorse democracy, in reality the effect of their pro-market policies is to discredit democracy. This happens in two ways: the market concentrates power in the hands of the rich; the discrediting of government deprives democracy of the means of corrective action.

We have seen the practical result of the emphasis on the market in the increasing inequality in the distribution of income and wealth in the US. We have also seen how the popularity of the President has created a false perception that the people, left to their own views, would rather see less government than more. The reverse is the case according to the public opinion polls. Democracy has been undermined both by the libertarian reliance on the market and by the discrediting of government at the hands of its leaders.

The only use that might be made of government in the simple Benthamite view of Hayek and Friedman is to procure by political means what cannot be obtained by economic means. Government has only a minimal instrumental value in defending the shores and punishing theft. Any other function makes government into the vehicle of improper individual aggrandizement. The answer to this argument depends not upon denying that government can alter the distribution of rewards in society in countermarket fashion, but in affirming that this is precisely its role and that civilization depends upon it.

The restoration of democracy requires that both ends of the problem be confronted. Fair and justifiable limits must be placed on the accumulation and uses of wealth toward the goal of making opportunity more widely available. Government regulation of the economy must be undertaken, not with the aim of preserving the advantages of the rich, but of increasing the ability of all citizens to participate in forming for themselves a secure and stable future. For most this will mean a large measure of freedom to engage in self-improvement and economic enterprise. For some it will mean government-provided employment opportunities. For all, it will mean that the government becomes the guarantor of survival and the initiator of standards, programmes, and forms of accountability that make individual attainment more likely. The arbitrariness of inheritance, position, accidental demands, and other vagaries of life in a state of nature must be reduced where doing so can yield a net advantage to the prospects of the least advantaged.

There must, as well, be a more sophisticated approach taken to democracy itself. Ultimately democracy is not simply majority rule over the decisions of government. It is an attainment of citizens in a social environment where, as Rousseau understood, the prerequisites of a civilized life are already in place. Democracy is a political art form and it is achieved by a discipline of civic consciousness, as well as by means of a climate of security and trust that government has to nurture.

Individualist conservatives would have us believe that the key to freedom is to prevent the domination of the market by government. The left must concede that command economies don't work either in encouraging growth or in enhancing democracy and the fair distribution of economic opportunity. Yet the reverse is equally true. The domination of the government by the market is similarly pernicious. A government that is too beholden to economic power becomes one more asset of the rich and well-placed in their ability to manipulate and exploit the poor.

Democracy requires a balance of the market and the government. The market's capacity for non-coercive decision-making is useful in all those instances where the distribution of opportunity is not fundamentally at issue. The capacity of democratic government to search out the common interest and redistribute the means of opportunity is unique. The failure of either institution will build up inequality and structural disadvantages for the least favoured in society.

As anthropologist Lewis Hyde pointed out in *The Gift*, no society and no individual can function at either extreme of the spectrum from purely contractual relations to purely charitable relations. The former is alienating and the latter foolish:

For where, on the one hand, there is no way to assert identity against the mass, and no opportunity for private gain, we lose the well-advertised benefits of a market society – its particular freedoms, its particular kind of innovation, its individual and material variety, and so on. But where the market alone rules . . . commerce becomes correctly associated with the fragmentation of community and the suppression of liveliness, fertility, and social feeling . . . we find ourselves unable to enter gracefully into nature, unable to draw community out of the mass, and, finally, unable to receive, contribute toward, and pass along the collective treasures we refer to as culture and tradition.[59]

The recrudescence of ideology discussed in this book will damage western society if it succeeds only in reviving the stereotypes at the heart of mythology about the market v. the government. It will serve some purpose if it opens up a fresher discussion of the relationship between these two institutional forms and the development of a truly human society.

Chapter Twelve

A VIEW FROM THE LEFT: GREAT BRITAIN

As we have tried to argue, the critique of post-war statist politics has placed the left on the defensive. In order to regain the initiative, it has to do two things. First of all, it has to counter the value basis of the conservative-capitalist critique and this we attempted to do in chapter 10. In this chapter we shall consider some of the ways in which the policies of the left could be brought to represent the values which we discussed earlier. The first thing that has to be done though is to show the enduring relevance of the left's traditional concern with distributive issues. Earlier we set out the moral case for saying that society has a moral responsibility for the outcomes of markets, and that in terms of both individual liberty and social justice there is a case for redistribution of resources within a framework which still allows a central role for the free market. In the first part of this chapter we shall argue that the way in which the British economy has developed under the impact of eight years of Thatcherism show the practical relevance of the moral case developed earlier. We go on to argue that issues of social justice and equality are still of concern to the electorate, as revealed in survey data, and that there is a need for the left to produce a coherent account of how it sees social justice and greater equality being combined with a commitment to the market. Finally, we argue that the policies of the left should be animated by ideas of citizenship, entitlment, and corresponding obligations, together with a greater commitment to decentralization as a way of rendering more accountable the behaviour of bureaucracies which will still be necessary, given the need to assume collective responsibility for market outcomes.

DISTRIBUTION v. THE TRICKLE-DOWN STRATEGY

The conservative-capitalist critic argues against equality on other than the abstract moral grounds which we have been considering. The argument here is as follows. The concern of the egalitarian is recognized as being with the poor and the least fortunate members of society. However, the free-market theorist will argue that the strategy for dealing with poverty is mistaken. The position of the poor will be improved much more effectively with the operation of the free market than it will under egalitarian, redistributive policies. If we can throw off the illusions of distributive politics and seek to secure a more productive and dynamic economy the position of the poor will be improved much more. Certainly a free-market economy will create inequalities, but this will not matter if the basic position of the poor is being improved.

This argument is certainly accepted by the present Conservative government in Britain. Mr Lawson, Chancellor of the Exchequer, said recently that one does not make the poor richer by making the rich poorer, and on a radio programme the day before the 1987 General Election, Mrs Thatcher put the case very eloquently when she said:

> Capitalism works by increasing what used to be the privileges of the few to become the daily necessities of the many. You have only got to look at the spread of all mod cons across the country to know that, or to look and see how prosperous the supermarkets are, the shops are, the stores are.[1]

We need therefore to consider the trickle-down effect, first, by considering its impact on the poor and, second, by looking at whether there are any necessary limits to the trickle-down strategy, particularly in relation to what Fred Hirsch in *The Social Limits To Growth* has called positional goods.[2]

First of all then, what have been the effects of the market-based strategy on the poor in Britain since 1979? In a speech in the early days of the government in 1979, Reg Prentice, then Minister of State at the Department of Health and Social Security, argued as follows: 'If you believe economic salvation can only be achieved by rewarding success and the national income is not increasing, then you have no alternative but to make the unsuccessful poorer.'[3]

Any kind of test of the trickle-down effect is very difficult, given the lack of a clear account of poverty from the market-conservative perspective. It seems on the one hand to be distinguished from absolute poverty in any strict sense by the absence of destitution and by the provision of subsistence – Sir Keith Joseph, for example, talks about capitalism producing a constantly rising minimum standard – but it is also emphatically distinguished from relative poverty which is frequently seen as just another way of talking about inequality. All that can be done in present circumstances is to refer to some of the figures about poverty and allow the reader to make up his or her own mind on the basis of the evidence about whether the trickle-down effect is producing a constantly rising minimum standard. This has to be considered against the recent statement by the Paymaster-General in the Commons when he said that: 'The Government are committed to helping all our citizens share in improved prospects, both in personal incomes and public services. This can only be achieved through the ability of an economy to create wealth.'[4]

It is certainly very unclear that this is happening to all our citizens, although it is abundantly clear that it is happening to some.

One way of trying to clarify the issue is to take two measures which seem to be incontrovertible measures of poverty, however else it may be defined, namely the numbers of people on Supplementary Benefit and the number of homeless families. In table 12.1 we indicate the changes in Supplementary Benefit levels from November 1978 to April 1987.

Since 1978 personal disposable income in Britain has risen by 122.5 per cent in money terms and by 14 per cent in real terms. Thus, as table 12.1 shows, compared with income in general, Supplementary Benefit levels have fallen from 61 per cent of disposable income per capita in 1978 to 53 per cent in 1987. Hence, using this measure of poverty, the incomes of the poorest groups in society have not kept up their share of the total disposable income in society.

Second, the number of people being drawn into Supplementary Benefit and hence into the group which is not sustaining its share in total national income has increased substantially. This percentage has increased by two-thirds, from about three million to about five million between 1978 and 1987. Of course, this indicates only the recipients of the benefits, not those who are dependent on

Table 12.1 Supplementary Benefit levels from November 1978 to April 1987

	%
Ordinary rate	
Single person	+95.5
Couple	+95.5
Long-term rate	
Single person	+94.2
Couple	+96.0
Retail price index	
Excluding housing	+86
All items	+96
Earnings	
Average gross earnings	+136
Disposal income per capita	+122.5

Source: A. Walker and C. Walker (1987) *The Growing Divide: A Social Audit 1979–1987*, London: Child Poverty Action Group

them. By 1984 it is estimated that about 7,729,000 people are now directly dependent on state benefit compared with five and three-quarter million in 1979.[5] These figures relate only up to 1984 and they are likely to have increased considerably since then.

If we take homelessness as a basic criterion of poverty, which it would be difficult to deny, whatever the other subtleties in assessing poverty, the figures are also alarming. In 1970 just more than 56,000 families were homeless. In 1985 the figure was marginally under 100,000 and is likely to have increased since. Hence, on these two measures of poverty, Supplementary Benefit and homelessness, the trickle-down mechanism has just not worked.[6]

Other measures show a similar story, although their interpretation will be disputed, just because they involve considerations of inequality in relation to poverty. However, if we take changes in

Table 12.2 Gross earnings (£ per week) adjusted for inflation at 1986 prices

	April 1979	*April 1986*	*% change*
Lowest decile	107.40	111.40	+ 3.7
Medium decile	166.40	185.40	+11.2
High decile	262.20	320.80	+22.3

Source: A. Walker and C. Walker (1987) *The Growing Divide: A Social Audit 1979–1987*, London: Child Poverty Action Group

the real level of gross earnings for the period 1979–86, we see the picture presented in table 12.2.

The market is clearly not working in a way to produce a constantly rising living standard for the poor unless an increase of 3.7 per cent, compared with 22.3 per cent for the best paid, is regarded as legitimate.

However, it is not only a matter of the market, it is also a matter of the government's own taxation policy which, consistent with the views we have discussed earlier, is an attempt to increase inequality as a basis for economic growth on the principle that the rich need to earn more to work harder, while the poor need to earn less. Between 1979 and 1986, the government gave away 8.1 billion pounds in tax cuts and benefits. Here is how these benefits were distributed:

(a) The poorest six million taxpayers received 8 per cent of the 8.1 billion.
(b) 20 per cent went to the richest 1 per cent.
(c) 22 per cent went to the richest 5 per cent.
(d) 50 per cent went to the richest 10 per cent.
(e) 66 per cent went to the richest 20 per cent of taxpayers.[7]

Again, the poorest sections of the population are bearing the burden of trying to create an enterprise culture but, as we have seen, the market mechanism in relation to the numbers thrown on to Supplementary Benefit is not working in the way assumed.

As we saw earlier, the market mechanism is celebrated by its adherents because it bypasses questions of distributive justice and this is clearly seen in the figures already given about the outcomes for individuals, but there is in Britain another example of the way in which the market has undercut issues of distributive equity, namely the outcomes between regions. Certainly some regions are doing very well out of the freeing of the market; others are doing very badly. This can be shown in various ways: the unequal distribution of employment prospects; the distribution of average earnings; the distribution of people on social security benefits.

Clearly the trickle-down effect of the employment opportunities in the market has been highly unequal in its results. A national government concerned with the futures of all people cannot fail to be worried by these consequences of the free market. The present government's rejection of distributive politics, however, makes it

Table 12.3 Regional unemployment January 1987

	% Registered unemployed
North	16.9
North-west	14.3
Yorks and Humberside	13.8
West Midlands	13.8
East Midlands	11.4
South-west	10.4
East Anglia	9.3
South-east	8.5
Northern Ireland	19.3
Scotland	15.1
Wales	14.3

Source: Employment Gazette (1987), March, London: Department of Employment

difficult for them to respond to these conclusions by making changes in macro-economic policy and in regional policy.

Similar points are borne out in the tables 12.4 and 12.5 concerning average earnings, the take-up of social-security benefit and the incidence of unemployment, all shown on a regional basis.

Table 12.4 Regional earnings of full-time workers: average earnings as a percentage of South-east average

Region	1979		1986	
	Men	Women	Men	Women
South-east	100.00	100.00	100.00	100.00
East Anglia	88.4	88.00	83.8	83.6
South-west	85.2	87.00	82.9	83.7
West Midlands	90.4	89.8	83.3	82.4
East Midlands	89.5	87.3	82.00	81.7
Yorkshire & Humberside	91.3	86.8	83.00	82.2
North-west	91.4	88.4	85.2	85.00
Wales	90.00	89.8	81.8	82.6
Scotland	93.3	88.3	86.5	84.4

Source: The New Earnings Survey (1979–87) London: Department of Employment

Again, the market is producing increased inequalities between the north and the south and brings into focus again the issue of the market versus distributive justice. If this trend continues, it is difficult to see how the market can be seen in the long term as a solvent of distributive dilemmas. Table 12.5 concerning regional equalities illustrates dependence on social security benefits between 1979/80

267

Table 12.5 Percentage of gross household income from Social Security, benefits

	1979–80	1983–4
South-east	9.4	9.7
East Anglia	11.00	15.1
South-west	14.2	13.2
East Midlands	10.8	13.5
West Midlands	11.1	15.00
Yorkshire and Humberside	15.1	16.7
North-west	14.00	17.00
North	15.7	20.00
Wales	15.5	19.5
Scotland	12.6	17.1
Northern Ireland	19.3	23.6

Source: *Family Expenditure Survey* (1980, 1985) London: Department of Employment

and 1983/4. The regional trend indicating the unequal distribution of the burdens of society through the free market is very clear.[8]

All of these figures show cumulatively that the trickle-down mechanism is not working as defenders of the free market hope and that at some point issues of distributive justice between individuals and regions are likely to reassert themselves. It is difficult to see how government can secure a common sense of citizenship if the market produces such radically unequal outcomes. However, it is central to the strategy of conservative capitalism to define citizenship in terms of the equal absence of coercion rather than in terms of resources and opportunities. As we have seen therefore, the trickle-down effect and a negative view of citizenship have been central to the argument of the individualist conservative, and each poses major questions.

We need to turn to the second part of the counter-argument, namely that there are ineradicable failures of supply in the market in relation to what Fred Hirsch in *The Social Limits to Growth* calls positional goods and welfare goods. We shall turn to the argument about positional goods first. This argument turns on an argument about the failure to supply. In this view not all goods can trickle down to the rest of society at the same level of value; rather the value of the goods is changed by the fact that some people consume them before others.

The argument is that one of the practical claims to legitimacy of the market order lay in the fact that it claims to be able to increase wealth more efficiently than socialism and, through the echelon advance or trickle-down mechanism, to benefit the worst off more effectively than socialism. In the absence of a more overtly distributive morality this promise seems crucial to the acceptability of markets. However, Hirsch argues that this argument is as seriously flawed as was the approach to egalitarian redistribution favoured by Crosland, because both of these strategies presuppose that all goods can be distributed more widely (the free-market conservatives)[9] or more equally (Crosland), at the same level of quality and the same level of value. In Hirsch's view this is false. Certainly some goods, electric fires and washing machines for example, can be consumed more widely or more equally without changing their quality or their value. But there are certain sorts of goods – what Hirsch calls positional goods – which cannot be more widely distributed without altering their economic value. The value of some sorts of goods to any individual depends upon the fact that only a limited number of people are consuming them.

An example will help to explain this. The paradigm case of a positional good might be taken to be standing on tiptoe in order to see a procession better. This is, however, a positional good in the sense that the value of doing it declines the more people take part in it. Similarly, tourism and having the benefit of secluded beaches or cottages are positional goods in this sense. It might be thought that, if these are the only examples of positional goods, the socialist could contemplate them with equanimity, just because they seem so marginal and unimportant. However, education is also a positional good for Hirsch in the sense that as an instrumental good, one that has a marketable value as opposed to being a means of self-fulfilment in a non-material way, the value of education depends to a great extent on its scarcity value. It cannot be distributed more equally without changing its value to those who consume it. So, in fact, instead of individuals', as in the trickle-down theory, being able to consume today the same educational goods which were reserved for the rich two generations ago, they do not consume the same good; the good has declined in value the more people have come to consume it.

Similarly education was a major weapon in the social democratic armoury for increasing equality and lessening social resentment, but again on the Hirsch analysis this has not turned out to be the case. Education is a positional good which cannot be distributed

269

more widely at the same level of value. Far from increasing equality and lessening tensions, the more equal distribution of education has led to the growth of credentialism, with more and higher qualifications being demanded for jobs which in previous generations may not have required qualifications at all. It would, of course, be comforting to think that the demand for qualifications was the result of the growing complexity of the jobs, but clearly in many instances this is not the case. Credentialism is a function of the paper chase and not the cause of it. In so far as this is true, it follows that a good deal of working-class demand for education is defensive in nature. Jobs which could be done in the past without qualifications now require them. The demand for educational expenditure could be seen as an attempt to secure access to the same jobs which in previous generations might not have needed publicly certified levels of educational attainment at all. As the American economist Lester Thurow has written:

> As the supply of educated labour increases individuals find that they must improve their education to defend their current income position. If they don't they will find their current jobs no longer open to them. Education becomes a good investment not because it would raise people's incomes above what they would have been if no one had increased his education, but rather because it raises their income above what it will be if others acquire an education and they do not.[10]

In this sense, education acts as a screening device for recruitment to unequal positions rather than as a Croslandite engine for equality.

The idea of positional goods and the social limits to growth which they imply pose two sorts of questions to political theory. For the Hayekian free-market theorist, it poses the problem of the legitimacy of the market order. They claim that we can dispense with raising distributional questions about the market because, if left unconstrained, the trickle-down effect will work, and we (including the poor) will become better off. This may still be true of material goods which can be consumed without positional advantage appearing, but is not true of positional goods such as education and leisure goods. If we all become richer in material terms, so that our basic needs become satisfied, then it is likely that attention will focus on the consumption of positional goods – an area where the trickle-down promise of the market is an illusion. It is likely that the failure to deliver the illusory promise will cause frustration and resentment and, because he turns his back on distributional questions, the free-market theorist has no theory about who should legitimately consume positional goods. That they are legitimately consumed by those whose market position enables them to consume them is about all that can be said. But this is not going to be sufficient. The failure of the promise is more likely to give rise to demands that opportunities for the consumption of these goods must be seen as fair and legitimate, and this makes socialist values which focus upon distribution more relevant than market-based principles.

Second, the positional-goods argument undermines what might be called the oblique approach to greater equality favoured during the 1950s and 1960s, which involved looking for greater equality through expenditure on health, education, and welfare rather than acting more directly on inequalities of income. In so far as these goods are positional in character, there is a flaw at the heart of this strategy. The scarcity engendered by positionality makes the whole business of scarcity much more acute than egalitarians of this period realized, and this is particularly so if the positionality of goods such as education is combined with the projected shortage of work opportunities which we discussed earlier.

In these circumstances, it is clear that socialist distributive values are more, not less relevant. While it is true that positional goods place limits on the extent of equality, it does mean that socialists have to be concerned with the legitimate consumption of goods which are socially scarce; we cannot just leave the allocation of these goods to the random effects of markets.

Hirsch concentrates his argument on the social rather than the physical limits to growth. But, leaving aside his strictures, even if we assume that the more doom-laden predictions related to the depletion of natural resources are overdrawn, and that in the sphere of material goods we can look forward to some incremental advance, it is doubtful that growth can play the role assigned to it by Crosland.[11] His strategy could be called a 'hidden hand' approach, in that it did not stress a direct attack on inequalities in the spheres of income and, to a lesser extent, wealth, but concentrated on removing the consequences of inequality by public spending in the sphere of education and welfare. However, recent evidence collected by Julian Le Grand in his *The Strategy of Equality*[12] suggests that, with inequalities of income and wealth, the better off will still be able to make better use of these services than the less well endowed, and that their impact upon equality has not been that great.

This problem will become even more stark if goods such as education are positional, because the better endowed will be able to make differentially better use of a service which already has a strong positional element within it. But, if we are to approach the problem of inequality in a more direct way by looking closely at policies for diminishing inequalities of income and wealth, we shall have to face the fact that we shall be accused of fostering inefficiency by disregarding incentives and concentrating our attention on distribution, when the real need is for competition and efficiency. We shall therefore have to confront directly that aspect of what Le Grand calls the 'ideology of inequality' which insists that there is a big trade-off to be made between equality and efficiency, particularly when we are talking about income and wealth, and that in the harsh world of the 1980s we have to choose efficiency rather than equality.

However, we argued in chapter 10 that arguments about efficiency and incentives in relation to equality are more complicated than they appear at first sight and that the trade-off indicated above is therefore more subtle and complex. The left has rather neglected issues of this sort in recent decades because of the belief in the 1950s and 1960s that economic growth would allow for greater equality via public spending in a way which did not involve a need to deal with tougher questions of the sort which we confront today when this view has to be defended against the conservative-capitalist critique. This approach is no longer adequate, partly because of the growth of the capitalist defence of inequality, partly because the strategy did not actually increase equality very much, and partly because it led to the growth of institutions which in the view of the right impeded the very growth on which the strategy depended.

CITIZENSHIP, EQUALITY, AND POLITICAL CULTURE

So far we have argued in favour of a conception of positive citizenship as against the conservative's negative view, of the centrality of distributive justice against the conservative view that social justice can be displaced by the trickle-down effect, and for the view that citizenship should be linked to an idea of equality which is sensitive to economic efficiency and incentives. However, while these may be theoretically cogent, they can be salient politically only if they tap values which people actually hold in British society. The fundamental question here is whether Thatcherism has changed political values in the population at large to the extent that a conception of egalitarian citizenship is now no longer a viable political project. Is there a sustained basis in public opinion for this conception of citizenship or has this been displaced by market-oriented values which would favour a negative and limited view of citizenship, based upon an extension of the market and further reductions in public expenditure, coupled with tax cuts? On the face of it, the resounding Conservative victory at the polls in June 1987 might lead one to the view that public attitudes may have changed and that the left has to either abandon its egalitarian and redistributive policies or face an indefinite period in the political wilderness. Such an assumption is very dubious, and we hope to be able to show that there is still strong public support for at least some elements of a citizenship approach, and that there is really quite sharp evidence that public values are still of an egalitarian sort. If this argument is correct, then it follows that the left can have some confidence that, if it can develop a coherent citizenship/rights strategy, it can once more win power and that the sources of the defeat of the left in 1987 lie elsewhere.

The sources of this optimism are to be found in survey evidence produced over the last two or three years in the *British Social Attitudes* surveys produced each year by Social and Community Planning Research (SCPR). Using the date assembled in these annual volumes we can discuss three aspects of the issues we have raised. They are:

(a) The extent of public support for welfare spending.
(b) The extent to which values have been changed in favour of a free market/limited government approach.
(c) The degree to which there is a favourable attitude towards egalitarian policies.

The SCPR evidence shows that there is still strong support for certain core areas of the welfare state such as health, education, and state pensions, even at the cost of higher taxation. In his chapter in *British Social Attitudes: The 1987 Report*,[13] Peter Taylor Gooby has produced the figures relating to attitudes to welfare (table 12.6).

What seems clear from these figures is that there is very little

Table 12.6   Public attitudes to welfare, 1983–6

	1983	1984	1985	1986
	%	%	%	%
Reduce taxes and spend less on health, education, and social benefits	9	6	6	5
Keep taxes and spending on these services at the same level as they are now	54	50	43	44
Increase taxes and spend more on health, education, and social benefits	32	39	45	46

Source: R. Jowell, S. Witherspoon, and L. Brook (eds) (1987) *British Social Attitudes: The 1987 Report*, Aldershot, Gower

support for a more draconian attempt to implement the programme of conservative capitalism and indeed that over the past few years support for growing public expenditure on resources for citizenship has increased to nearly half the population. Hence this does not support the view that conservative capitalism in Britain has produced a fundamental change in values.

However, it has to be recognized that support for increased public expenditure is not indiscriminate. This can be shown from the tables 12.7–12.15.

Table 12.7   Highest priority for extra government spending

	1983	1984	1985	1986
	%	%	%	%
Health	37	51	47	47
Education	24	20	23	27
Help for industry	16	10	8	8
Housing	7	6	8	7
Social security benefits	6	7	5	5

Source: R. Jowell, S. Witherspoon, and L. Brook (eds) (1987) *British Social Attitudes: The 1987 Report*, Aldershot: Gower

Again this shows that the Conservatives' electoral success can hardly be based upon a fundamental change in public values, but equally it shows that attitudes to public spending are rather discriminative, with housing and social security spending very low on the list of priorities. This is also confirmed by table 12.8:

Table 12.8 Highest priority for extra social benefit spending

	1983	1984	1985	1986
	%	%	%	%
Retirement pensions	41	43	41	40
Benefits for disabled	24	21	26	25
Benefits for unemployed	18	18	16	16
Child benefits	8	9	10	11
Benefits for single parents	8	7	6	7

Source: R. Jowell, S. Witherspoon, and L. Brook (eds.) (1987) *British Social Attitudes: the 1987 Report*, Aldershot: Gower

This discrimination is not a straight reflection of party identification but exists to varying degrees across the political spectrum as the tables 12.9 and 12.10 show.

Table 12.9 Highest priority for extra spending according to political party

	Conservative		*Alliance*		*Labour*	
	1983	1986	1983	1986	1983	1986
	%	%	%	%	%	%
Retirement pensions	40	46	40	37	41	37
Benefits for disabled	30	29	24	27	19	20
Benefits for unemployed	11	11	20	17	25	22
Child benefit	7	8	7	10	8	13
Benefits for single parents	11	6	6	8	6	7

Source: R. Jowell, S. Witherspoon, and L. Brook (eds) (1987 *British Social Attitudes: The 1987 Report*. Aldershot: Gower

So although there are differences, the main message is that there is considerable cross-party support for some of the resources necessary for citizenship compared with others. Two things follow from this in terms of the general thesis of the book. One is that there is no deep-seated support for the full Conservative capitalist programme in relation to welfare, citizenship, and social justice. The second is that there is a public-value basis only for a limited range of welfare resources for citizenship. Later we shall discuss the impact that this might have on the social basis of citizenship.

At the same time, there is not a great deal of agreement about the relative or citizenship approach to poverty where poverty is not defined in terms of subsistence, but rather in terms of the ability to live according to a standard considered to be normal by the majority of citizens (table 12.10).

Table 12.10 Responses to question 'Would you say someone in Britain *was* or *was not* in poverty if:

	Yes	No
They had enough to buy the things they really needed but not enough to buy the things most people take for granted	25	72
They had enough to eat and live, but not enough to buy other things they needed	55	43
They had not got enough to eat and live without getting into debt	95	3

Source: R. Jowell, S. Witherspoon, and L. Brook (eds) (1987) *British Social Attitudes: The 1987 Report*, Aldershot: Gower

Again the issues behind these figures are to some degree shared across parties, although there is more support among Labour identifiers for the relative view of poverty.

Table 12.11

	Conservative	Alliance	Labour
	%	%	%
Agree with a relative conception of poverty	19	22	33

Source: R. Jowell, S. Witherspoon, and L. Brook (eds) (1987) *British Social Attitudes: The 1987 Report*, Aldershot: Gower

So, there is certainly a mixed message here for both proponents and critics of conservative capitalism, but the main point for the moment is that there is not much support for the full Conservative capitalist project. However, a socialist approach to citizenship rights has to take account of the negative features revealed in these figures.

The issues at stake here can be put in another way too, namely the extent to which there is support for government intervention in and indeed control of market forces. For example, in the 1985 survey the figures in table 12.12 emerged in response to questions about the role of government in relation to the market.

Table 12.12 Support for economic controls

	Support	Oppose
	%	%
Control wages by legislation	42	53
Control prices by legislation	66	30
Introducing import controls	67	27

Source: R. Jowell (ed.) (1986) British Social Attitudes: The 1986 Report, Aldershot: Gower

[handwritten margin note: but what happens in H of C? despite public opinion]

These are dramatic, not to say draconian, policies and, apart from wage control, receive majority support. Again the inference to be drawn is that the conservative-capitalist message about the virtues of the free market has not produced a fundamental shift in values in favour of the market.

However, while this may be true, socialists have to tackle two issues which flow from this. The first is that socialists wish to see citizenship in terms of greater equality rather than of a residual form of basic welfarism, and again this needs to be considered against public values. After the 1987 election there were many suggestions that, because social values had been changed in a capitalist way, the Labour Party should abandon its commitment to greater equality and redistribution. So clearly coming to a view about this is of central political importance. Again, however, the survey evidence over more than one year suggests that egalitarian values have not been displaced by free-market ones and indeed that egalitarian sentiments are expressed in terms of the direct issue of income inequalities.

This is vital in another way too, as we shall see, in that it does seem that equality is the political value which most clearly separates right and left in politics and that there would be grave political dangers in the left's abandoning its commitment to greater equality, given the contribution which this makes to its identity. To abandon an egalitarian perspective would not only be unjustified in the light of the survey evidence, but would also put at risk the political identity of the Labour Party. In British Social Attitudes: The 1987 Report, respondents were asked for their views on the following issues:

1 Government should redistribute income from the better off to those who are less well off.
2 Big business benefits owners at the expense of workers.
3 Ordinary people do not get their fair share of the nation's wealth.
4 There is one law for the rich and one for the poor.
5 Management will always try to get the better of employees if it gets the chance.

Agreement or disagreement with these propositions was then ranked on a linked five-point scale, ranging from 'Agree strongly' to 'Disagree strongly'. A score of 1 was given to indicate strong agreement with the propositions listed above. Thus the strongest egalitarians who agree with all five above would have a score of 5; strongly anti-egalitarians would have a score of 25. These scores were then divided by the number of propositions so that the strongest egalitarians had a score of 1; the strongest anti-egalitarians a score of 5. The results are shown in table 12.13.

Table 12.13   Egalitarian scale

Average position:	Total	Conservative	Party identification Alliance	Labour
	%	%	%	%
Strongly egalitarian				
1 point	11	2	10	21
2 points	40	25	37	54
3 points	32	40	38	20
4 points	13	27	12	20
Strongly anti-egalitarian				
5 points	1	3	–	–

Source: R. Jowell, S. Witherspoon, and L. Brook (eds) (1987) *British Social Attitudes: The 1987 Report*, Aldershot: Gower

Various things follow from this: 83 per cent of respondents had moderate-to-strong egalitarian sentiments (although only 11 per cent had fully egalitarian attitudes); three-quarters of Labour identifiers had egalitarian sentiments and no anti-egalitarian ones, and indeed a quarter of Conservative identifiers had moderate-to-strong egalitarian preferences. Again this would seem to indicate that the conservative-capitalist critique of egalitarian values has not bitten all that deeply and that there is a strong reservoir of egalitarian

sentiments on which the left can call in defence of an egalitarian
approach to citizenship.

As we saw earlier, one of the central features of conservative
capitalism has been its defence of inequality and, in particular,
inequality of income. The Labour Party too has often been wary of
advocating redistributive policies preferring very often, as we saw
in the case of Crosland and others, to improve the position of the
worst-off members of society by using public expenditure to improve
the 'social wage' and thus avoiding direct redistribution. However,
the 1984 survey (table 12.14) shows that there is a good deal of
egalitarian sentiment in terms of the direct distribution of income.[14]

Table 12.14 Percentage of total responses to the question: 'Thinking of
income levels in Britain today, would you say that the gap between those
with high incomes and those with low incomes is too large, about right, or
too small?

	%
Too large	72
About right	22
Too small	3
Don't know	2

Source: R. Jowell and C. Airey (eds) (1984) *British Social Attitudes: The 1984 Report*, Aldershot:
Gower

Of course, this might be predictable in manual social classes, but,
even when the figures are disaggregated, many of those in social
classes 1/2 thought that the gap was too large. In the 1987 report
similar attitudes were revealed. Overall 69 per cent thought that it
was the responsibility of government to reduce income differences
between the rich and the poor. Disaggregated by party, the figures
are shown in table 12.15.

Table 12.15 Percentage of total responses to the question: 'Do you think
it should or should not be the government's responsibility to reduce income
differences between the rich and poor?

	Conservative	Alliance	Labour
	%	%	%
Definitely/probably should	47	73	87
Probably/definitely should not	46	22	6

Source: R. Jowell and C. Airey (eds) (1984) *British Social Attitudes: The 1984 Report*, Aldershot:
Gower

Among the non-aligned there were 66 per cent in favour of redistribution. Hence the General Election victory of Mrs Thatcher in 1987 can hardly be put down to a fundamental change in values on the part of the public. It presumably had more to do with the prevailing sense of well-being for those in work, the unpopularity of Labour's defence policy, and the activities of some Labour local councils which have received wide publicity. However, there is no basis on this evidence for a widespread retreat from distributive values.

CITIZENSHIP, AGENCY, AND RIGHTS

As we have seen, free-market conservatism cannot effectively displace distributive concerns in politics. Its vaunted trickle-down effect, which is central to its legitimacy, is not working and is creating social and regional divisions, and is in danger of producing an under class, features which are of as great a concern of traditionalist, one-nation Conservatives as they are to socialists. In addition, as we have seen, there are public attitudes which do favour both greater equality and redistribution and which are also favourable to forms of public expenditure which secure the economic and social basis of citizenship, albeit not in an indiscriminate manner. The central need on the left therefore is to draw upon these values in a way which will link them to a conception of social citizenship and allow the arguments in favour of a more equal society to be developed in a more coherent and cogent manner than has been the case in the past twenty years. In doing so, the left can draw upon a central feature of the British political tradition which free-market conservatism has yet to displace, that which has its roots in the development of Social or New Liberalism (20) in the late nineteenth century and which has had a major influence on left-wing thought in Britain, particularly that which has focused on the contribution of R. H. Tawney and those who have followed him. However, there is no doubt that this tradition is in need of updating and rethinking in much the same way as the free-market conservatives have rethought and updated the tradition of classical liberalism. This is now a matter of urgency. The rethinking of this tradition was not really necessary in the period of the post-war boom when it seemed that social and economic rights could be extended indefinitely by means of economic growth, a strategy which was central to the revisionism of Crosland, Jay, and Gaitskell. However, it does seem likely that some of the policies which seemed to be implied in this strategy, particularly in relation to the role of the state and the growth of the importance of interest groups, may well have had a negative effect on growth and thus impeded the very conditions for its own success. The left should have the responsibility to accept some aspects of the supply-side critique here and to rethink policies in relation to citizenship in the light of this.

Indeed the idea of citizenship may itself be important here. One of the advantages which Reagan and Thatcher have had in trying to confront interest groups has been their ability to appeal to something beyond interest groups – in each case an appeal to patriotism, placing the idea of the needs of Britain or America above that of sectional interests. On the left this could be the function of the idea of citizenship, placing this as a common value against which the pressures from interest groups could be countered. The demands of interest groups could be counterposed to those of citizenship to see whether interest-group pressures would extend rather than limit a conception of citizenship and agency. An approach of this sort could be used as a countervailing value to the potential fragmentation on the left in favour of a rainbow coalition of interest groups. This strategy, which has been important to the left in Britain and the United States, has not been successful and there is a clear danger of incoherence in that interest-group values are not capable of being harmonized into a coherent programme, as the General Election in Britain in 1983 demonstrated. In addition, there is an urgent economic reason for seeking a different and more common-value basis for politics on the left, namely the cogent arguments developed on the right by public-choice theorists about the baleful economic effects of interest groups on economic performance. There is some truth in this diagnosis, and to base left-wing politics on interest groups would be a failure to learn from this. Citizenship and its associated needs could be one way forward in an attempt to stake out an ideological positon which would transcend the fragmentation which is implicit in the politics of interest groups. However, before this can be done, we need to have a coherent idea of what citizenship implies at both the level of values and of policy; only then can it act in the countervailing way we have suggested.

Many of the assumptions about citizenship which were important in socialist thinking immediately after the war, for example, in the writings of Marshall and Titmuss, were predicated on assumptions about social solidarity which reflected the wartime experience. There is a central need now to rethink the idea of citizenship in a more individualistic age. This will require bringing ideas about citizenship into a clearer relationship with the market which, despite the defects we have discussed, must play a major role in a socialist society as a more efficient way than politics of allocating many resources. In addition, while, as we shall argue, collective provision is of central importance to the maintenance of citizenship, in a more individualistic society, with a variety of goals, the justification of collective provision will have to be much more instrumental than it was in previous periods of socialist thought. It must be in terms of what it can contribute to individual freedom and agency rather than being seen as an intrinsic good. The basis of this latter attitude seems to have been fatally undermined, partly as the result of some of the forms which collective provision has taken, particularly in the nationalized industries since the war, and partly as the result of growing affluence and the break-up of neighbourhoods which may have sustained collective values. Many of the left rightly wish that this was not so, but nostalgia for what for the moment at least seem to be past ways of life cannot be the basis for political rethinking, however unpleasant this may be.

Some of the main features of the value basis of citizenship have already been discussed in chapter 10 on the market and the state; however, it is important at this point to bring together some of these ideas and look at their potential impact on policy. One of the central features of our earlier discussion was the emphasis on the idea of agency and the necessary goods of agency. We saw that the free-market conservative was able to define citizenship in negative terms, that is, in terms of the framework of law and order which would secure the greatest amount of mutual non-coercion, and this is clearly very important, but we argued at that point that to see citizenship in this narrow way rested upon a very limited under-standing of the nature of liberty, namely as the absence of coercion. However, as we saw, there are grave limitations to this approach. What we are interested in is that range of resources which are necessary conditions of following any plan of life at all. There are certain generic goods which people in a society such as ours need in order to be able to act effectively as agents, and these generic goods will certainly involve freedom from coercion and thus a need for a framework of law, but they will also involve a decent level of education, health care, income, and security. These are common needs which we have as citizens and it is these common resources which are directly the concern of the state. The free-market conservative rightly places a lot of emphasis on equal freedom but the freedom in question is a purely formal one. The left are as much interested in the conditions which are necessary to exercise that freedom. While capitalism may secure equal negative freedom for all, although this is itself a dubious claim, it cannot secure an equal or even fair distribution of the worth of liberty, those goods which are necessary for such freedoms to be exercised. It is common ground between the free-market right and the left that the state should guarantee freedom; the divide comes over what is necessary to secure this. So on the left it becomes a central and ineradicable role for the state to secure a more equitable distribution of the worth of liberty. The key problem for the left, in the light of this role for the state, is to reconcile this concern with social justice and the distribution of the conditions of freedom with a view of the state which will not actually seek to secure social justice in ways that decrease freedom and create other political inequalities of power, particularly in relation to the professional and bureaucratic delivery of services to meet generic needs. It is at this stage particularly that a great deal of rethinking has to be done on the left in terms of the type and scope of service delivery through the state, and in particular whether benefits should be provided in cash rather than in kind, and indeed whether we could move away from a benefit culture to some degree through a guaranteed-income scheme.

One way in which this should proceed is to consider whether existing patterns of welfare delivery meet the underlying values of citizenship on which their justification rests. Do existing forms of welfare provision enable people to live lives shaped by their own values and purposes? Do they create a sense of independence? Are they too reliant on the discretionary power of bureaucracies and professionals? Have these debates been conducted too much in the terms set by producer-interest groups in the welfare field rather than by the common values of citizenship? Does greater equality in terms of the needs of citizenship require greater selectivity and targeting of welfare goods in the sense that, if we wish to create greater equality of resources, this will require targeting welfare expenditure on those with fewest resources? One way in which these issues could be addressed in relation to the underlying values of citizenship would be to consider them in terms of ideas about rights, and the corresponding duties of citizenship, and the extent to which ideas about rights could lead to empowering individuals at the expense of state and welfare bureaucracies.

The idea of defining welfare benefits in terms of rights could act as a constraint on bureaucracies and professional groups in that this would limit the area of discretion available to the latter. If certain welfare benefits were defined in terms of strict entitlement, this would limit the power of professionals both to use bureaucratic discretion and would indeed limit the scope of the interaction between client and professional. This might be particularly important in the context of welfare and social security.

There are clearly difficulties involved in defining access to some goods in terms of rights, but for the moment there are grounds for thinking that this would limit professional and bureaucratic power. It would make a reality of citizenship in securing to all individuals, in a way that the market cannot, the necessary means of exercising positive and participatory citizenship. Examples of this could range from social-security entitlements to the example given by Peter Hain in *The Democratic Alternative*: where a council failed to do a repair to a council flat within a specified time, the tenant would have the right to have it done privately and send the bill to the council.[15]

In addition to being defined in terms of rights, many benefits could be given in cash rather than in kind or, where this is not possible, in terms of vouchers as a cash surrogate, which would be an alternative way of describing the example given by Hain. The argument in favour of cash benefits is as follows: provision in terms of cash will allow recipients to spend their money in their own way and this will enhance their opportunity to live a life shaped by their own purposes. It will also be a good learning mechanism in a society in which the management of income is crucial to success and status, and thus meet a point often made by the dependency theorists. In such a way this will circumscribe the opportunities for professional and bureaucratic paternalism, while at the same time creating the possibility of independence. One large question here, in the British context, is whether the basic resources necessary for citizenship would best be supplied through a minimum-income guarantee. There are two ways of approaching this. The first is through the idea of a guaranteed minimum wage, an approach which the Labour

Party has certainly found attractive. Roy Hattersley, for example, argues for it in *Choose Freedom*, in the context of a more general thesis about incomes policy.[16] The other alternative is a guaranteed income through the social-security system which would require some merging of the tax and benefits system. Clearly both are rather long-term proposals. The advantage of a minimum income rather than the minimum wage is that it would not involve the degree of interference in the market which minimum-wage legislation would involve. It would be secured through the tax and social security system rather than through direct interference in what firms believe they are able to pay. However, in the British context, defining a basic positive right to citizenship in this way seems to be an obvious and potentially less bureaucratic way of securing the rights of citizenship than other alternatives.

Citizenship values must always challenge the assumptions of professionals that what are, ultimately, very often issues of morality and ways in which people choose to live their lives can be turned over to professional expertise and adjudication. Only in this way will the counter-argument from the free-market side, that welfare delivery limits freedom, entrenches paternalism, and confers professional power, be countered. If the left believes in the fair value of freedom for citizens, issues of this sort have to be tackled.

If we are in favour of equal freedom, then there must be scope for genuine choice within state-provided services, whether in the field of health or education. For example, if we are to have a state educational system run on egalitarian grounds, there can be no possible basis for restricting the opportunities of schools to have diverse patterns of subjects and specialism, so long as these are not bought at the expense of others, and so long as they do not limit the capacity to develop the basis of common citizenship in a free society. This might require a common curriculum based upon what are taken in our society to be the basic educational needs for common citizenship, and it would also limit the opportunity to set up forms of education which run against these values and which might restrict the capacity of children to develop a sense of their own independence and liberty. Beyond this common basis, however, there should be scope for different styles and traditions. If it is to take freedom seriously, the left must be more responsive to diversity in education within the boundaries set by the common values of citizenship which, as we have already argued, will involve a commitment to personal freedom, but we should be clear that this is likely to involve some conflict with professional groups; if we look forward to a society of citizens, then we must resist the basic features of citizenship being turned into a matter which professional groups can dominate.

The same could be argued in relation to health care, and a limit must be placed on the professional power of doctors outside the strictly clinical field, which is much narrower than the sphere over which such power is currently exercised, and, as in the case of education, could be an aid to choice and to efficiency. In each case, however, the crucial thing is to reduce the power of producer-interest groups and increase that of citizens. This again could mean giving patients the right to be treated outside their own area if treatment is available there more quickly. We have to find ways of giving consumers the power of choice within the state sector in order to make the choice, which currently depends on going out of the state sector into the market, more of a reality for all. However, proposals of this sort will require a challenge to the power of producer-interest groups within the state sector. On the whole, the traditional attitude of the left in Britain has either been to accept the claims of expertise, and thus the power of producer-interest groups, or to seek to restrict it by political or administrative means.

However, bearing in mind the public-choice critique of bureaucracy outline in chapter 3, we should not place all our confidence in political solutions to such problems. Clearly one way to give political and democratic control more purchase on bureaucratic structures would be to decentralize them into smaller and more locally based units, and there have been some examples of the attempt to do this in the welfare fields, promoted by Labour councils in Walsall, Sheffield, and Islington. Clearly smaller and locally based bureaucracies might, in principle, be more susceptible to democratic control than large ones. However, it is important too to limit control and discretion in other ways too, particularly by giving people entitlements and empowering consumers of bureaucratically delivered services.

In addition there will be a need to have a more welcoming attitude towards voluntary groups and agencies. It should be no part of the socialism of the future that the state should be the only deliverer of services, as opposed to the idea that the state would guarantee a framework of secure provision for all and allow voluntary agencies a role in neighbourhoods. The state, as Lindblom has said, is all thumbs and no fingers,[17] and one way of putting this point in the welfare field would be to say that, of course, the state has a duty to meet needs on a secure and predictable basis as rights, but also to say that there is always likely to be a gap between the needs of particular individuals and what the state can provide as a matter of general policy. It cannot be discriminating enough and there will always be a place for the voluntary sector. This should not be squeezed out as the result of over-optimistic assumptions about the capacity of the state to be discriminating enough and the over-professionalization of welfare which discounts voluntary help.

The point about decentralization is important too in fields such as planning. As we saw in chapter 3, there are very strong epistemological arguments which can be mounted against the idea of centralized planning, while at the same time in chapter 10 we saw, in the discussion of the issue of small decision-making, that the market, left to itself, may produce outcomes, based upon small decisions, which are actually unwanted. So there is a need on the left to reconcile these two things. One way in which this could be done would be to decentralize planning a good deal and to open up planning to a greater degree of democratic citizen involvement. Again there are, or at least were, signs that this was happening on the left before the abolition of the metropolitan counties by the Thatcher government. The greater London Enterprise Board was reasonably successful in the field of local planning. The decentralization of planning, when combined to a commitment to an ineradicable role for the market, could overcome many of the epistemological strictures of Hayek and others who have argued against centralized forms of planning. There is, of course, the important question of how local planning outcomes would fit into a national economic strategy, and therefore the relationship between the state and local authorities, but it must be central to such a relationship that, while the state clearly has national responsibilities, it cannot itself formulate detailed planning proposals for the economy from the top down. If planning is to occur, it has to have as its basis local initiatives if the left is to avoid the cogent questions posed by the Hayekians about the possibility of centralized planning.

CITIZENSHIP AND RIGHTS

The obvious problem with defining citizenship in terms of entitlement to positive resources is that these resources are finite. It will be remembered from chapter 3 that this was one of the major reasons why the conservative capitalist wishes to reject the socialist idea that there can be a right to resources. In their view traditional civil and political rights do not imply the provision of resources but, on the contrary, require the government to stay its hand and not to interfere with what is claimed under the right. Thus, in the case of rights to freedom of speech and association, the duty of government is to stay its own hand in terms of interference, rather than providing positive resources for the fulfilment of the right. However, as we saw, this difference is not categorical as the critic seems to think. First of all, in the world in which we live, these rights do need resources to protect them and indeed the resources needed to secure a right to be protected from murder, from the infringement of privacy, from interference with freedom of all sorts will have to be subject of political negotiation. The amount of resources we should as a society put into protecting these rights will be a matter of political judgement and will vary from time to time. If this is so, there cannot be any clear distinction between positive and negative rights. The free-market conservative will argue that rights, such as privacy and the security of the person, are somehow beyond politics, and thus beyond negotiation and interests, but this really is not so. We have to come to some political agreement about how much in the way of resources has to be put into protecting these rights. If this is the case, there is no difference of principle between these rights and social and economic rights. To argue, as Rose and Peters do in the passage quoted in chapter 3,[18] that social and economic rights bespeak the language of bargaining and bribes, whereas civil and political rights do not, is to neglect the resource implications of the latter and the extent to which these resources have to be negotiated through political processes. The socialist will want to argue that, if we are all equally citizens, then we have to see that our rights are defined in as equal a way as possible, and that there is as fair an allocation of resources between individuals to defend these rights as we can manage. Clearly all rights will come up against resource constraints, and thus political questions about the distribution of resources to meet rights will come up. The way to approach this is through a conception of social justice of the sort which we discussed in the previous chapter. At the moment we do not have equal rights to physical security, even in the narrow sense conceived by the capitalist, because some people can buy their way into greater security and live behind protected environments and neighbourhoods. Many people, who may in fact be the most vulnerable, cannot do this. It must therefore be central to the socialist argument that, if we are equal as citizens having equal rights to freedom and security, there must be a fairer distribution of the resources necessary to protect these rights between individuals and not take refuge in the sophistical argument that one sort of right does not require resources, whereas another does, drawing the conclusion that only the former are genuine rights.

As we saw in chapter 3, one feature of the approach of modern conservatism in relation to Workfare proposals is that citizenship involves obligations as well as rights. That, if we live in a democratic society, citizenship cannot be seen in a purely passive way, in terms of merely demanding rights, but rather that claiming a right from society implies obligations to that society too. In the conservative view this means that if one has a right to income support, one has a duty to seek work and to acquire the skills necessary to enter the labour market. As we saw, there are many difficulties with this in terms of the conservative capitalist's own theory of the state, and in any case in Britain at the moment, with current levels of unemployment, a Workfare programme would be a cruel deception. Nevertheless there is something here from which the socialist should learn or rather relearn, namely that citizenship does involve obligations as well as rights. We say relearn, because certainly this has been part of the British socialist tradition and of those forms of thought which have contributed to the formation of that political outlook, such as the development of Social Liberalism based upon Idealist philosophy. This had a major influence upon Tawney, whose work was permeated by the idea of mutual obligation. There is nothing intrinsic to a socialist conception of rights to say that, if I demand something as a right from the community, I do not have corresponding obligations. In the case of work this might well mean that, under a government which adopted policies to restore full employment, there could be an obligation to undertake training in order to enter the labour market if one were able-bodied enough to do so. For the socialist tradition labour is a means to self-respect and fulfilment, and it is also the means whereby the wealth is created to meet the common needs of citizens and to provide for their liberty. One cannot consistently claim these rights and be indifferent to the means whereby they are sustained, i.e. productive labour. It could certainly be part of the way in which the idea of socialist citizenship is rethought, that there should be a corresponding duty to seek work or to train for the labour market in return for an income guarantee until work could be found. Clearly any such approach would not apply to those unable to work and to others, such as single parents, because of the potential effect on children.

There could be other benefits too. If a right to income guarantee is linked to discharging social obligations, this could overcome some of the lack of enthusiasm for unemployment benefit which was noted in *British Social Attitudes: The 1986 Report* which was discussed earlier in the chapter. Indeed it could overcome a more general problem in relation to social rights, namely that, within a society in which capitalist ideas are very strong, it is very difficult to get people to accept that they have rights to things which they have not paid for. For certain kinds of benefits this can be achieved through a pure insurance approach, but the idea of discharging obligations as a correlative to having a right to resources could be another means whereby this deep-seated idea is overcome. This may well appear very abstract and theoretical, but it relates directly to practical politics in that a future Labour government would be very unlikely to dismantle the Manpower Services Commission, and one way in which its work could be directed would be in the way suggested above. At the moment the ideas tentatively suggested above are likely to be seen on the left as coercive or even, to use some of the language used in Parliament, as slave labour. However, this is clearly not so. First of all, as we have suggested, the idea of duties correlating with citizenship rights does have a place within the British socialist tradition and there could be a form of minimal and residual provision for anyone who decided to opt out of social obligations, with much more generous provision for those who choose to take their social obligations seriously.

Many people on the left have a strong feeling for the idea of community or fraternity, a notion which is notoriously difficult to apply to a complex society, but the idea that we have common needs which are to be understood as rights, and that these common needs produce common obligations towards one another, is one way of trying to make sense of this value on the left. It is a long way from the form of community which Hayek and others see as a form of tribalism in which it is assumed that community can exist only with shared substantive goals and purposes. Rather the form of community which is salient in the modern world is one in which we accept that peoples' purposes and values differ and they will have different ends to pursue, but in which we do recognize that, in order to act as agents in the pursuit of such ends, we have to have a high degree of collective provision; but that such collective provision, if it is to be a right, has to involve common obligations; and that at the end of the day there has to be some sanction to secure the performance of those common obligations; and that this is a central role of government in a socialist society. While these ideas are inherently controversial, they are put forward in the firm belief that the rise of conservative capitalism is much more than an ephemeral phenomenon associated with Mrs Thatcher and Ronald Reagan, and that its analysis of modern society has to some extent to be taken seriously and learned from on the left. This process has taken too long already and, until some unpalatable ideas and issues are directly confronted, the left will remain on the defensive for the foreseeable future. However, we shall have to accept that a society of citizens will require hard thinking about the shape of those institutions which will both enhance and reflect such values.

NOTES

1 CONSERVATIVE CAPITALISM AS IDEOLOGY

1 Daniel Patrick Moynihan (1986) 'Political AIDS', *The New Republic*, 26 May: 18.
2 See John Joseph Wallis (1984) 'The birth of the old federalism: financing the New Deal, 1932–1940', *Journal of Economic History*, XLIV (1): 139–59.
3 The question was 'From which level of government do you feel you get the most for your money – federal, state, or local?'. See US Advisory Commission on Intergovernmental Relations (ACIR) (1984) *1984 Changing Public Attitudes on Government and Taxes*, S-13, Washington, DC: Government Printing Office: 1–4. Cf. Kenneth Palmer and Alex Pattakos (1984) 'The state of American Federalism', *Publius: The Journal of Federalism*, 15 (2): 1–17.
4 See Samuel Beer (1982) *Britain Against Itself: The Political Contradictions of Collectivism*, New York: Norton; especially pp. 100–1.
5 See Peter Hall (1986) *Governing the Economy: The Politics of State Intervention in Britain and France*, New York: Oxford University Press: 29. For a statement of the 'government overload' thesis regarding British politics, see Samuel Beer, *op. cit.*
6 See the use of this phrase by Kenneth Dolbeare and Patricia Dolbeare in (1976) *American Ideologies: The Competing Political Beliefs of the 1970s*, Chicago: Rand McNally, 3rd edn: 57–61. Cf. the more extended discussion in chapter 2.
7 Cf. A. James Reichley (1981) *Conservatives in an Age of Change: The Nixon and Ford Administrations*, Washington, DC: Brookings Institution.
8 Consequently, in Britain, the term 'liberal' retains its classical connotations and is sometimes used to describe the *laissez-faire* tendency in the Thatcher coterie. See Desmond King (1987) *The New Right: Politics, Markets, and Citizenship*, Homewood, Ill.: Dorsey Press and London: Macmillan, and David Green (1987) *The New Conservatism*, New York: St Martin's Press, where the term 'liberal' is used interchangeably with 'libertarian'.

292

9 As Robert Lane points out, they are 'separate and alternative methods of co-ordinating production and distributing goods; neither is merely the disguised servant of the other'. Robert Lane (1986) 'Market justice, political justice', *American Political Science Review*, 80 (2): 383.

10 Michael Novak (1982) *The Spirit of Democratic Capitalism*, New York, NY: Simon & Schuster.

11 Summarized in Robert Alford (1983) 'The Reagan budgets and the contradiction between capitalism and democracy' in Mark Kann (ed.) (1983) *The Future of American Democracy: Views from the Left*, Philadelphia: Temple University Press: 22–53. Cf. Frances Fox Piven and Richard Cloward (1982) *The New Class War*, New York: Random House.

12 Piven and Cloward, *op. cit.*

13 Kevin Phillips (1982) *Post-Conservative America: People, Politics, and Ideology in a Time of Crisis*, New York: Vintage: 47, on the history of the term. Cf. Nick Bosanquet (1983) *After the New Right*, London: Heinemann.

14 A. James Reichley, *op. cit.*, 3. While his definition is useful, and his study of conservatism in the Nixon–Ford years immensely informative, we do not follow his use of Martin Seliger's distinction between 'ideational' and 'positional' conservatism. We feel it is more useful to emphasize how a belief in inequality underlies both libertarian and traditional conservatism (and ideational and positional conservatism) and to trace out the differing policy consequences of each ideological variant.

15 See Norman Luttbeg and Michael Gant (1985) 'The failure of liberal/ conservative ideology as a cognitive structure', *Public Opinion Quarterly*, 49, Spring: 80–93, specifically 91.

16 This revisionist line of research is in response to Philip Converse's earlier and very influential work, reported in Angus Campbell *et al.* (1980) *The American Voter*, Chicago: University of Chicago Press. See Mark Peffley and Jon Hurwitz (1985) 'A hierarchical model of attitude constraint', *American Journal of Political Science*, 29 (4): 885. Cf. William Jacoby (1986) 'Levels of conceptualization and reliance on the liberal-conservative continuum', *Journal of Politics*, 48 (2): 423–32.

17 See Murray Edelman (1964) *The Symbolic Uses of Politics*, Urbana, Ill.: University of Illinois Press.

18 Bruce Moon and William Dixon (1985) 'Politics, the state, and basic human needs', *American Journal of Political Science*, 29 (4): 689.

2 THE POLITICAL ECONOMY OF CONSERVATIVE CAPITALISM

1 For a detailed account of this in Britain see W. H. Greenleaf (1983) *The Ideological Heritage*, vol. 2 of *The British Political Tradition*, London: Methuen.

2 Nigel Lawson (1980) *The New Conservatism*, London: Centre for Policy Studies.

3 Keith Joseph (1976) *Stranded on the Middle Ground*, London: Centre for Policy Studies: 7.

4 J. M. Keynes (1973) *General Theory of Employment, Interest and Money*, London: Macmillan: 89.

5 ibid., 379.

6 Milton Friedman and Rose Friedman (1980) *Free to Choose: A Personal Statement*, New York: Avon and London: Secker & Warburg and Penguin.

7 For a very good account of how the Labour Party approached these issues in the light of Keynesian theories, see E. Durbin (1985) *New Jerusalems: The Labour Party and the Economics of Democratic Socialism*, London: Routledge & Kegan Paul.

8 Keith Middlemas (1986) *Power Competition and the State*, vol. 1, London: Macmillan: 93.

9 ibid., 95.

10 *Full Employment in a Free Society* (1944) Cmnd 6527, London: HMSO.

11 Middlemas, *op. cit.*, 87.

12 See George Gilder (1982) *Wealth and Poverty*, London: Buchan & Enright: xvii. Some of these figures are members of the Mont Pelerin Society, founded after the war by F. A. Hayek.

13 Margaret Thatcher, foreword to Keith Joseph (no date) *Monetarism is not Enough*, London: Centre for Policy Studies.

14 Samuel Brittan (1983) *The Role and Limits of Government*, London: Temple Smith: 135. Part 2 of this book is one of the best non-technical accounts of monetarism.

15 ibid., 256.

16 David Stockman (1985) *The Triumph of Politics: The Crisis in American Government and How It Affects the World*, New York: Coronet: 9.

17 ibid., 253.

18 ibid., 135.

19 ibid., 35.

20 J. Wanniski (1979) *The Way the World Works*, New York: Basic Books; J. Wanniski 'Taxes, revenues and the Laffer Curve', *Public Interest*, 50: 3–16.

21 Stockman, *op. cit.*, 42–3.

22 For further discussion of this, see T. B. Edsall (1984) *The New Politics of Inequality*, New York: W. W. Norton.

23 Alan Walters (1986) *Britain's Economic Renaissance: Margaret Thatcher's Economic Reforms 1979–84*, New York: Oxford University Press.

24 Stockman, *op. cit.*, 9.

25 ibid., 41.

26 Walters, *op. cit.*, 41.

27 ibid., 36.

28 David Friedman (1978) *The Machinery of Freedom*, New Rochelle, NY: Arlington House: 116.

29 See A. Vincent and R. Plant (1984) *Philosophy, Politics and Citizenship*, Oxford: Blackwell.

30 J. O'Connor (1973) *The Fiscal Crisis of the State*, New York: St Martin's Press.
31 J. Habermas (1976) *Legitimation Crisis*, London: Heinemann.
32 ibid., 81.

3 THE CRITIQUE OF THE WELFARE STATE

1 Powell was an early apostle of monetarism within the Conservative Party.
2 M. Holmes (1985) *The First Thatcher Government*, Brighton: Wheatsheaf, chapter 5.
3 See the discussion of this in F. A. Hayek (1960) *The Constitution of Liberty*, London: Routledge, chapter 19.
4 Keith Joseph (1976) *Stranded on the Middle Ground*, London: Centre for Policy Studies: 32.
5 Keith Joseph and Jonathan Sumption (1979) *Equality*, London: Murray; Milton Friedman (1962) *Capitalism and Freedom*, Chicago: University of Chicago Press.
6 This strategy is clearly at work in the major social democratic writings of the post-war period such as Anthony Crosland (1956) *The Future of Socialism*, London: Jonathan Cape and Douglas Jay (1962) *Socialism in the New Society*, London: Longman. It is also to be found in Crosland (1975) *Social Democracy in Europe*, London: Fabian Society, by which time many of the assumptions behind *The Future of Socialism* were beginning to look much less plausible, although he died before the traumas of the late 1970s and early 1980s.
7 Margaret Thatcher (1977) *Let Our Children Grow Tall*, London: Centre for Policy Studies.
8 Joseph and Sumption, *op. cit.*, 47.
9 Milton Friedman and Rose Friedman (1980) *Free to Choose: A Personal Statement*, New York: Avon and London: Secker & Warburg and Penguin: 60–1.
10 Joseph and Sumption, *op. cit.*, 48.
11 See F. A. Hayek (1960) *The Constitution of Liberty*, London: Routledge: 17:

> The confusion of liberty with power with liberty in its original meaning leads to the identification of liberty with wealth; and this makes it possible to exploit all the appeal which the word liberty carries in support of a demand for the redistribution of wealth.

For examples of exactly the kind of thing Hayek decries, see the following: Roy Hattersley (1987) *Choose Freedom*, London: Penguin; Bryan Gould (1985) *Socialism and Equality*, London: Macmillan; Raymond Plant (1984) *Equality, Markets, and the State*, London: Fabian Society.
12 F. A. Hayek (1976) *The Mirage of Social Justice*, vol. 2 of *Law, Legislation and Liberty*, London: Routledge: 69.
13 See Hayek, *The Constitution of Liberty*, chapter 19; Keith Joseph (no

date) *Monetarism is not Enough*, London: Centre for Policy Studies, passim; Margaret Thatcher in foreword to Joseph, *op. cit.*: 9.

14 Hayek, *The Mirage of Social Justice*: 65.

15 Joseph and Sumption, *op. cit.*, 1.

16 George Gilder (1982) *Wealth and Poverty*, London: Buchan & Enright.

17 Joseph, *Stranded on the Middle Ground*: 75–6.

18 Hayek, *The Constitution of Liberty*: 93; Joseph and Sumption, *op. cit.*, 15ff.; Thatcher, in foreword to Joseph, *op. cit.*, 4.

19 Joseph, *Stranded on the Middle Ground*: 76.

20 ibid., 77.

21 Crosland, *Social Democracy in Europe*.

22 In *Stranded on the Middle Ground* Joseph discussed the meaning of a minimum standard as follows:

> An absolute standard of means are defined by reference to the actual needs of the poor and not by reference to the expenditure of those who are not poor. A family is poor if it cannot afford to eat. . . . A person who enjoys a standard of living equal to that of a medieval baron cannot be described as poor for the sole reason that he has chanced to be born into a society where the great majority can live like medieval kings. By any absolute standard there is very little poverty in Britain today.

Joseph's words in *Equality* (pp. 27–8) demonstrate that the conservative capitalist regards relative poverty as another form of inequality. The crucial issue which Joseph and Sumption neglect here is whether those at the bottom of society are able to share in some minimal standard of citizenship and do the sorts of things which most people do not regard as luxuries, but as part and parcel of an everyday way of life, such as being able to give gifts at birthdays and Christmas, to have some escape from routine life through leisure, etc. For the detailed justification of this argument see Peter Townsend (1979) *Poverty in the United Kingdom: A Survey of Household Resources and Standards of Living*, London: Penguin. We discuss the citizenship approach to distribution in chapter 12.

23 T. H. Marshall (1950) *Citizenship and Social Class*, Cambridge: Cambridge University Press.

24 Margaret Thatcher, in foreword to Joseph, *op. cit.*, 10.

25 R. Rose and G. Peters (1978) *Can Government Go Bankrupt?*, London: Macmillan: 238.

26 Enoch Powell (John Wood (ed.)) (1972) *Still to Decide*, London: Elliot Right Way: 27. Compare also:

> Politics is thus caught in a vicious circle. Violence feeds on social grievances which derive from unjustifiable rights. The result is that ever wider and deeper state intervention is demanded while the state has itself become the source, as well as the focus of social grievances. (p. 27)

27 Maurice Cranston (1973) *What Rights are Human Rights?*, London:

Bodley Head. For further discussion see R. Plant, H. Lesser, and P. Taylor-Gooby (1981) *Political Philosophy and Social Welfare*, London: Routledge & Kegan Paul and R. Plant 'Needs, rights, and agency' in D. Galligan and D. Sampford (eds) (1985) *Laws, Rights, and the Welfare State*, London: Croom Helm.

28 Joseph, *Stranded on the Middle Ground*: 71.

29 *A Second Selsdon Group Manifesto* (1977) London: Selsdon Group: 3.

30 For a further discussion of this see chapter 12.

31 This view has been clearly endorsed by Mrs Thatcher; see the *Guardian*, 11 June 1987.

32 Joseph, *Stranded on the Middle Ground*: 70.

33 John Kenneth Galbraith (1968) *The New Industrial State*, London: Penguin: 6.

34 Joseph, *Stranded on the Middle Ground*: 59.

35 William Niskanen (1973) *Bureaucracy – Servant or Master? Lessons from America*: London: Hobart Publications. This essay was published by the Institute of Economic Affairs together with a commentary by Nicholas Ridley (among others). Mr Ridley is now Secretary of State for the Environment and in this comment on Niskanen he called it 'a paper of devastating importance'. In October 1983 Mrs Thatcher wrote in *Economic Affairs* (the journal of the IEA): 'All our policies are firmly grounded on these ideas which have been developed with such imagination in your journal.' For a different perspective, see David Beetham (1987) *Bureaucracy*, Milton Keynes: Open University Press.

36 This critique is endorsed by Nigel Lawson (1980) *The New Conservatism*, London: Centre for Policy Studies, in which he looks back further than Hegel:

> We are all imperfect – even the most high minded civil servant. Academic work is still in its infancy on the economics of bureaucracy; but it is already clear that it promises to be a fruitful field. The civil servants and middle class welfare administrators are far from selfless Platonic guardians of popular mythology: they are a major interest group in their own right. (*op. cit.*: 8)

Compare Margaret Thatcher, foreword to Joseph, *op. cit.*, 53.

37 John Gray (1984) *Hayek on Liberty*, Oxford: Blackwell: 73.

38 ibid.

39 ibid.

40 Joseph, *Stranded on the Middle Ground*: 59.

41 Robert Dahl (1982) *Dilemmas of Pluralist Democracies*, New Haven: Yale University Press: 1. Compare Samuel Brittan (1983) *The Role and Limits of Government*, London: Temple Smith: 76.

42 ibid.

43 Samuel Brittan (1977) *The Economic Consequences of Democracy*: London: Temple Smith. See also his essay, 'Hayek, freedom and interest groups' in *The Role and Limits of Government*.

44 Samuel Beer (1982) *Britain Against Itself: The Political Contradictions of Collectivism*, New York: Norton, chapters 1 and 2.

45 Anthony King (1976) 'The problem of overload' in *Why is Britain Becoming Harder to Govern?*, London: BBC Publications: 15.
46 ibid.
47 Margaret Thatcher, foreword to Joseph, *op. cit.*, 74.
48 Lawrence Mead (1986) *Beyond Entitlement: The Social Obligations of Citizenship*, New York: Free Press; Charles Murray (1984) *Losing Ground: American Social Policy 1950–1980*, New York: Basic Books.
49 American Enterprise Institute (1987) *A Community of Self-Reliance: The New Consensus on Family and Welfare*, Milwaukee: AEI: xiv.
50 ibid., 5.
51 See A. Vincent and R. Plant (1984) *Philosophy, Politics and Citizenship*, Oxford: Blackwell.
52 Gilder, *op. cit.*, 51.
53 Michael Heseltine (1987) *Where There's a Will*, 2nd edn, London: Hutchinson.
54 Frances Fox Piven and Richard Cloward (1987) *The Mean Season: The Attack Upon Welfare*.

4 TRADITIONALISTS AND INDIVIDUALISTS: CONFLICT IN THE MOVEMENT

1 For a detailed account of these two traditions see W. H. Greenleaf (1983) *The Ideological Heritage*, vol. 2 of *The British Political Tradition*, London: Methuen.
2 A more extended definitional discussion may be found in Kenneth Hoover (1986) *Ideology and Political Life*, Monterey, Calif.: Brooks/ Cole, chapters 3 and 4; and in Raymond Plant (1974) *Community and Ideology*, London: Routledge & Kegan Paul.
3 Samuel Huntington (1957) 'Conservatism as an ideology', *American Political Science Review*, 51 (2): 454–5.
4 George Nash (1979) *The Conservative Intellectual Movement in America Since 1945*, New York: Basic Books: 81–2) has labelled these two conservative variants as 'traditionalist' and 'libertarian'. In deference to the association of the term 'libertarian' with libertine sexual attitudes in Britain and the particular meanings given to the term 'liberal' in the United States, we have followed the practice of identifying this strand in modern conservatism as 'individualist conservatism'. Cf. Kenneth Hoover (1987) 'The rise of conservative capitalism' in *Comparative Studies in Society and History*, 29 (2): 245–68, and the exchange between the author and Desmond King in *Comparative Studies in Society and History* (forthcoming issue). On the phrase 'individualist conservatism' see Kenneth Dolbeare and Patricia Dolbeare (1976) *American Ideologies: The Competing Beliefs of the 1970s*, 3rd edn, Chicago: Rand McNally: 57–62. Robert Behrens locates the fault line in the Conservative Party between the Ditchers who have bought into the post-war politics of statism, and the Diehards who insist on the 'true faith' of the free market and personal responsibility. The individualist-traditionalist distinction differs in assessing the

NOTES

historical dimension of this split and its impact on current policy.
Traditionalism, in our view, is compatible with statism of the sort
practised in Britain up to 1979; and the faith of the Diehards, as
Behrens allows, is an adaptation of utilitarianism and *laissez-faire*,
not the conservative tradition. Cf. Behrens (1979) 'Diehards and
Ditchers in contemporary conservative politics', *Political Quarterly*, 50
(3): 287–8, 292, and (1980) *The Conservative Party from Heath to Thatcher*,
London: Saxon House: 7–9, 39. For additional terminology used in
the analysis of developments in Great Britain, see the distinction
between the 'New right' and the 'Tory far right' in Patrick Dunleavy
'Analysing British politics' in Henry Drucker (ed.) (1983) *Developments
in British Politics*, New York: St Martin's Press: 292–3; the discussion
of 'Drys' and 'Wets' in Ronald Butt (1983) 'Thatcherissima: the
politics of Thatcherism', *Policy Review*, 26 (3): 30–5; and Julian
Critchley's term for libertarians, the 'arditti', in (1985) *Westminster
Blues*, London: Hamish Hamilton: 77. Cf. Lon Felker and Robert
Thompson (1983) 'The intellectual roots of economic conservatism in
the Reagan and Thatcher administrations', *Journal of the North
Carolina Political Science Association*, 3 (1): 38–55.

5 See David Green's treatment of these sources in Green (1987) *The
New Conservatism*, New York: St Martin's Press, and the review by
Kenneth Hoover in the *American Political Science Review*, 82 (2): 612.
For nuances in the argument cf. Tibor Machan (ed.) (1974) *The
Libertarian Alternative*, Chicago: Nelson-Hall: 499; George H. Nash, *op.
cit.*, 16–18, 32–3; Noel K. O'Sullivan (1976) *Conservatism*, New York:
St Martin's Press: 27.

6 Robert Nisbet (1962) *Community and Power*, New York: Oxford
University Press: xii.

7 ibid. Cf. Robert Nisbet (1975) *The Twilight of Authority*, New York:
Oxford University Press.

8 Francis Pym (1984) *The Politics of Consent*, London: Hamish Hamilton.
Cf. William Keegan (1984) *Mrs Thatcher's Economic Experiment*,
London: Allen Lane, on the doctrinal infighting.

9 Joseph Lelyveld (1985) 'Thatcher government upset over a critical
church report', *New York Times*, 2 December. The report was *Faith in
the City: a Report of the Archbishop of Canterbury's Commission on Urban
Priority Areas*, London: Church House Publishing, 1985.

10 Martin Durham (1985) 'Family, morality, and the New Right',
Parliamentary Affairs: A Journal of Comparative Politics, 38 (2): 180–91.

11 Survey reported in Norman Ornstein (1987) 'How to win in '88: meld
the unmeldable', *US News and World Report*, 12 October: 31–3.

12 Milton Friedman and Rose Friedman (1980) *Free to Choose: A Personal
Statement*, New York: Avon and London: Secker & Warburg and
Penguin: 281.

13 Robert Behrens (1980) *The Conservative Party from Heath to Thatcher:
Policies and Politics 1974–1979*, Westmead: Saxon House: 13. This is a
more dynamic conception of traditional conservatism than Samuel
Huntington finds in the American version, where the traditionalist

299

is seen more simply as 'one who stands by established institutions'. Samuel Huntington, *op. cit.*, 161.

14 David Stockman (1986) *The Triumph of Politics: The Crisis in American Politics and How It Affects the World*, New York: Harper & Row: 409.
15 ibid.
16 Ralph Miliband (1978) 'A state of de-subordination', *British Journal of Sociology*, 29 (4): 402.
17 Samuel Beer (1982) *Britain Against Itself: The Political Contradictions of Collectivism*, New York: Norton: 194–7. Cf. William Harbour (1982) *The Foundations of Conservative Thought*, Notre Dame: University of Notre Dame Press: 185.
18 A problem Adam Smith was vaguely aware of but did not address. See Martin Carnoy (1984) *The State and Political Theory*, Princeton, NJ: Princeton University Press: 29.
19 See Charles Leathers (1984) 'Thatcher-Reagan conservatism and Schumpeter's prognosis for capitalism', *Review of Social Economy*, 4 (1): 28–9.
20 Beer, *op. cit.*: 126–31. Cf. Richard Viguerie's mix of libertarianism and populism in (1983) *The Establishment v. the People*, Chicago: Regnery Gateway.
21 Frances Fox Piven and Richard Cloward (1982) *The New Class War*, New York: Random House: 23. Cf. Robert Alford 'The Reagan budgets and the contradiction between capitalism and democracy' in Mark Kann (ed.) (1983) *The Future of American Democracy: Views from the Left*, Philadelphia: Temple University Press: 47–8, on Daniel Bell's argument of the same kind; and Samuel Beer's argument about 'pluralist stagnation' in Britain, *op. cit.*, 100–1.
22 Friedman and Friedman, *op. cit.*, 90.
23 John Hoskyns (1984) 'Conservatism is not enough', *Political Quarterly*, 55 (1): 10–11. Cf. Peter Riddell (1986) *The Thatcher Government*, updated edition, Oxford: Blackwell: 54. The government is also criticized by the individualist conservatives for being 'inadequately radical'. See Hugh Thomas, Chairman of the (Conservative) Centre for Social Studies, (1984) 'The fruits of conservatism', *New Society*, 67 (13): 435–6.
24 David Walker (1984) 'Thatcher faces revolt on student aid', *Chronicle of Higher Education*, December: 1.
25 Garry Wills (1979) *Confessions of a Conservative*, London: Penguin: 124.
26 Richard Viguerie, *op. cit.*, 8–9.
27 Keith Middlemas (1980) *Politics in Industrial Society: The Experience of the British System Since 1911*, London: André Deutsch.
28 Robert Behrens (1977) *The Conservative Party in Opposition*, Coventry: Lanchester Polytechnic: 17–18.
29 For a sampling of these claims see W. H. Greenleaf (1983) *The Rise of Collectivism*, vol. 1 of *The British Political Tradition*, London: Methuen: 161–3; Robert Behrens, 'Diehards and Ditchers': 286–95.
30 William Harbour, *op. cit.*, 186–7. Cf. Beer's citation in *Britain Against Herself*: 173–4, of the sentiment of a prominent Tory MP of

traditionalist background that 'political advice, derived from liberal economic theory . . . leaves governors and its own adherents always frustrated at the distance between their model of the world and reality'.

31 Philip Norton and Arthur Aughey (1981) *Conservatism and Conservatism*, London: Temple Smith: 285.

32 Susan Tolchin and Martin Tolchin (1983) *Dismantling America: The Rush to Deregulate*, New York: Houghton Mifflin: 255; cf. 'State regulators rush in where Washington no longer treads: will the New Federalism create a fifty-headed hydra?', *Businessweek*, 19 September 1983: 124 *et seq.*.

33 Patrick Dunleavy and R. A. W. Rhodes (1983) 'Beyond Whitehall' in Henry Drucker (gen. ed.) *Developments in British Politics*: 126–8. Robert Behrens points out that anti-devolutionists were generally found on the free-market side, though there were exceptions. See Behrens, *The Conservative Party in Opposition*: 19–20.

34 Timothy Conlan cites ten cases where structural devolution lost out to Reagan's prescriptive policy goals: 'Federalism and competing values in the Reagan administration', paper at the annual meeting of the American Political Science Association, Washington, DC, September 1984. Cf. Alfred Light (1983) 'Federalism, FERC v. Mississippi, and product liability reform', *Publius: The Journal of Federalism*, 13, spring: 85–96.

35 Cited by R. W. Apple (1985) 'Thatcher barely escapes defeat as 48 Conservative MPs rebel', *New York Times*, 24 July.

36 Donald Shell (1985) 'The House of Lords and the Thatcher government', *Parliamentary Affairs*, 38, winter: 16–32.

37 Cf. A. James Reichley, (1981) *Conservatives in an Age of Change: The Nixon and Ford Administrations*, Washington, DC: Brookings Institution: 13–14, 21, 415–16.

38 Sheldon Wolin (1976) 'The new conservatives', *New York Review of Books*, 5 February: 6.

39 Joel Krieger may be right that 'Toryism was transformed as the party's ethos shifted from the playing fields of Eton to the housing estates of Grantham', but suburban traditionalism is no oxymoron: (1986) *Reagan, Thatcher, and the Politics of Decline*, New York: Oxford University Press: 63.

5 THE RISE OF CONSERVATIVE CAPITALISM IN THE UNITED STATES

1 Lou Cannon (1984) *Reagan*, New York: Putnam.

2 ibid., 184. Cf. Frank Levy (1977) 'What Ronald Reagan can teach the US about welfare reform', Urban Institute.

3 Daniel Patrick Moynihan (1973) *The Politics of a Guaranteed Income: The Nixon Administration and the Family Assistance Plan*, New York: Vintage: 110.

4 ibid., 214–15.

5 A. James Reichley (1981) *Conservatives in an Age of Change: The Nixon*

and Ford Administrations, Washington, DC: Brookings Institution: 71–2, 169.

6 Moynihan, *op. cit.*, 62.

7 ibid., 374–5; Christopher Leman (1980) *The Collapse of Welfare Reform*, Cambridge, Mass.: MIT Press: 92.

8 Cannon, *op. cit.*, 178–9.

9 Reichley, *op. cit.*, 150.

10 It is interesting to note that Senator Ribicoff's version of FAP failed among Democrats as well. The only category that favoured it were the 'Liberals', 14 to 1. The 'Regulars', 'Centrists', and 'Traditionalists' were all opposed (6 to 4, 12 to 1, and 9 nil). Reichley, *op. cit.*, 150–1. Cf. Moynihan, *op. cit.*, 127.

11 See M. Stanton Evans' salute to Reagan and Carleson in 'Dark horses', *National Review*, 30, 23 June 1978: 793.

12 This proposal has made the otherwise much applauded economist suspect among some libertarians, and Friedman has returned the favour by refusing to characterize his views as libertarian. Cf. Reichley, *op. cit.*, 135.

13 Reichley, *op. cit.*, 151–2. Cf. David Stockman (1985) *The Triumph of Politics: The Crisis in American Government and How It Affects the World*, New York: Harper & Row: 110–11.

14 Cannon, *op. cit.*, 202–7.

15 Richard Williamson (1981) '1980: the Reagan Campaign – harbinger of a revised federalism', *Publius: The Journal of Federalism*, 11, summer: 149–50.

16 Structural reforms were much more popular than the cuts in anti-poverty programmes. Cf. John Robinson and John Fleishman (1984) 'Ideological trends in American public opinion', *Annals of the American Academy of Political and Social Science*, 472, March: 56–60; (1981) 'Public receptive to New Federalism', *Gallup Report*: 2–9.

17 Cf. Robert Pear (1982) '3 key aides reshape welfare policy', *New York Times*, 26 April; on AFDC, Linda Demkovich (1982) 'Medicaid for welfare; a controversial swap', *National Journal (NJ)*: 363; on CDBG, Catherine Lovell (1983) 'CDBG: the role of federal requirements', *Publius: The Journal of Federalism* 13: 94; on hunger, Linda Demkovich (1983) 'Hunger in America: is its resurgence real or is evidence exaggerated?', *NJ*: 2051; on Social Security, Linda Demkovich (1982) 'Team player Schweiker may be paying a high price for loyalty to Reagan', *NJ*: 849; on Medicaid, (1982) 'A weekly checklist of major issues', *NJ*: 303; on urban policy, (1982) 'Inside Washington', *NJ*: 1119; and on ending federal programmes for the cities, (1981) *Nation's Cities Weekly*, 4 (1) 25 May: 1–2.

18 Robert Carleson and Kevin R. Hopkins (1981) 'Whose responsibility is social responsibility? The Reagan rationale', *Public Welfare*, 8, fall: 9, 13–14. Cf. Associated Press (1986) 'Reagan blasts welfare programs', 16 February. Reagan cites his experience as Governor in instituting a Workfare programme that allegedly put 76,000 welfare recipients into private jobs as a model for the nation. The success

of that programme, and the numbers involved, are sharply disputed. See *New York Times* (1986) 'Reagan's 70's program of "Workfare" disputed', 12 April. However, the notion of linking welfare to work has been tried with some success in other states – the limit is the availability of jobs.

19 Public Welfare (1981) 'Whose responsibility is social responsibility? An opposing view', 8, fall: 9.

20 Stockman, *op. cit.*, 24.

21 In Claude Barfield (1981) *Rethinking Federalism*, Washington, DC: American Enterprise Institute: 81. About Carleson see *National Journal* (1982) 'A weekly checklist of major issues', 7: 268. Cf. *Nation's Business* (1973) 'Lightening the welfare load', August: 17 *et seq.*

22 In James Reston (1984) 'Discussing the bugs in the machinery', an interview with David A. Stockman, *New York Times*, 12 April. Cf. Barfield, *op. cit.*: 82; Stockman (1975) 'The social pork barrel', *Public Interest*, 39, spring: 3–30.

23 In his account of his intellectual odyssey through Marxism to 'intellectual conservatism', Stockman at one point describes himself as a libertarian. However, he also claims to be an 'idealist' as well – a combination that, in policy terms, comes out as traditional conservatism on questions of governmental benefits and libertarianism on matters of social and economic regulation. See David Stockman, *op. cit.*, 40, 49. Cf. William Greider (1981) 'The education of David Stockman', *Atlantic Monthly*, December: 51–2.

24 See William Greider, *op. cit.*, 27–54. Cf. David Stockman, *op. cit.*, 6.

25 Richard Williamson (1983) 'The 1982 New Federalism negotiations', *Publius: The Journal of Federalism*, 13: 27–8.

26 John Kessel (1984) 'The structures of the Reagan White House', *American Journal of Political Science*, 28 (2): 235–6.

27 Stockman, *op. cit.*, 40, 323, 347–8, 363–4.

28 Cannon, *op. cit.*, 194.

29 However, the safety net is of smaller size in Reagan's view. The Urban Institute reported that changes proposed in Reagan's 1981 budget document would have cut programmes for 'early retirees, disabled workers or retiree's dependent children under Social Security; workers unemployed longer than thirteen weeks; the typical welfare recipient (who has income other than welfare); and recipients of noncash aid regardless of their income'. Cited in Ronnie Dugger (1983) *On Reagan: The Man and his Presidency*, New York: McGraw-Hill: 301.

30 Stephen Gettinger (1986) 'Partisanship hit new high in 99th Congress', *Congressional Quarterly Weekly Reports*, 44 (46), 15 November: 2901–6.

31 Steve Blakely (1986) 'Conservatives: a rise in unity but not victories', *Congressional Quarterly Weekly Report*, 44 (46), 15 November: 2907–12.

32 Julie Rovner (1987) 'Reagan endorses revised GOP welfare plan', *Congressional Quarterly Weekly Report*, 45 (32), 8 August: 1811.

33 Benjamin Ward (1979) *The Conservative Economic World View*, New York: Basic Books: 29.

34 See *Wall Street Journal* (1981) 'Change in mood: wave of mergers stirs only mild opposition, but benefits are hazy', 23 July: 1.

35 Associated Press (1982) 'FTC drops antitrust case against three cereal firms', 17 January. Cf. Steven Surdell (1984) 'Mergers under the Reagan Justice Department: redefining section 7 of the Clayton Act', *Journal of Legislation*, 11, summer: 421–40.

36 Robert Hershey (1982) 'New merger rules to scrutinize markets', *New York Times*, 2 April: 31 (note).

37 Data for *Mergers and Acquisitions Magazine*, cited in Kenneth Gilpin (1986) 'Wave of mergers likely to continue', *New York Times*, 29 December: 26.

38 Lydia Chavez (1982) 'New merger wave rolls ever stronger', *New York Times*, 14 November, sect. 3, p. Fl, col. 2.

39 Robert Hershey, *op. cit.*.

40 *New York Times* (1984) ''47 anti-trust rule disavowed', 20 June: 31.

41 *Wall Street Journal op. cit.*

42 Wallace C. Peterson (1985) 'The US "Welfare State" and the conservative counterrevolution', *Journal of Economic Issues*, 19 (3), September: 639.

43 The military build-up was also the end of the 'Reagan Revolution' in the sense that Reagan was supposed to have stood for a reduction in the cost of government. David Stockman dates the split between rhetoric and reality to 11 September 1981 when it became clear that Secretary Weinberger was to have his way on military expansion regardless of the deficit projections. See Stockman, *op. cit.*, 299.

44 Stockman, *op. cit.*, postcript to the 1987 paperback edn, New York: Avon Books: p. 449.

45 Quoted in Peter Kilborn (1987) 'Where the Reagan revolution went awry', *New York Times*, 8 November: 1. Niskanen was, until 1985, a member of the President's Council of Economic Advisers, and is now the President of the libertarian Cato Institute.

6 THE IMPACT OF CONSERVATIVE CAPITALISM IN THE UNITED STATES

1 Richard Nathan and Fred Doolittle (1984) 'Reagan's surprising domestic achievement', *Wall Street Journal*, 18 September: 28.

2 John Weicher, American Enterprise Institute (1984) 'Welfare "reforms" will stick', *Chicago Tribune*, 16 August: 27.

3 D. Lee Bawden and John Palmer (1984) 'Social policy' in Palmer and Isabel Sawhill (eds) *The Reagan Record*, Cambridge, Mass.: Ballinger Press: 201.

4 ibid., 185–6.

5 US Congress, House Committee on Ways and Means (1984) 'Effects of the Omnibus Budget Reconciliation Act of 1981 (OBRA) welfare changes and the recession on poverty', Committee Print for the Subcommittee on Oversight and Subcommittee on Public Assistance and Unemployment Compensation, US GPO, 25 July: table A.

NOTES

6 ibid., 12.
7 Marilyn Power (1984) 'Falling through the "safety net": women, economic crisis, and Reaganomics', *Feminist Studies*, 10, spring, 1: 37.
8 See Center on Budget and Policy Priorities (1984) *Taxing the Poor*, April, Washington, DC.
9 Joint Committee on Taxation (1985) 'Federal tax treatment of individuals below the poverty level' (JCS-18–85), Joint Committee print by the staff of the Committee, US GPO, 14 June: 3.
10 Congressional Budget Office projections, February 1983, cited in 'The combined effects of major changes in federal taxes and spending programs since 1981', staff memorandum, April 1984, prepared by the staff of the Human Resources and Community Development and Tax Analysis Division of the Congressional Budget Office.
11 *Newsweek*, 9 September 1985: 24. This is the lowest percentage recorded for the bottom 40 per cent since the Census Bureau began collecting this data in 1947.
12 Joint Economic Committee, 99th Cong., 1st sess. (1985) 'Family income in America', 28 November. Cf. Sheldon Danziger and Peter Gottschalk (1986) 'Families with children have fared worst', *Challenge*, 29, March-April: 40–7.
13 Robert Pear (1987) 'Poverty rate dips as the median family income rises', *New York Times*, 31 July: 12.
14 Marilyn Moon and Isabel Sawhill (1984) 'Family incomes: gainers and losers' in Palmer and Sawhill, *op. cit.*, table 10.5, p. 329, and table 10.6, p. 333.
15 Sheldon Danziger and Peter Gottschalk (1987) 'Renewing the war on poverty: target support at children and families', *New York Times*, 22 March, sect. F, p. 2.
16 Sheldon Danziger and Peter Gottschalk (1985) 'The impact of budget cuts and economic conditions on poverty', *Journal of Public Policy Analysis and Management*: 587–93.
17 Reported by the Associated Press (1986) 'Mayors seek federal aid to curb poverty in cities', in the *New York Times*, 19 December: 15.
18 ibid.
19 Sheldon Danziger and Peter Gottschalk (1983) 'The measurement of poverty', *American Behavioral Scientist*, 26 (6), July/August: 739.
20 Joann Lublin (1984) 'Declining housing aid worsens the struggle for many poor people', *Wall Street Journal*, 204 (44), 31 August: 1, 10.
21 Observation by Molly Orshansky, cited in Harrison Donnelly (1981) 'Experts differ on how many are poor', *Congressional Quarterly Weekly Report*, 39, 18 April: 669.
22 Wallace C. Peterson (1985) 'The US "Welfare State" and the Counterrevolution', *Journal of Economic Issues*, 19 (3), September: table 6, p. 618.
23 'Tax burden found to rise for the poor', Milwaukee Journal, 11 November 1987: 1, 6. The study was carried out by the Congressional Budget Office.
24 *AFL-CIO News* (1986), 31 (28), 12 July: 1.

---

25 Cf. Louis Uchitelle (1987) 'America's army of non-workers', *New York Times*, 27 September: 1.
26 Kenneth Noble (1985) 'Study finds 60 per cent of 11 million who lost jobs got new ones', *New York Times*, 6 February.
27 Jim Hightower (1987) 'Where greed, unofficially blessed by Reagan, has led', *New York Times*, 21 June: sect. E, p. 25.
28 ibid. Cf. Susan Shank and Steven Haugen (1987) 'The employment situation during 1986: job gains continue, unemployment dips', *Monthly Labor Review*, US Department of Labor, Bureau of Labor Statistics, 110 (2), February: 3–10.
29 Barry Bluestone and Bennett Harrison (1986) 'The great American job machine: the proliferation of low-wage employment in the US economy', a study prepared for the Joint Economic Committee of the US Congress, December 1986. The number of poor people who live on welfare has increased by 19 per cent since 1975, while the number of *working* poor has increased by 52 per cent – almost all of it since 1979. See 'America's hidden poor', *US News and World Report*, 11 January 1988: 20.
30 Sheldon Danziger 'Families with children have fared worst': 44.
31 John Herbers (1987) 'Poverty of Blacks spreads in cities', *New York Times*, 26 January: 1, 13.
32 See, for example, Charles A. Murray (1983) 'The two wars against poverty: economic growth and the Great Society', *Public Interest*, fall: 3–16.
33 A summary of recent research on this dilemma may be found in Jan Mason, John Wodarksi, and T. M. Jim Parham (1985) 'Work and welfare: a re-evaluation of AFDC', *Social Work*, 30 (3): 200–1.
34 Marilyn Power, *op. cit.*, 43–4.
35 Wallace C. Peterson, *op. cit.*: table 1, p. 606.
36 See Robert Pear (1987) 'Reagan's critics', *New York Times*, 22 October, 1. Also James Lebherz (1986) 'US falling deeper into debt', *Washington Post*, 13 July.
37 Cf. Wallace C. Peterson, *op. cit.*, 611–12.
38 Elizabeth Wehr (1986) 'Gramm-Rudman both disappoints and succeeds', *Congressional Quarterly Weekly Reports*, 44 (46): 2881.
39 See David Stockman (1986) *The Triumph of Politics*, New York: Harper & Row: 231, 250, 403, 409–10.
40 David Stockman (1975) 'The social pork barrel', *Public Interest*, 39, spring: 27.
41 William Greider (1981) 'The education of David Stockman', *Atlantic Monthly*, December: 50.
42 Paul Blustein (1986) 'Stockman terms Regan "destructive" as Reagan adviser', *Wall Street Journal*, 21 April: 30. Cf. *Wall Street Journal* (1986) 'Goodbye to all that', editorial, 11 July: 24.
43 In the galley proofs of Stockman's book the point is made even more strongly: 'The $800 billion worth of deficits *were the results of* his [Reagan's] deficit spending [emphasis mine].' That comment, along with several others critical of administration officials, was softened in a

final editing by Mr Stockman. See Sidney Blumenthal (1986) 'Stockman, cutting the unkindest', *Washington Post*, 15 July. Reagan, however, proposed major cuts in welfare programmes in his 1986 budget – both parties in Congress rejected his proposals.

44 Stockman, *The Triumph of Politics*: 250.

45 Leonard Silk (1986) 'Stockman role in "Revolution" ', *New York Times*, 16 April: D2.

46 John Cranford (1987) 'Trade bill: partial remedy for complex problem', *Congressional Quarterly Weekly Reports*, 45 (17), 25 April: 769.

47 Senator Dole, then Republican Senate Majority leader, criticized the Reagan administration's 1983 effort to revive the New Federalism agenda by consolidating various low- and moderate-income-assistance proposals into four block grants on the grounds that important federal programmes, such as maternal and child-health services, could be undermined if they were 'shuffled off into some block grant'. Cited in Robert Pear (1983) 'Stockman calls revenue sharing best way to aid poor and jobless', *New York Times*, 5 March: 9.

48 Cited in Rich Jaroslovsky (1982) 'White House strives to combat the feeling that Reagan is unfair', *Wall Street Journal*, 10 June: 1.

49 William Woodside (1986) 'For the record', excerpts reported in the *Washington Post*, 18 July, from a speech given at a Greater Washington Research Center luncheon, 17 June 1986.

50 Reported in the *New York Times* (1986) 'Catholic bishops say US must do more for the poor', 13 November: 1.

51 Washington Post News Service (1986) 'Huge Black-White wealth gap found', 10 July.

52 Based on Justice Department data.

53 See Robert Pear (1982) 'Questions and answers on helping the "truly needy" ', *New York Times*, 2 April.

54 ibid.

55 See US Advisory Commission on Intergovernmental Relations (ACIR) (1984) *Significant Features of Fiscal Federalism, 1984 Edition*. Cf. Kenneth Palmer and Alex Pattakos (1985) 'The state of American Federalism: 1984', *Publius: The Journal of Federalism*, 15, summer: 1–17.

56 See Palmer and Pattakos, *op. cit.*, 2.

57 From an estimated $98.8 billion in fiscal year 1984 to $102.2 billion in fiscal year 1985. See Palmer and Pattakos, *op. cit.*, 6.

58 Sarah Liebschutz (1985) 'The national minimum drinking-age law', *Publius: The Journal of Federalism*, 15, summer: 39–51.

59 Susan Golonka (1985) 'Whatever happened to Federalism?', *Intergovernmental Perspective*, 11, winter: 14.

60 David Beam and Margaret Wrightson (1984) 'Intergovernmental regulatory relief: the fourth face of the New Federalism', paper presented at the 1985 American Political Science Association Convention, Washington, DC, 2 September.

61 Timothy Conlan (1986) 'Federalism and competing values in the

Reagan administration', *Publius: The Journal of Federalism*, 16, winter: 37.

62 ibid., 38–9.

63 US Conference of Governors (1986) 'Federalism and the States, 1986', February.

64 James Perry (1987) 'Controversial as ever, Mrs Thatcher begins drive for third term', *Wall Street Journal*, 68 (147), 12 May: 1, 20.

65 See Palmer and Pattakos, *op. cit.*, 4–5, 13. Cf. US ACIR (1984) *op. cit.*

66 See Debra Stewart (1985) 'State and local initiatives in the federal system, *Publius: The Journal of Federalism*, 15, summer: 81–95.

67 John Herbers (1988) 'The new federalism: unplanned, innovative, and here to stay', *Governing the States and Localities* (Congressional Quarterly), 1 (1): 33.

68 Cf. 'High tide for conservatives, but some fear what follows', *New York Times*, 13 October 1987: 1.

7 THE RISE OF CONSERVATIVE CAPITALISM IN BRITAIN

1 Although one has to remember that Mr Heath came to power in 1970 on a vigorously free-market anti-lame-duck industrial policy and it was only in 1972 that the pressure of events led to a fundamental change in direction, Lord Blake in his *The Conservative Party from Peel to Thatcher*, London: Fontana, 1985, argues that the origins of Thatcherism lay in Heathism before 1972 but does go on to say that 'There has been a real change in Conservative ideology since the 1964 election', p. 367.

2 See A. T. Peacock and J. Wiseman (1967) *The Growth of Public Expenditure in the United Kingdom*, New York: Oxford University Press, and the *Annual Register of Statistics*, 117, London: HMSO.

3 Taken from W. H. Greenleaf (1983) *The Rise of Collectivism*, vol. 1 of *The British Political Tradition*, London: Methuen: 36.

4 A. J. P. Taylor (1965) *English History 1914–45*, London: Oxford University Press: 1.

5 Keith Joseph (1976) *Stranded on the Middle Ground*, London: Centre for Policy Studies: 28.

6 Keith Joseph (no date) *Monetarism is Not Enough*, London: Centre for Policy Studies: 8.

7 Nigel Lawson (1980) *The New Conservatism*, London: Centre for Policy Studies: 10.

8 ibid., 11.

9 Peacock and Wiseman, *op. cit.*

10 R. A. Butler (1947) *About the Industrial Charter*, London: Conservative Political Centre: 6.

11 In 1987 the Chancellor, Mr Lawson, effectively downgraded the Council.

12 Joseph, *Monetarism is Not Enough*: 7.

13 Lawson, *op. cit.*, 12.

14 Joseph, *Monetarism is Not Enough*: 9.
15 Lawson, *op. cit.*, 3.
16 Enoch Powell and Angus Maude (1954) *Change is Our Ally*, London: Conservative Political Centre: 25–6.
17 Anthony Crosland (1956) *The Future of Socialism*, London: Jonathan Cape. For an assessment of Crosland's contribution to British socialism in the postwar period, see D. Lipsey and D. Leonard (1981) *The Socialist Agenda: Crosland's Legacy*, London: Jonathan Cape.
18 The so-called Barber Boom, after the Chancellor Anthony Barber, now Lord Barber.
19 *Labour Party Conference Record* (1976) London.
20 The letter contained the following important passage which should be read in conjunction with chapter 2 of the current work:

> The Government intends in the years ahead a continuing and substantial reduction in the share of resources taken by public expenditure. It is also part of the strategy to reduce the public sector borrowing requirement so as to establish a monetary condition which will help the growth in output.

Quoted in S. Brittan (1983) *The Role and Limits of Government*, London: Temple Smith: 239. There is no doubt that monetarist views were brought towards the centre of the political agenda by the 1976–9 Callaghan government.
21 Joseph, *Stranded on the Middle Ground*: passim.
22 Joseph, *Monetarism is Not Enough*: 13.
23 ibid., 14.
24 See the judgement of Lord Blake cited in note 1.

8 THE IMPLEMENTATION OF CONSERVATIVE CAPITALISM IN BRITAIN

1 *Financial Statement and Budget Report, 1980–81* (1980) London: HMSO.
2 S. Brittan (1983) *The Role and Limits of Government*, London: Temple Smith: 248.
3 *Report of the Treasury and Civil Service Select Committee* (1982) December.
4 *Sunday Express* (1983) 9 October.
5 *Independent* (1987) 24 July.
6 Samuel Brittan (1987) 'The economy: traumatic rather than radical' in (1987) *The Thatcher Years*, London: *Financial Times*.
7 *The Times* (1982) 30 June and (1983) 7 October.
8 For a very good discussion indeed by a radical free marketeer, see John Burton (1985) *Why No Cuts?*, London: Institute of Economic Affairs.
9 E. G. Patrick Minford (1984) 'State expenditure: a study in waste', *Economic Affairs*, 4 (3).
10 See Burton, *op. cit.*, 88. He also gives examples of the same thing from the United States.
11 Peter Riddell (1985) *The Thatcher Government*, Oxford: Blackwell: 154.

12 See the discussion in chapter 3.
13 See S. Brittan, *The Role and Limits of Government*: passim.
14 For further discussion see chapter 12.
15 Milton Friedman and Rose Friedman (1980) *Free to Choose*, New York: Avon and London: Secker & Warburg and Penguin: chapter 6.
16 For this argument see the speech by Mrs Rumbold, Minister of State at the Department of Education, reported in the *Independent*, 30 July 1987.
17 For a leftwing view of vouchers in an American context, see B. Barber (1984) *Strong Democracy*, Berkeley: University of California Press: chapter 10.
18 For further detail see Riddell, *op. cit.*, 148.

9 PRIVATIZATION IN BRITAIN

1 John Moore (1986) 'The success of privatisation' in J. Kay, C. Mayer, and D. Thompson (eds) *Privatisation and Deregulation*, Oxford: Oxford University Press: 94.
2 See the critique of bureaucracy in chapter 3.
3 Moore, *op. cit.*, 95.
4 M. Beesley and S. Littlechild (1986) 'Privatisation: problems and priorities' in Kay, Mayer, and Thompson, *op. cit.*, 43.
5 Compare Moore, *op. cit.*, 89:

> Public sector trades unions' experience of previous administrations has given their leaders a taste of political power without responsibility. They are all too ready to seek to involve government in the interests of their own political objectives if not in the interests of their members. Privatisation decisively breaks this political link.

6 ibid., 83.
7 Cited in chapter 3. See also Keith Joseph (no date) *Monetarism is Not Enough*, London: Centre for Policy Studies: 14.
8 Moore, *op. cit.*, 89.
9 Quoted in *The Thatcher Years*, London: Financial Times: p. 46.
10 ibid., 46–7.

10 THE MARKET AND THE STATE

1 F. A. Hayek (1979) *The Mirage of Social Justice*, vol. 2 of *Law, Legislation and Liberty*, London: Routledge & Kegan Paul: passim.
2 See R. Plant (1985) 'Welfare and the value of liberty' in *Government and Opposition*, 20 (3).
3 F. A. Hayek (1960) *The Constitution of Liberty*, London: Routledge, 136.
4 ibid., 129.
5 John Rawls (1972) *A Theory of Justice*, Cambridge, Mass.: Harvard University Press: 204.
6 G. B. MacCallum (1967) 'Negative and positive freedom', *Philosophical Review*, 76.
7 For a more detailed elaboration of these ideas, reference could be

made to A. Gewirth (1978) *Reason and Morality*, Chicago: University of Chicago Press; R. Plant, H. Lesser, and P. Taylor-Gooby (1981), *Political Philosophy and Social Welfare: Essays on the Normative Basis of Welfare Provision*, London: Routledge & Kegan Paul; R. Plant (1985) 'Needs, agency, and rights in law' in D. Galligan and C. Sampford (eds) (1985) *Rights and the Welfare State*, London: Croom Helm. For a political interpretation see Roy Hattersley (1987) *Choose Freedom*, London: Penguin.

8 ibid.
9 The issues at stake here go back a very long way. Hegel probably first identified clearly the problem of a common citizenship against a background of material inequality. Vide R. Plant (1983) *Hegel*, Oxford: Blackwell: chapter 9.
10 John Rawls, *op. cit.*, 226.
11 For a discussion see T. Morris (1980) 'The crimes of the powerful' in A. Bottoms and R. Preston (eds) (1980) *The Coming Penal Crisis*, Glasgow: Scottish Academic Press.
12 R. Plant (1984) *Equality, Markets and the State*, Fabian Society pamphlet.
13 David Green (1987) *The New Right*, New York: St Martin's Press and London: Macmillan.
14 ibid., 128.
15 ibid.
16 Treasury Green Paper (1984) Cmnd 9189, London: HMSO: 14.
17 For the salience of Rawls' ideas to Labour Party views about social justice, see R. Plant (1981) 'Democratic socialism and equality' in D. Leonard and D. Lipsey (1981) *The Socialist Agenda: Crosland's Legacy*, London, Jonathan Cape; Anthony Crosland (1974) *Socialism Now and Other Essays*, London: Cape; Bryan Gould (1985) *Socialism and Freedom*, London: Macmillan; Roy Hattersley (1987) *Choose Freedom*, Harmondsworth: Penguin.
18 Of course, free-market critics will argue that this cannot be done, because no consensus will be available about the limits of welfare. The conservative has as much of a problem securing consensus about the minimum level of welfare expenditure, given that this is supposed to go beyond the bare prevention of destitution.
19 Sir Keith Joseph and Jonathan Sumption (1979) *Equality*, London: Murray: 29:

> Equality of opportunity is a neutral concept. It does not set up any particular social arrangement as a desirable goal but merely requires the absence of artificial constraints on individual achievement.

20 As such, it is defended by Hayek, *The Mirage of Social Justice*; Milton Friedman and Rose Friedman (1980) *Free to Choose: A Personal Statement*, New York: Avon and London: Secker & Warburg and Penguin; Margaret Thatcher (1977) *Let Our Children Grow Tall*, London: Centre for Policy Studies; Joseph and Sumption, *op. cit.*.
21 Sir Keith Joseph and Jonathan Sumption, trading on the work of

Coleman and Jencks in the United States, argue that 'At no point in their lives are men equal in ability and capacity to exploit the opportunities which all equally enjoy. Nor at any time in their lives can they be made to do so'. *op. cit.*, 35. (J. Coleman (1973) 'Equality of opportunity and equality of results', *Harvard Educational Review*, 43. C. Jencks (1972) *A Reassessment of the Effects of Family and Schooling in America*, London: Allen Lane.)

22 This is the Jencks argument that Joseph rejects. He calls it an ideological argument. This seems odd, given the usual hostility of the right to labelling arguments as ideological (see Kenneth Minogue (1986) *Alien Powers: The Pure Theory of Ideology*, New York: St Martin's Press). It is, in fact, a straightforward moral argument about how far people should derive benefits or suffer burdens as the result of factors such as genetic endowment or fortunate family background for which they bear little or no responsibility. See Rawls, *op. cit.*, passim, and Anthony Crosland, *The Future of Socialism*, passim.

23 As is argued by Rawls and Crosland. See Plant, *Democratic Socialism and Equality*; Plant (1984) *Equality, Markets and the State*, London: Fabian Society; Bernard Crick (1987) *Socialism*, Milton Keynes: Open University Press.

24 J. Le Grand (1982) *The Strategy of Equality*, London: Allen & Unwin.

25 Anthony Crosland, *The Future of Socialism*, passim.

26 ibid.

27 Rawls, *op. cit.*, 102; Crosland, *The Future of Socialism*: 144, 168; Crosland, *Socialism Now and Other Essays*: 15.

28 Compare Thatcher, *op. cit.*, passim.

29 See Joseph and Sumption, *op. cit.*.

30 Joseph and Sumption, *op. cit.*. What renders a particular distribution of wealth fair or unfair is not the distribution itself, but how it arose. Since inequality arises from the operation of innumerable preferences, it cannot be evil, unless the preferences are themselves evil. This view is clearly indebted to Robert Nozick (1973) *Anarchy, State and Utopia*, particularly the celebrated Wilt Chamberlain example which is designed to show that the end-state or patterned principles of social justice are not compatible with the free exercise of choice. Joseph and Sumption do not use Nozick's own example but invent a parallel one, namely Geebert von Charabanc, a celebrated musician who derived similar benefits from the free play of preferences as Nozick's Wilt Chamberlain.

31 Note that Joseph and Sumption regard this outcome as just.

32 For further discussion of this central issue, see G. A. Cohen (1978) 'Robert Nozick and Wilt Chamberlain: how patterns preserve liberty' in J. Arthur and W. H. Shaw (eds) (1978) *Justice and Economic Distribution*, Englewood Cliffs, NJ: Prentice-Hall.

33 F. Hirsch (1977) *The Social Limits to Growth*, London: Routledge & Kegan Paul: 182; R. Plant (1983) 'Hirsch, Hayek, and Habermas: dilemmas of distribution' in A. Ellis and K. Kumar (eds) (1983)

Dilemmas of Liberal Democracies, London and New York: Tavistock: 45–64.

34 J. Goldthorpe (1974) 'Social inequality and society integration' in D. Wedderburn (ed.) (1974) *Poverty, Inequality and Class Structure*, Cambridge: Cambridge University Press: 228.

35 Samuel Brittan (1977) *Economic Consequences of Democracy*, London: M. T. Smith: 272. For an argument about the role of political philosophy in grounding judgements about distribution, see R. Dahl (1982) *Dilemmas of Pluralist Democracies*, New Haven: Yale University Press.

36 I. Kristol (1970) 'When virtue loses all her loveliness', *The Public Interest*, 21: 250–1.

37 Hayek, *The Mirage of Social Justice*: 74.

38 R. Titmuss (1971) *The Gift Relationship*, London: Allen & Unwin.

39 Ian Gilmour (1978) *Inside Right*, London: Quartet: 117.

40 Christopher Lasch (1986) in *New Statesman*, 29 August; (1980) *The Culture of Narcissism*, London: Abacus.

41 In August 1987 the Centre for Policy Studies published a pamphlet on Victorian values which is a good indication of the way in which the right is concerned to reject the applicability of values to the market mechanism, while seeking to encourage a particular set of values in private life.

11 A VIEW FROM THE LEFT: THE UNITED STATES

1 Gar Alperovitz and Jeff Faux (1984) *Rebuilding America: A Blueprint for the New Economy*, New York: Pantheon: 77–8.

2 Sheldon Danziger and Eugene Smolensky (eds) (1985) 'Income transfer policies and the poor: a cross-national perspective', *Journal of Social Policy* (special issue) 14 (2), July: introduction, p. 259. The reference is to studies by Michael O'Higgins of Great Britain and Danziger, Gottschalk, and Smolensky in the same issue.

3 ibid., 262.

4 Wallace C. Peterson and Paul S. Estenson (1985) 'The recovery: supply-side or Keynesian?', *Journal of Post Keynesian Economics*, 7 (4), summer: 447–62.

5 See Peter Gottschalk and Terry Malone (1985) 'Involuntary terminations, unemployment and job matching – a test of job search theory', *Journal of Labor Economics*, 3 (2): 102–23. Cf. Peter Gottschalk (1982) 'Earnings mobility – permanent change or transitory fluctuations', *Review of Economics and Statistics*, 64 (3): 450–6.

6 Peterson and Estenson, *op. cit.*, 461.

7 For a discussion of the 'arithmetic' politics of Reagan in forming a coalition, see Joel Krieger (1986) *Reagan, Thatcher, and the Politics of Decline*, New York: Oxford University Press: 150–1.

8 The percentage of people in the Harris Poll who think that government can be trusted to 'do what is right' most of the time or always increased from 25 per cent in 1980 to 45 per cent in 1984, an improvement to be sure, though the level in 1972 was 61 per cent,

and in 1964 it was 76 per cent. David Gergen (1985) 'Following the leaders', *Public Opinion*, 8 (3), June/July: 16–57.
9 Seymour Martin Lipset (1986) 'The anomalies of American politics', *PS*, 2, spring: 229. Cf. Gergen, *op. cit.*, 55–6.
10 Cited in John Dillin (1983) 'The ideological struggle for control of the Republican Party', *Christian Science Monitor*, 22 December: 3, 5.
11 Murray Edelman (1971) *Political as Symbolic Action: Mass Arousal and Quiescence*, Chicago: Markham: especially 4–7, 23–4, 56–61, 82–3, 180–1.
12 Cf. Murray Edelman (1964) *The Symbolic Uses of Politics*, Urbana, Ill.: University of Illinois Press: 30–4.
13 David Stockman's postscript to the paperback edition (1987) of *The Triumph of Politics*, New York: Avon, as reported by the Washington Post News Service, 'Stockman takes new swipe at Reagan' in the *Milwaukee Journal*, 28 December 1986: 4a.
14 While the Democrats were regaining control of the Senate in the 1986 elections, they were also losing a number of important governorships.
15 Samuel Bowles and Herbert Gintis (1982) 'The crisis of liberal democratic capitalism: the case of the United States', *Politics and Society*, 2: 1, 61–4.
16 This is the general argument of Bowles and Gintis, Przeworski and Wallerstein, and others. Cf. Helene Slessarev (1984) 'Two Great Society programs in an age of Reaganomics', paper presented to the Midwest Political Science Convention, April 1984: 3–5. The argument is placed in the context of response to economic decline by Joel Krieger (1986) *Reagan, Thatcher and the Politics of Decline*, New York: Oxford University Press: 139.
17 Cf. British traditionalist Roger Scruton (1980) *The Meaning of Conservatism*, Totowa, NJ: Barnes & Noble: 127–8, and American traditionalist Russell Kirk (1962) 'The problem of community' in *A Program for Conservatives*, Chicago: Regnery: chapter 6, 140–2.
18 This argument is developed by Ben Fine and Laurence Harris (1985) *The Peculiarities of the British Economy*, London: Lawrence & Wishart.
19 Cf. Andrew Gamble (1981) *Britain in Decline: Economic Policy, Political Strategy and the British State*, Boston: Beacon Press: 220.
20 Cf. Patrick Wright (1985) *On Living in an Old Country*, London: Verso New Left Books.
21 See 'Laxalt moving closer to candidacy' (1986) *Washington Post* Writers Group, 29 July: 8.
22 Jan Mason, John Wodarski, and T. M. Jim Parham (1985) 'Work and welfare: a re-evaluation of AFDC', *Social Work*, 30 (3): 197–9.
23 For a fuller exploration of the relationships between identity and politics, see Kenneth Hoover (1976) *A Politics of Identity*, Urbana, Ill.: University of Illinois Press: especially chapters 5 and 6. Cf. Sheldon Wolin (1976) 'The New Conservatives', *New York Review of Books*, 5 February: 6–11.
24 Sheldon Wolin, *op. cit.*, 6, 8.
25 For a thorough summary and analysis of the reasons why government

is seen as less just than the market-place, see Robert Lane (1986) 'Market justice, political justice', *American Political Science Review*, 80 (2), June: 383–402.

26 Lane, *op. cit.*, 392.
27 ibid.
28 Seymour Martin Lipset (1986) 'The anomalies of American politics', *PS*, 19 (2), spring: 228. Cf. Lipset (1979) *The First New Nation: The United States in Historical and Comparative Perspective*, New York: Norton.
29 Lane, *op. cit.*, 389, 391, 399.
30 C. B. Macpherson (1965) *The Real World of Democracy*, New York: Oxford University Press: 54, makes the point:

> Human beings are sufficiently unequal in strength and skill that if you put them into an unlimited contest for possessions, some will not only get more than others, but will get control of the means of labour to which the others must have access. The others then cannot be fully human even in the restricted sense of being able to get possessions, let alone in the original sense of being able to use their faculties in purposive creative activity. So in choosing to make the essence of man the striving for possessions, we make it impossible for many men to be fully human.

31 On the ambivalence of public opinion, see the discussion of thirty years of National Opinion Research Center data in Daniel Patrick Moynihan (1973) *The Politics of a Guaranteed Income*, New York: Vintage: 87.
32 Several of these alternatives are explored by Martin Carnoy, Derek Shearer, and Russell Rumberger (1983) *A New Social Contract*, New York: Harper & Row: chapters 7 and 8; and by Kenneth Dolbeare (1984) *Democracy at Risk: The Politics of Economic Renewal*, Chatham, NJ: Chatham House: chapters 7–10.
33 In Lane, *op. cit.*: 392.
34 In US Advisory Commission on Intergovernmental Relations (ACIR) (1984) *1984 Changing Public Attitudes on Government and Taxes*, S-13, Washington, DC: US Government Printing Office: 3, table 4.
35 On the productivity of non-defence governmental investments in jobs, see the data assembled by Marton Carnoy, Derek Shearer, and Russell Rumberger in *op. cit.*, 160–5.
36 Reported by the Congressional Budget Office based on data in the Budget of the United States Government in 'AFL-CIO reviews the issues', Report no. 8, 14 November 1986: 2.
37 See Daniel Patrick Moynihan (1973) *The Politics of a Guaranteed Income*, New York: Vintage: 131.
38 Recommended in 'The family: preserving America's future', a Reagan Administration report cited in Associated Press (1986) 'Democrats assail White House report on the family', 14 November.
39 Data from a staff study prepared for the Joint Economic Committee of Congress and reported to David Perlman (1987) 'Faltering economy drives families into poverty', *AFL-CIO*, 3 January: 1.

40 There is an intriguing example of how producer co-operatives can work in the more than sixty industrial co-operatives found in Mondragon in the Basque country of northern Spain. Henk Thomas and Chris Logan (1982) *Mondragon*, London: Allen & Unwin.

41 For an assessment of producer co-operatives see Jenny Thornley (1982) *Workers' Co-operatives: Jobs and Dreams*, London: Heinemann Educational; Thomas and Logan, *op. cit.*; Saul Estrin, Derek Jones, and Jan Svejnar (1987) 'The productivity effects of worker participation: producer co-operatives in western economies', *Journal of Comparative Economics*, 11: 40–61; and Keith Bradley (1986) 'Employee-ownership and economic decline in western industrial democracies', *Journal of Management Studies*, 23 (1), January: 51–71.

42 See Robert Zager (1978) 'Managing guaranteed employment', *Harvard Business Review*, 56 (3): 103–15.

43 See Thomas Peters and Robert Waterman, Jr, (1982) *In Search of Excellence: Lessons from America's Best Run Companies*, New York: Harper & Row.

44 Moynihan, *op. cit.*, 17.

45 Moynihan, *op. cit.*, 22.

46 Krieger, *op. cit.*, 137–9.

47 The principal content for the concept of human development discussed here is provided by Erik Erikson (1953) *Childhood and Society*, New York: Norton, and (1968) *Identity: Youth and Crisis*, New York: Norton. For a more specific discussion of the political implications of these ideas, see Hoover, *op. cit.*, chapters 5 and 6.

48 Lane, *op. cit.*, 385.

49 US ACIR, *op. cit.*, table 6, p. 5.

50 Theodore Lowi (1979) *The End of Liberalism: The Second Republic of the United States*, New York: Norton.

51 Lane, *op. cit.*, 390–1.

52 US Congress, Joint Economic Committee (1986) 'The concentration of wealth in the United States: trends in the distribution of wealth among American families', by the Democratic staff of the Joint Economic Committee, based on data, analysis, and additional assistance provided by James D. Smith, Program Director, Economic Behavior Program, Survey Research Center, University of Michigan, July. Data drawn from US Federal Reserve studies and the US Census Bureau's *Current Population Reports*.

53 ibid., 36. There was considerable controversy over the publication of this study since part of it emphasized the sharply increased rate of wealth holding among the top half of 1 per cent (the 'super rich' in the Committee's terms). A task force was organized by the Treasury Department to discredit the study and it was claimed that there was an error in data collection for this category. The study was re-issued by the Federal Reserve, though without including any data from families worth more than $60 million, considerably below the assets of the *Fortune* five-hundred-richest-families list. Consequently we have not reported the findings concerning the top *half* of 1 per cent. This

additional information was provided by Scott Lilly, Staff Director for the Joint Economic Committee.

54 US Congress, Join Economic Committee, *op. cit.*, 23.
55 ibid., 29.
56 The pretransfer poverty rate is about where it was in 1965. Sheldon Danziger and Peter Gottschalk (1983) 'The measurement of poverty', *American Behavioral Scientist*, 26 (6), July/August: 753–4. Cf. Danziger and Gottschalk (1987) 'Renewing the war on poverty: target support at children and families', *New York Times*, 22 March: sect. F, p. 2.
57 Gamble, *op. cit.*, 223.
58 Krieger, *op. cit.*, 189.
59 Lewis Hyde (1979) *The Gift: Imagination and the Erotic Life of Property*, New York: Vintage: 38–9.

12 A VIEW FROM THE LEFT: GREAT BRITAIN

1 *Guardian*, 11 June 1987.
2 F. Hirsch (1977) *The Social Limits to Growth*, London: Routledge & Kegan Paul.
3 A. Walker and C. Walker (1987) *The Growing Divide: A Social Audit 1979–1987*, London: Child Poverty Action Group: 8.
4 *Hansard*, House of Commons debates, 6 April 1987, Cls 42–3.
5 Walker and Walker, *op. cit.*, 22–3.
6 ibid., 24–5.
7 ibid., 31.
8 The three tables just discussed are further analysed in Walker and Walker, *op. cit.*
9 Keith Joseph and Jonathan Sumption (1979) *Equality*, London: Murray: 35.
10 Lester Thurow (1977) 'Education and economic equality' in J. Karable and A. H. Halsey (1977) *Power and Ideology in Education*, Oxford: Oxford University Press.
11 Anthony Crosland (1956) *The Future of Socialism*, London: Jonathan Cape and (1975) *Social Democracy in Europe*, London: Fabian Society.
12 J. Le Grand (1982) *The Strategy of Equality*, London: Allen & Unwin.
13 P. Taylor Gooby (1987) 'Citizenship and welfare', in R. Jowell, S. Witherspoon, and L. Brook (eds), *British Social Attitudes: the 1987 Report*, Aldershot: Gower.
14 R. Jowell (ed.), *British Social Attitudes: the 1984 Report*, Aldershot: Gower.
15 Peter Hain (1984) *The Democratic Alternative*, Harmondsworth: Penguin.
16 Roy Hattersley (1987) *Choose Freedom*, Harmondsworth: Penguin.
17 C. Lindblom (1977) *Politics and Markets*, New York: Basic Books.
18 R. Rose and G. Peters (1978) *Can Government Go Bankrupt?*, London: Macmillan.

AFTERWORD

We will never know for certain how much the victory of the new right – both in America and in Britain – was a product of its irresistible ideas and how much it was the result of chance, high class organization, and the incompetence of its opponent. Certainly, on both sides of the Atlantic, the libertarian, radical, progressive movements were in profound disarray. The Democratic Party (rendered unrepresentative in much of its old constituency by the McGovern reforms) and Labour (similarly debilitated by the constitution changes of the early 1980s) made victory easy for Ronald Reagan and Margaret Thatcher. And welfare capitalism, in all its forms, had grown profoundly boring. It had delivered. But it had not delivered enough. The people wanted something which was more exciting. For a moment, what Kenneth Hoover and Raymond Plant call 'conservative capitalism' was seductively attractive.

In both countries, the anti-state rhetoric was often stronger than anti-state legislation. But in Britain, despite the government retaining powers which the American right equated with communism, the conscious rejection of collective responsibility and corporate action has dominated almost a full decade of legislation. Inequality is celebrated as the manifestation of a free society. The market is extolled as possessing *all* the answers to *every* economic question. Supply-side economies – interpreted as an assault on the power of the trade unions, reduction in tax rates, and the rejection of regional employment policies – are exalted whilst demand management is derided. There is a conscious and considered campaign against comprehensive welfare provision. The magic word is 'choice'. Its incantation is said to turn lead into gold and water into wine.

318

Commentators have, inevitably, related the passion of the ideological commitment to the achievement of political success. The idea that victory at the polls is no more than coincidental to the espousal of the free-market ethic is too subtle for the average British political commentator. Margaret Thatcher's victory has become the triumph for Hayek, Nozick, and von Mises. Her definition of freedom – the absence of government restraint and nothing more – has become the standard definition of liberty. The trickle-down effect – making the poor the automatic beneficiaries of increasing wealth amongst the advantaged minority – is accepted as conventional wisdom by journalists who have never examined the theory but regard the notion that vast disparities of wealth are in the interest of the over-privileged as attractive and comforting. Romantics insist that Margaret Thatcher won because she cornered the market in ideas. The corollary was, of course, that the left lost because of its intellectual bankruptcy.

The contention that the left does not possess an ideological position which matches, for consistency, coherence, and contemporary relevance, the theories of 'conservative capitalism' are clearly nonsense – at least, if it is the existence rather than the adoption of a philosophy which is regarded as important. There is a convincing theory of freedom and equality that seems tailor-made for modern radicals. The problem is the reluctance of modern radicals (at least within the United Kingdom) to adopt it. No one in Britain has done more than Raymond Plant to rehabilitate the notion that to succeed, perhaps even to survive, the Labour Party needs to possess a theoretical framework within which to build its practical policies. The creation by the radical left of its own values inevitably requires the 'critical appraisal' of the theories of the new right, which their often jejune ideas have not previously received.

Central to the argument is the role of the market. 'Until the left confronts the intellectual self-confidence of the free-market right' (p. 205), that argument will be won and lost by default. It would be foolish to pretend that, even when battle is properly joined, the confrontation will result in an easy victory for the left. The market theories of the new right possess the immense attraction of an intellectual tyranny. They are iron laws which apply in all circumstances and always produce the most beneficial results because beneficial results are defined as being what the market produces. The left is bound to take up the unheroic position that, in the pursuit of its related goals of freedom and equality, markets may sometimes be a help and may sometimes be a hindrance. It is not a theory in support of which men and women take to the streets or crouch behind barricades.

When Hoover and Plant consider 'the nature of the left's response to the changed agenda . . . away from public collective provision towards private market provision' (p. 205), they are examining a record of intellectual success but political failure. Politicians of the left, taking it for granted that they are against the market in all its forms (and in favour of something called planning, which they do not define) have never made a frontal assault on the market's moral legitimacy and all the jujus that go with it. Capitalist conservatives assert that the market being neutral, it is foolish to complain about its amoral allocation of resources. It is not neutral: it is biased in favour of the rich. And there is no reason in logic or morality why a compassionate society should not seek to change even a random system of distribution, if it unreasonably disadvantages some members of society. It is necessary for the politicians of the left to begin the destruction of the nonsensical mysticism with which the market has been surrounded.

For until they do – thus beginning to fight if not to win the battle of ideas – the voters will continue to believe in the market's supreme importance and will continue to elect the party which supports it. Hoover and Plant tell us that

> in a culture where self-interest is assumed to be the universal motivator, the intrinsic public appeal of the market-place is that in the market-place . . . self-interest is thought to be both fruitful for the common good and policed by competition. . . . Rewards in the market-place are perceived to be earned, whilst politically determined rewards are the result of 'political muscle'.
>
> (p. 245)

The left has to rehabilitate the idea of government action without reviving the calumny that it believes in an all-powerful state in which goods and services are allocated by biased and incompetent bureaucrats. The new idea is complicated, but it is essential to an ideological revival of the left. The market has to be made to work for some object, not treated as if it provided all the answers itself.

Running parallel to the argument about markets, is the dispute about citizenship and rights. The capitalist conservative will argue, with the certainty of a simple theory, that the citizen is entitled to the level of protection against external aggression and internal turmoil which allows all members of society to pursue their competitive self-interest. On the left the argument is diametrically different. Indeed, the socialist notion of freedom, far from being no more than the absence of restraint, requires the state to organize in such a way that new opportunities (crudely described as 'freedom to') are made available to all its members.

It is a wholly reputable political theory which can be justified in terms of overall efficiency as well as the extension of the sum of liberty – real liberty which provides men and women with the power to exercise their freedoms which are only theoretically available in less egalitarian societies than those which socialists hope to create. But the extensions of 'agency' – the ability to do those things which men and women are free to do – have to accommodate the hard facts of economic life.

> The obvious problem with defining citizenship in terms of entitlement to positive resources is that these resources are finite. . . . Clearly all rights will come up against resource restraints, and thus political questions about the distribution of resources to meet rights will come up.
>
> (p. 288)

The main task now facing politicians of the left is to provide and to popularize an acceptable theory of distribution which is both consistent with egalitarian principles of socialism and with the realities of the modern economy. The right is fortunate enough (and sufficiently attracted by the charms of simplicity) to espouse the market and nothing but the market. On the left we have to start arguing not against the market but for the market properly constrained and circumscribed. It is a difficult theory to popularize but it does suffer from the considerable merit of being intellectually respectable, and morally right.

Roy Hattersley MP
Deputy Leader of the Labour Party

INDEX

328

government officials, salary
increases 88
government transfers: dependence
on 237; redistribution 116–19
Gramm-Rudman-Hollings
legislation 122–3
Gray, John 61–2, 297 n37, 297 n38,
297 n39
Great Society 96, 97, 121, 257
Great War 133
Greater London Enterprise Board
287
Green, David 214–16, 292 n8, 299
n5, 311 n13, 311 n14, 311 n15
Greenleaf, W. H. 293 n1, 298 n1,
300 n29, 308 n3
Greider, William 124, 303 n23, 303
n24, 306 n41
Griffiths Report 177
gross earnings, real level 265–6
growth, social limits 270, 271
guaranteed employment 247–50
guaranteed income programmes
243
guaranteed minimum wage 284–5
Guardian 317 n1

Habermas, J. 40, 234, 295 n31, 295
n32
Hain, Peter 284, 317 n15
Hall, Peter 292 n5
Hansard 317 n4
Harbour, William 300 n17, 300 n30
Harris, Laurence 314 n18
Harris, Lord 27
Harrison, Bennett 306 n29
Hattersley, Roy 285, 295 n11, 311
n7, 311 n17, 317 n16, 318–21
Haugen, Steven 306 n28
Hayek, F. A. von 9, 18, 21, 35–6,
44, 45, 56, 77, 82, 93, 180, 190,
219, 226, 229, 294 n12, 295 n3,
295 n11, 295 n12, 295 n13, 296
n14, 296 n18, 310 n1, 310 n3, 310
n4, 311 n20, 313 n37; on

coercion 207; on inequality 56;
on interest groups 63, 66; on
justice 214; on knowledge 59, 74;
on liberty 46–7, 208, 209; on
planning 143, 287; on publicly
provided housing 62; role of
government 259; on social justice
48, 49, 231, 232; on
unforeseeable economic
outcomes 206–7
Healey, Denis 146, 156, 196
health care, choice within 286
health expenditure, demand 43, 44
health insurance, compulsory 176
health policy 176–8
health service 162, 165
Heath, Edward 60, 81, 132, 146,
308 n1
Heath government 151, 152, 181,
186, 195
Hegel, G. W. F. 60, 63, 297 n36,
311 n9
Herbers, John 131, 306 n31, 308
n67
Heritage Foundation 27
Hershey, Robert 304 n36, 304 n39
Heseltine, Michael 72, 298 n53
high-spending councils 168
higher education, state funding 164
Hightower, Jim 306 n27
Hirsch, Fred 227, 229, 263, 268,
269, 312 n33, 317 n2
Holmes, M. 295 n2
homelessness 116, 265
Hoover, Kenneth 298 n2, 298 n4,
299 n5, 314 n23, 316 n47
Hoover, President Herbert 96
Hoover Institute 27
Hopkins, Kevin R. 302 n18
Hoskyns, Sir John 84, 300 n23
hospital services, contracting out
177–8
hospital stay, payment 176
House of Commons, Treasury and